Skywalker

Close Encounters on the appalachian trail

By Bill Walker

Indigo Publishing Group, LLC

Publisher	Henry S. Beers
Associate Publisher	Richard J. Hutto
Associate Publisher	Rick L. Nolte
Executive Vice President	Robert G. Aldrich
Operations Manager	Gary G. Pulliam
Editor-in-Chief	Joni Woolf
Designer	Audra George
Marketing & Media	Mary Robinson

Library of Congress Control Number: 2007941445

ISBN: (13 digit) 9781460999424
      (10 digit) 1460999428

In Memory of

My father, the late Duncan Walker Jr. (1922-2004), who would have thought trying to hike the entire Appalachian Trail was a nutty idea, but who would have been my biggest fan anyway.

Dedication

To the literally tens of thousands of volunteers, "trail angels," and members of local trail clubs who maintain the Appalachian Trail and form part of its unique culture.

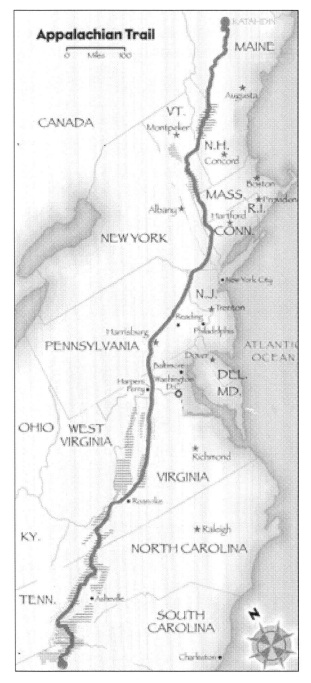

Appalachian Trail from Georgia to Maine.

part I

"There is a tide in the affairs of men which, taken at the flood, leads on to fortune. Omitted, all their voyages end in shadows and miseries."
— **Brutus, in Shakespeare's Julius Caesar**

chapter 1

On the third afternoon in Shenandoah National Park I was trooping along contentedly. The sounds of bird chirps and the soothing flow of wind in the treetops lent a carefree atmosphere. Suddenly, I heard something to my left that gave me the feeling that whatever made the noise was large. I turned quickly and saw in the fern bushes a large black bear looking at me, not twenty yards away. I stopped in my tracks as it ran across the trail in front of me. *Great, I finally got a good glimpse of a bear and it ran just like many people had said it would.* But then this bear stopped, right on the trail, about twenty-five yards in front of me. It slowly sauntered down the trail away from me and disappeared around the bend. I watched in rapt attention.

I was tense, but not petrified. But my condition rapidly changed from the former to the latter when the bear suddenly reappeared on the trail, walking very slowly in my direction. I felt helpless, even cheated. Everybody had promised me they were afraid of humans and would run. But this bear didn't look afraid and wasn't running.

So there I was in a standoff with a bear. It assumed a crouching position and I got the distinct impression it had been through this drill many times before. I utilized my "bear training," and began speaking back and forth to myself, and even to the bear while waving my hiking pole (and potential weapon) in the air. It was very low to the ground, but looked much bigger and wider at the stomach from a head-on view than it had appeared when it was running sideways toward the trail. God knows what all was stored in that stomach.

So what in the world was I doing in a standoff with the king of the Appalachian food chain?

***

"Bill, have you heard of the Appalachian Trail?" Tara asked.

"Yeah, it starts in Georgia — my home state." I replied. "Why?"

"Oh, you've got to read Bill Bryson's latest book." she said. "He and this crazy friend of his, Katz, tried to hike the entire trail."

"But doesn't that trail run almost the length of America?" I asked in amazement.

"Yes," she giggled.

I was living in London, England, in 1998 and was shocked at the strong undercurrent of anti-Americanism. The transplanted American author, Bill Bryson, had developed a huge following among the British with his own brand of anti-American mockery. Nonetheless, I had read a couple of Bryson's books with a combination of dismay and mirth, and made an immediate mental note to read this one — for a special reason.

***

I had a long history as a *streetwalker*. I had lived in Chicago from 1985 to 1995, and had worked downtown as a futures trader at the Chicago Board of Trade. After a few years I had figured out the best way to avoid the paralyzing city traffic was to walk home. At first I began walking until I passed over the Chicago River, at which point I would catch the bus for the remainder of the trip home. After a few months I found the walk so cathartic that I began walking all four miles home every day. People I had ridden the bus with for years asked me at work what in the heck I was doing walking, often in the freezing cold, straight up the bus line after being on my feet on all day. But I enjoyed the notoriety, and, better yet, saved one dollar per day in bus tokens.

In 1995 I got a job in London and reveled in trooping all over the west end of that historic, old city, often to the consternation of male and female companions. After leaving London in 1999 I lived in four Latin American countries over the next four years. In each country I continued this habit of walking what I then considered to be long distances of several miles at a time. I had come to love walking.

***

And so it was with special interest that I read Bill Bryson's book about his Appalachian Trail adventures. Bryson and Katz, his hapless high school sidekick, both in their mid-forties, had set off to hike the entire trail, but ran into one problem after another. During their fourth week in the Great Smoky Mountains — after days of slogging through mud, slush, and even snow — they bailed out and took a bus to Shenandoah National Park in northern Virginia. From there they challenged the trail for a couple hundred more miles, until a spooky encounter with a phantom bear shooed them once more. They disbanded, but reconstituted their partnership in Maine where, in the Hundred Mile Wilderness, Katz got lost. After a frightening search they happened upon each other the next morning. That was the final straw: They immediately took the nearest side trail back to civilization. Overall, they had actually hiked only about seven hundred of the trail's almost 2,200 miles.

A light bulb went off in my head when I read in Bryson's book that of the approximately four million people who hike some portion of the Appalachian Trail (AT) each year, approximately two thousand start off with the objective of being "thru-hikers." A thru-hiker is someone who hikes the entire 2,175 mile trail in one year.

I immediately decided I wanted to attempt a thru-hike, despite a daunting statistic: Ninety percent of the two thousand drop out along the way.

For the next six years, no matter where I lived, the idea of thru-hiking the Appalachian Trail haunted and beckoned me. Despite my now relentless habit of striding seemingly endless miles through big cities, the cold fact was that I had never even spent a night in the woods. Many times during these years I'd wake up in the middle of the night to use the bathroom and imagine what it would be like waking up like that in the deep woods. Would I be able to sleep out there?

And then there was the obvious, looming question: *Was I strong enough and determined enough to walk 2,175 miles in mostly rugged, mountainous terrain from the north Georgia mountains, where the trail begins, to Mount Katahdin in north central Maine*? It is usually too cold to start off in the southern Appalachians before late March, and one needs to arrive in northern Maine by early October to beat winter. Thus, a thru-hiker has a window of opportunity of a bit over six months. Instead of the several pedestrian miles per day I was accustomed to walking, I would daily need to cover considerably longer distances in mostly mountainous terrain, hauling a fully provisioned backpack. If I tried it I would be taking on — in my mid-forties — a challenge on a vastly different scale and of a completely different character than anything I had attempted up to that point.

On November 19, 2004, my father died. The year before his death I had mentioned the possibility of trying to hike the entire Appalachian Trail. He was incredulous. Later that afternoon, while exercising on his patio, an electrical storm chased me into his house. "What do you do on the AT when the lightning is cracking like this?" I mused.

"Hide under a bear," he deadpanned in his trademark ironic tone.

Within weeks of his death I made my decision. Despite my lack of hiking experience and some serious doubts about my capability for such a monumental journey, I was going to give it my all in 2005 — I would hike the entire Appalachian Trail.

***

It seemed logical to start my preparation by finding the best hiking equipment — something about which I knew almost nothing. I had never owned even the most basic items, such as a sleeping bag, a tent, or a backpack. I didn't even know what to take. Everyone said REI is the premier company in the outdoor equipment business, and I was determined to spend whatever it took to gain the greatest odds of success on this quixotic journey.

Once inside REI's main Atlanta store I realized that purchasing outdoor equipment involved more decisions than I had ever fathomed. Everything was further complicated by a most unusual personal characteristic — I'm 6' 11". When I started looking at tents, it immediately became clear that my long frame wouldn't fit in any one-person tent. A very upbeat employee from Georgia Tech then showed me a two-person tent, but it was two-and-a-half pounds heavier than any one-person tent. Worse yet, even the two-person tent seemed claustrophobic, and I wondered if I'd be able to sleep in it.

Undecided, I walked over and muttered to the sales assistant in the boots section. He happened to be a former AT thru-hiker. "What you need is a bivy sack," he said enthusiastically. "They're lighter weight, and you can sleep anywhere you want."

"Oh, yeah," I responded with my hopes lifted. We rushed across the store to look at some bivy sacks. But, upon seeing how prophylactic they appeared, my lifted hopes were soon dashed.

Noticing my existential crisis, a nice, willowy brunette sales assistant approached. "You would probably be perfect for a tarp," she said sincerely. "They're open on both sides so you won't feel claustrophobic. Also, they're lighter than either bivy sacks or tents."

"Could you show me one?" I pleaded. We went over and started fumbling through them. But when the Georgia Tech student noticed this he came over and said, "Dude. Tarps are much tougher to set up than tents. Also, they don't protect you from bugs and cold weather. I've used both. Trust me on this."

Reluctantly, I finally decided on the two-person tent and bought a pair of boots and a backpack after similarly baffling discussions with still more REI personnel. This first of several shopping trips set a pattern. I was unusually vulnerable to the equipment recommendation of whichever "expert" I was speaking with at the time. Usually, I just ended up following the suggestion of the last person I spoke with. I was the easiest lay in town.

***

From the beginning *he* seemed *different*. He was a professor of childhood education at Lee's McRae College in his daytime job. But what Warren Doyle was most renowned for was having hiked the entire Appalachian Trail a record *thirteen* times — that's 28,275 miles, which is more than the earth's circumference — and for being one of the trail's epic personalities. He once even held the record for the fastest thru-hike of the entire AT — sixty-six days! So it was probably safe to say he was different.

I had signed up for his four-day Appalachian Trail Institute seminar in Banner Elk, North Carolina on *how* to thru-hike the AT. Naturally, I was quite curious as to what such a person was like. In his mid-fifties, and with a vibrant, flowing, white beard covering a bespectacled demeanor, Dr. Doyle was of a short, powerful build. But surprisingly he didn't *appear* to be in great physical shape. After brief salutations he quickly led us to the university lunch hall as I closely observed his walking stride — quite unexceptional.

But once the formal seminar began it quickly became clear that the key to the real Doyle lay not in any exceptional physical characteristic, but in his deeply held philosophy of the so-called "outdoor lifestyle." "Walking the AT is not recreation," he began. "It is an education and a job. And walking the entire AT is not 'going on a hike,' but a journey with deeper ramifications."

"The trail is inherently difficult," he said with great conviction, and he went to great lengths to demonstrate just that. Various 'Doylisms' included:

During the seventh straight day of rain a drenched hiker should exclaim: "Great, the streams are full of drinking water."

During the third straight week of mosquitoes and black flies: "At least they aren't wasps."

And when you are dehydrated or have the runs: "Ho! Ha! Who cares? This is the song of the trail!"

He said there were two main reasons people drop off the trail. They try to go too fast, and they carry too much weight. In a line that I was to repeat many times in moments of duress, Doyle said, "There is no way you can go too slow on the uphills." This made sense when he pointed out that many more calories are burned going up a hill at a fast pace than at a slow pace. "And it's all about calories out there."

The second point — of not carrying too much weight — was a personal obsession for Warren. In short, he was an ultra-minimalist. He spoke rhapsodically about the advantages of a lighter tarp versus a tent. "That's a no-brainer," he said.

As for hiking boots, there were no ifs, ands, or buts. One should never, ever wear them, but rather something much lighter. "I went to a garage sale once," he recalled fondly, "and bought five pairs of used sneakers for a total of six dollars. They carried me all the way from Georgia to Maine."

And I just didn't know what to make of suggestions such as this one: "Instead of purchasing mittens, we could save weight by just using our spare pair of socks when our hands got cold." After all, *who wants to be known as the hiker with the smelly hands?*

On the second afternoon he drove us in his recently purchased $350 car to the AT, which is about ten miles from Lee's McRae College. It was my first look at the trail. Amy's too. She was a fifty-four-year-old Singaporean woman who had extensive experience as a cross-country skier above the Arctic Circle in Norway. Of Chinese extraction, Amy had been preparing for years, in Confucian-like fashion, to thru-hike the AT. The AT is marked by two-by-six inch white-blazes spray painted on trees and rocks. When Amy saw her first blaze she lost her vaunted self-control and began jumping for joy. Meanwhile, I insecurely bolted up the mountain ahead of the others and made sure I "beat" them to the top. My classmates were impressed by my speed. Warren wasn't.

"It's much better to be a smart hiker than a strong hiker," he said with great conviction. The next morning in class he strongly emphasized that we had not attempted anything difficult yet: "The mountains in New Hampshire and Maine will be more difficult by a factor of seven or eight," he solemnly intoned.

My persistent questions revealed a wide range of insecurities about many basics, such as equipment, food, water, and bears. The other hikers in the class were obviously much better versed in these matters than I was, which made my ignorance stick out like a sore thumb. "The trail is about discomfort, not comfort," Warren bore in. "Leave your emotional fat at home." After one particularly vexing question he even looked at me and said softly, "Why don't you just try a section this year?"

These weren't reassuring words coming from the person who'd spent more time on the AT than any other human. My humble reply was, "I know I'm an underdog. But this might be my only chance to ever attempt a thru-hike, and I'm going to go as far as I possibly can."

At one point or another everyone in the class probed for some comforting crutch to rely on, such as asking if Virginia is easier than North Carolina. Affecting a brusque manner Warren would shoot back, "No, it's less difficult than North Carolina." When he spoke of the importance of not taking days off I asked, "What if you have sharp stomach pains?" "You hike," he shot back.

One of the members of Warren's prior expeditions told us, "There is nothing that turns Warren on like watching somebody vomit and then get up and start hiking again."

Listening to all this I thought: *No wonder this guy has been able to hike the damn trail thirteen times. I just want to thru-hike once and spend the rest of my life bragging about it, instead of endlessly re-enacting it.*

As we prepared to depart Warren spoke movingly of the gratitude and reverence he held for the AT. "I have respect for everybody out there," he said, "as long as they aren't damaging the trail or another hiker in some way." He ended the four-day seminar by saying, "If your goal is to hike the entire trail, then do it. Unfulfilled dreams are bad."

***

I drove up I-81, through the Blue Ridge Mountains to my sister's house, which was near the AT in northern Virginia. Warren had been looking directly at me when he strongly suggested we take a couple long practice hikes. I closely studied the official AT data book he had given me and found a fourteen-mile stretch from Highway 7, where my sister could drop me off, to a road crossing on West Virginia Highway 9, where she would pick me up that afternoon. I hadn't yet bought all the necessary equipment so I loaded my backpack with twenty pounds of books, along with some sandwiches.

The topography in an area aptly called "the Roller Coaster" was quite demanding the first few miles, and I immediately began wondering if I could make the fourteen miles to Keys Gap before dark. Then it leveled off, and I began making better time. An eerie silence reigned, and I didn't see or hear a single other living creature all day in the dormant winter forest. Combined with the blanket of late winter snow, and surrounded by mountains on all four sides as far one could see, it was a magical scene.

I arrived at Keys Gap on West Virginia Highway 9 at four in the afternoon, having hiked fourteen miles in seven hours.

I had been wondering for several years whether the whole AT idea was gigantic folly, so my adrenaline was rushing upon completion of the day's task. Looking at the data book I saw that the next road crossing was at the historic city of Harper's Ferry, which was also the headquarters of the Appalachian Trail Conference. I quickly called my sister on the cell phone and notified her, without allowing time for a response, that I was continuing to Harper's Ferry.

I later learned that she had then called my mother about what I was doing and they did some simple arithmetic. I had averaged two miles per hour the first seven hours. It was four o'clock and it would be completely dark in northern Virginia by six o'clock. That meant that at the pace I had maintained so far there was time to hike at most four more miles before dark. But it is 5.7 miles from Keys Gap to Harper's Ferry. Further, I didn't have a flashlight, sleeping bag, or tent with me, and heavy snow was in the forecast for the evening.

Off I went, hoping the trail would be as easy as it had been the last five miles. But, it wasn't. The gentle inclines became more pronounced. As I headed up the mountain I began doing the same arithmetic my mother and sister had done and realized I had a time problem. At that point a thought crept into my mind that would reappear on several occasions in the next six months. Regardless of how I felt, and fatigue was indeed setting in, *I had to make it*.

The terrain became much rockier, which was a problem because my boots were beginning to kill me. I stumbled over rocks and roots, and cried out as I hurried. But there was no time for a break as the sun began to fall below the hills and the temperature dropped.

The data book showed that at the four-mile mark the trail reached the top of Loudon Heights at which point there was a steep descent into Harper's Ferry. It was too late to turn around, and it was now getting dark. My hopes rested on reaching that hilltop and then heading toward the lights of Harper's Ferry, in case I lost the trail. I was slowed by the rugged terrain and my throbbing feet; the point of maximum concern came after traveling what seemed like a quarter mile without seeing a blaze. Was I off the trail and, if so, what would I do? It even occurred to me that if I went much farther without seeing a white blaze that I might have to abandon my backpack in order to get to Harper's Ferry before pitch black dark. Why had I packed books, rather than a flashlight? Instead of preparing for a twenty-mile hike, I had packed for a sedate picnic.

Finally, I saw two posts ahead. Squinting hopefully, I read *Loudon Heights* on the right and *Harper's Ferry* 1.7 miles on the left. Looking below to the left I could make out lights shining way below and even hear the distant roar of the Shenandoah River. Greatly relieved, I bounded down the steep descent into Harper's Ferry, frequently veering off the trail, whose blazes were almost invisible in the enveloping darkness. Improved morale, however, didn't change the fact that my feet had gone from consistent pain to indescribable agony as I continued stumbling over rocks and roots and screaming in anguish.

In total darkness I finally reached the river and highway and luckily saw the path to the steps of the bridge leading over the majestic Shenandoah River. Following the AT blazes that run across the bridge, I saw a Comfort Inn and called my sister. "She's already gone out in the car looking for you," her eleven-year-old daughter informed me.

"That was stupid," my sister barked out the second she found me. Then she called my mother in Georgia who gave me a much more comprehensive lecture on my stupidity.

That night I had to drag myself up my sister's stairs. The next day my two big toenails were black and blue (I would eventually lose them), and I spent most of the day in bed, while six inches of snow fell outside. While it was encouraging that I had been able to go 19.7 miles in one day — with a backpack — it was also a glimpse into what a mess a person could get into with poor judgment. And it was sobering to think that this was what I would be doing on a daily basis, followed by spending my nights out there.

***

On the way home from Virginia to Georgia I stopped again at REI in Atlanta. Dutifully, per Warren Doyle's advice, I exchanged my tent for a tarp and my boots for some mid-cut trail shoes. But I had no idea if I was actually making the right decisions.

I began the homestretch of preparation by moving into my mother's house in Macon, Georgia. Having always been too thin for my extreme height, I was desperately trying to gain as much weight and strength as possible as quickly as possible. My mother was feeding me prodigiously and I was drinking high-calorie, enriched drinks. Finally, I was able to get my weight to 212 pounds, the highest of my life. And while I have never been an impressive physical specimen, the months of training at Gold's Gym had me in the best condition of my life.

The real possibility of bear encounters was another concern that loomed in the recesses of my mind. To the great amusement of friends I even visited the dancing bear act when the circus came to town. I wanted to see how their bear trainer handled the two bears. Fred, the male, was much larger than Ginger, and the trainer gave him plentiful helpings of honey after the acts. But all I could think was that if I see one of these enormous mammals out in the woods alone there wouldn't be a fence between us, and I wouldn't have a bottle of honey handy either.

After it was over I sauntered over by the trainers to chat. "Do you have any suggestions about how to respond if I see a bear on the Appalachian Trail?" I asked.

"A wild bear, you mean?" she clarified.

"Well, yeah, out in the woods, in case I run into one," I stammered.

"Gee, I don't know," she said to my disappointment. "It's probably best to stand up on your tiptoes and wave things in the air to make yourself look more fearsome. That, and try talking to him if he starts approaching you."
I was hoping for something more reassuring than her answer. Was I really going to stand on my tiptoes and wave something at a bear, or would I just follow instinct and hightail it?

The final big item on my shopping list was a sleeping bag. REI didn't have any seven-foot-long down sleeping bags, so I ordered one named "the Ponderosa" from Western Mountaineering in California *for $438.* At that price it had better keep me warm!

The sleeping bag arrived on March 26 which meant everything was in place to leave as planned on April 1. But there was one problem. I didn't feel ready. I called several friends to see if anybody could be convinced to go, at least for awhile, but they all demurred. I still had never spent a single night outside, and wondered if I had what it took to head off alone into the woods for six months, take what comes. It was at this point that a lack of resolution led to my first major blunder.

***

Warren Doyle had a practice hike scheduled from April 1 to April 4, starting in Ceres, Virginia. It was a grueling march of seventy-four miles in four days. Those who completed it were eligible to go on his "expedition," which was van-assisted. I called Warren and asked permission to try out. "Why are you suddenly interested in this?" he asked, dubiously.

Nonetheless, he warily assented.

What followed was a comedy of errors. First, I arrived late and missed the "Circle of Dreams." This was a huddle in which expedition members solemnly yearn to make it all the way to Mount Katahdin in Maine. Then, I got caught red-handed violating the prohibition against eating anything but cold food for the four-day march. Finally, the weather was so diabolical on the second evening that I told Warren that I would have to sleep inside my car because of fear of hypothermia.

"Then, you're not going on the expedition," he fired back.

Before we parted ways he said, "Bill, this is a major journey you are about to undertake, and *you don't appear to be ready.*" When I thanked him for his honesty, he said "It's not me that's telling you. It's the *trail* telling you."

When I arrived home two days early on Monday afternoon, April 4, my mother laughed knowingly at my vague explanation of what had happened. I then endured another lecture to attempt just a section, culminated with the question, "Why set yourself up for failure?"

I replied softly, "I'm starting this Sunday," and went upstairs to bed, exhausted.

I still hadn't ever spent a full night outside and decided to spend the night of Tuesday, April 5, out on my mother's lawn. Since there weren't two trees the right distance apart to set up my tarp, I just threw the sleeping bag on the ground, cowboy style, and tried to sleep. After about two or three hours of uneven sleep I woke up cold, with tensed-up neck muscles, and was unable to get back to sleep. At first light the next morning I went back inside and got three or four hours of deep, lusty sleep in my soft, warm bed.

When I woke up I decided I needed a sleeping bag with the "full mummy" feature, to fully envelop my neck and the back of my head. So I called Western Mountaineering and asked if I could switch it out for a full-mummy, seven-foot, down-filled bag. The saleswoman got the manager on the line: Yes, they could finish one called *"the Badger"* in a couple hours and overnight it to me. When it arrived on Thursday, April 7, I tried it out on the rug inside, but had no idea how well I would be able to sleep in it.

The last couple days I spent loading my backpack and agonizing over which items were absolutely necessary and which weighed more than the benefits. I was especially sensitive to my cold nature. Two sets of long johns, a balaklava and stocking cap, a fleece vest, two rain jackets, rain pants, and four pairs of socks made the cut. But also heavily influenced by Warren Doyle's minimalist philosophy, a stove, a camera, underwear, and even a watch, fell by the wayside. And I would only have the one shirt and pair of pants on me every day. I was "ready."

There was no denying I was very much the novice hiker.
Here I am making the agonizing decision of what to carry
the day before departure.

part II

"The woods are lovely, dark, and deep." — **Robert Frost**

Chapter 2

Daniel Boone described the southern Appalachians as "so wild and horrored that it is impossible to behold them without terror."

The southern terminus of the AT is at Springer Mountain, in north Georgia, seventy-six miles south of the North Carolina border. Just getting there can be complicated, as it lies right in the middle of the Chattahoochee Valley National Forest, nowhere near a town of any note. My mother volunteered to drive me to this remote spot. The irony of a seventy-year-old mother dropping her forty-four-year-old son off into the mountains for a six-month journey didn't elude me. As the formidable north Georgia mountains began to appear in the distance it occurred to me that many hikers from outside the South probably had a different image of Georgia and were in for quite a surprise.

Driving up U.S. Forest Service Road (USFS) 42 our eyes widened as we wound our way up the narrow, steep mountainous, dirt road that dropped off precipitously on the outside. Between "oohs" and "ahs," my mother renewed her lecture that this should be considered a two-week adventure, and I should be proud to do that much.

Finally, we arrived at the trailhead parking lot, and I was relieved to see several people unloading backpacks. It was about 1 o'clock, and the weather was gorgeous. I asked a couple people where exactly the trail began. The summit of Springer Mountain was nine-tenths of a mile hiking south from the parking lot — the trail then went straight back down through the parking lot and continued north. I decided to hike south up to the starting point without a backpack and come right back down to the parking lot.

At the top of Springer Mountain a "ridge runner" named Glenn was giving an orientation lecture to a group of hikers and asked me to join in. His theme was "low-impact hiking," which minimizes humans' effect on the environment. He so belabored the point of digging six-inch "cat holes" to bury our feces and toilet paper that our necks became sore from nodding. It seemed especially ironic that animals have more rights than humans in this regard.

Then he segued to the subject of bears. I listened closely as he spoke in deliberate fashion: "Bears have seven times greater sense of smell than bloodhounds. *It is incumbent on you to hang a 'bear bag'* (a food bag suspended out of the reach of bears) *every evening at your chosen campsite.*"

Oops, another task at which I was incompetent and, thus, had been amenable to Warren Doyle's counsel to just keep my food bag with me at night.

"And one final thing"

I tried to remain calm around everybody here on opening day. But the truth is I really wondered what in the world I was getting into.

— Glenn paused for gravity — "there's a certain amount of glorification attached to thru-hikers. Some start thinking they are the only people on the trail and want to dominate it. All other hikers — day hikers or section hikers — have the same rights as you." I was too green to have any sort of attitude or a swagger, but would eventually learn the basis for his remarks.

I then went over and signed the register for thru-hikers. I was number 1,093. The obvious question was how many of these hikers would still be headed north come September.

***

Back in the parking lot I found my mother with some newfound friends. She introduced me to a late-twentyish fellow named Justin, and his girlfriend. Tattoo-covered and bedecked with a headband and long flowing hair, Justin seemed an unlikely friend for my more traditional mother. But they hit it off.

I introduced myself as "Skywalker." This had seemed like an obvious trail name, given my height and surname of Walker. People often ask me how a thru-hiker gets a trail name. As best I can tell about half choose their own, and the rest get tagged by others. It seemed like a good idea to name myself and not risk picking up some unflattering name such as Snot Rag, Rat Puke, or Puss Gut, three thru-hikers I would meet farther up the trail.

Justin and his girlfriend had a tearful parting and he headed off down the trail. Then a middle-age, upbeat looking fellow passed through the parking lot and stopped to introduce himself as "Scottie Too Lite." My mother, being partial to resume talk, immediately had all the essentials down. Scottie had worked at IBM in Connecticut for thirty-three years, until a recent corporate restructuring. He would be one of many such victims of corporate downsizing I would meet on the trail. In fact I would soon notice a clear pattern of the trail being heavily populated with people having gone through a major life change such as graduation, divorce, or retirement.

About this time, three attractive girls from Chicago showed up in what appeared to be designer hiking clothing. The oldest one, at about twenty-two, came over and asked a couple questions at which point my mother began to elicit biography information. "I have a certificate for outdoor excellence," she said. "I'm in charge of safely getting my younger sisters to the finish."

"Have they hiked before?" my mother asked.

"Barely," she said rolling her eyes.

"So you're leading your inexperienced younger sisters almost two thousand, two hundred miles through the mountains to northern Maine?" I asked in disbelief.

"We'll get there," she said stoutly. From what I later heard they barely made it to North Carolina.

As hikers streamed through the parking lot and headed north — hopefully to Maine — it was clear I was entering a whole new world. Growing up I had spent nice Sunday afternoons like this at the golf course, before going home for dinner, a shower, and sleep. But here people were spending a nice Sunday afternoon hiking in the mountains, followed by God knows what.

My mother and I hugged as I worried about her trip back down the steep, rugged U.S. Forest Service Road. Looking around at mountains as far as the eye could see she said, "Bill, I'll have dinner ready for you next Saturday night. Don't let pride get in the way of good judgment." And then I departed.

Quickly, I caught up with long-haired Justin. He was adjusting his back pack, which looked to be twice the size of mine. His most visible accoutrement was a bulky dagger sheathed to his side. This was a surprise because I hadn't even considered bringing a weapon. What more, there seemed a basic assymetry to his strategy. With his impressively muscled physique, Justin should have been able fend off any possible human attackers without any weapon, but this knife couldn't possibly keep a mauling bear at bay for long. Nonetheless, eager to make my first real trail friend, I followed him along the trail. In a sense this was following a lifelong pattern of standing or walking behind shorter people, and I was to continue it much of the way on the AT.

Justin appeared, unlike me, to be well-schooled in the wilderness and preferred solitude. While solitude is obviously part of the bargain on the AT, this springtime Sunday saw hikers galore all over the trail. Most everyone appeared clean, well decked-out, and upbeat — not a surprise given that it was opening day. It was a scene not to be witnessed again.

Out of a combination of shared camaraderie, curiosity, and insecurity, I was trying to talk a bit with everyone possible. Adding to the buoyant atmosphere was some quite friendly terrain that wound along Stover Creek. In 1958 the trail's southern terminus had been moved twenty miles north from Mount Oglethorpe because of overdevelopment, and the change seemed fortuitous.

At the 7.6-mile mark Justin and I came to a sign pointing to the Hawk Mountain Shelter. One look over there showed a scene out of Grand Central Station. As a true babe in the woods I was heavily influenced by Warren Doyle's iconoclastic bias ("people farting, snoring, mice running rampant") against these nocturnal gathering points. And, given Justin's solitary instincts, we trudged on.

But then I began to feel winded going up Hawk Mountain and said, "Ha, Justin. You wanna' take a quickie?"

"It's getting late," he said. "I'm gonna keep going and scout out a campsite."

"I'll try to catch up with you," I said, feeling a bit forlorn.

Unsure of myself, but trying to remain calm because this was going to be my life for the next six months, I cut my break short and caught Justin as he was descending Hawk Mountain. We decided to spend the night right there at the gap.

My biggest weakness as a long-distance hiker was not in walking, but in camping. The first thing ninety-five percent of hikers do upon making camp is cook. But I didn't have a stove. So, as Justin pulled all sorts of cooking gadgets and culinary delights out of his backpack to prepare a meal, I began nibbling on pop tarts, bagels and peanut butter. I wasn't feeling sorry for myself, but Justin apparently was.

"Ha, man, let me cook you some noodles and make you some hot tea or something," he said, concerned. "You gotta' eat better than that." But I declined. It seemed unfair to eat something another hiker had carried all day. (I would later alter this principle, modestly).

As we sat on a log nibbling away, a trim young mid-twentyish hiker, wearing a wide-brim straw hat, approached. "You guys mind if I camp with you?" he asked.

"Sure," we replied.

Despite Justin's counterculture appearance he went by the book in his campsite preparations. "I took an Outward Bound (wilderness-preparation school) course," he said, "and just do this stuff out of habit."

When I started to put my food bag back in my backpack he said, "Gimme ya'll's food bags," and commenced setting up an elaborate roping system to hang our food out of reach of any nocturnal visitors.

Justin built a fire, and the three of us warmed ourselves and talked like close friends. Justin was a singer, as evidenced by his deep, soulful delivery. "Man, I'm really glad to be hiking with you two," he said movingly. And then in words I would remember hauntingly, he added, "I'm really uncomfortable in crowds. They freak me out."

Seth was a twenty-five-year-old English teacher from West Virginia, and this was his second straight try on the AT, after being struck down by injury in Virginia the previous year. "This year is going to be different," he said confidently.

When it was time to go to sleep, Justin said, "Did ya'll see that sunrise this morning? It was red."

"What's that mean?" I asked.

"Foul weather soon."

With a bit of anxiety stirring, I decided it was necessary to set up my tarp. I found a couple trees the right distance apart to attach the strings, although the ground was slanted, which meant sleeping at an angle. But after watching me flail around, trying to erect an effective shelter, Seth got the message. He quickly showed me a more user-friendly way to do it. It wasn't the Hilton Hotel, but appeared capable of warding off rain.

This would be the night with them I would most fondly remember when, a few months later, one of us was still ambling up the trail, one had suddenly and surprisingly gotten off, and one had *died* in the most tragic way imagineable.

***

On the third day we faced Blood Mountain, the highest point on the AT in Georgia. The southern Appalachians are a natural mystery. Stretching from north Georgia to southern Virginia are about eighty-five mountains (including Blood Mountain), known as balds. Their summits are treeless, in spite of being below timberline, which is about 7,000 feet at these southern lattitudes. Even the Cherokees, who dominated the area for centuries, were baffled by these balds.

The dark, leaden sky looked ominous. Justin and Seth, exhibiting more equanimity than me, were scattered along the trail separately taking snack breaks. But I anxiously tried hurrying up the mountain as the visibility worsened. Warren Doyle had specifically warned about clearing exposed areas in high winds, poor visibility, and rain. Indeed, this would be my first taste of just how harshly the winds can blow at high elevations.

Blood Mountain was impressively steep, and I ran into my first "false summit" — clearing an area that appears to be the summit of a mountain only to find another summit ahead. One big concern at the higher altitudes is the lack of blazes, usually due to the dearth of trees. Thus, it was a relief when the Blood Mountain Shelter came into view out of the dense fog.

Inside the shelter, attempting to warm up, was a big, hefty fellow named "Study Break." He was taking a semester off from the University of Pennsylvania Medical School to attempt hiking the AT. I tried bundling up in all three corners of the shelter to stay warm, but it was useless. The shelter was exposed to the high winds, and it was necessary to get out of there quickly.

For the first time it wasn't clear where to go, as Study Break and I started off in one direction, then another. Finally, identifying a badly faded blaze on a rock, we started the 2.5-mile descent into Neel's Gap. I kept hiding in the rhododendron bushes to shield myself from the wind while Study Break caught up. But he kept warning, "I'm slower than Christmas,

Skywalker. Don't wait on me." It soon became clear that he was correct, and I hurried to get to a lower elevation.

I was amazed after one thousand feet of descent to see how much the intensity of the wind had waned and the visibility improved. Soon I was at Neel's Gap. The archway, with a blaze painted on top, at the Cherokee Outdoor Center there is the only place on the entire AT where the trail runs *through* a building.

Justin and Seth soon arrived. "Did ya'll meet Study Break?" I asked.

"Yeah," Justin laughed. "He'll be down by dinnertime."

It was only one o'clock, so we went inside to see if they had any "real" food, and gorged ourselves on the available fare of microwaveable hamburgers and ice cream sandwiches.

When I went back outside Study Break had arrived in high spirits after a five-day walk from Springer Mountain — a trip that had taken everybody else three days.

"I'm first going to call my wife," he announced buoyantly, "and let her know I haven't been eaten by a bear yet."

I had gone thirty-one and seven-tenths miles in three days without feeling overly taxed. But I was feeling impatient and set my sights on going all-out starting the next day.

***

Hypothermia refers to any condition in which the core body temperature falls below a level at which it can carry out its normal bodily functions. It can happen at any time of the year, even on a seventy-degree summer day. In fact, hypothermia is actually more likely when the temperature is above freezing. And it's a killer, make no single mistake about it. In the 1990s an average of seven hundred, fifty-four people per year died from hypothermia.

The common thread in most hypothermia stories is human error of some sort. Stories are legion of outdoorsmen dying with their backpacks full of clothes. At forty degrees a human head may lose half of its heat production. The process is insidious and can kill in minutes. The key is to avoid letting even mild hypothermia begin.

***

Wednesday, April 13, I awoke restlessly at four o'clock, anxious to leave early and cover a lot of miles. But it was raining, and I wanted the owner of the Cherokee Outdoor Center, Lyle Wilson, to do a "pack shake" before I started, so I waited around. Wilson advertised that he could reduce a hiker's backpack weight by an average of ten pounds.

He proceeded to rearrange my pack in dizzying fashion as I stood over him, tensed up. My biggest concern was whether I would be able to remember how to pack everything once back on the trail.

His manner was so self-assured that when he said a Thermarest self-inflated pad was an absolute necessity (Warren Doyle had said just the opposite), I relented. But the Thermarest was only six feet long — almost a foot shorter than me. Meanwhile, the Ridge Rest sleeping pad I had traveled all around Atlanta looking for, but would now be giving up, was seven feet. "No problem," he said when I pointed this out. "I'll just cut off a foot from your Ridge Rest that we're getting rid of, and you can put it at the end of your new Thermarest."

A week later at a shelter in North Carolina a hiker right next to me pulled out the remaining six feet of my ridge rest for her sleeping pad. I swear to God.

We went through a few more songs and dances as my eyes got wider and wider from being told that this or that item would be highly beneficial (I thought this was about reducing weight!). This guy really knew how to ring the cash register. And this was the point in the journey when hikers were the most vulnerable and flush with cash.

So it was ten-thirty in the morning, instead of the intended eight o'clock, before I finally left Neel's Gap, and this would begin to loom more fateful as the day drew on. There was a light drizzle from dark clouds overhead, but the sky seemed clear both east and west, so I was optimistic. It would prove to be the first of many awful weather-related prognostications on my part.

The section ahead was known as difficult, but I felt good. Determined to make good time I gave polite, but brief, salutations to other hikers on the trail. At three o'clock, I arrived at Low Gap Shelter having made eleven miles in four and a half hours. Better yet, the familiar faces of Justin and Seth were on hand, as well as an elusive redheaded fella' named Beeker. We sat there dutifully eating "trail food," as everyone who had been laid up at Neel's Gap by the previous day's rain started trickling in.

Vertical Jerry, appropriately named, pulled out a copy of the *Companion Data Book* and chortled, "Oh, great. Look at this. 'Shelter closed in summer of 2000 due to continued trouble with bears. A 2000 thru-hiker reported waking in the shelter to find a black bear straddling him.'" That, of course, drew wry remarks from various quarters.

"This doesn't look like my type scene developing here," Justin whispered.

"Yeah, I'm thinking about going," I said.

The big wild card was the weather. I was cold when sitting still and didn't think I could stay warm by remaining at this shelter. Beeker was the only one committed to going the full nine miles to Unicoi Gap on Georgia Highway 75. He claimed the trail runs fairly flat along an old forest service road and then over a small hill and down to the road. This was a surprise since the data book showed sharply undulating topography for the rest of the time in Georgia. But I was later to learn that Beeker made up for his social unease by telling people exactly what they wanted to hear. He planned to hitchhike into Helen, Georgia, a Bavarian style village, and spend the night in a motel. Now, there was an enticing plan — my first twenty-mile day, followed by a full-night's sleep in a warm bed. My heart said yes, after feeling a bit shackled the first three days. After all, a thru-hiker's mantra is "no rain, no pain, no Maine."

I headed off in the threatening weather. When I turned the first corner water was unexpectedly shooting out of a big rock face, probably due to all the recent rain. I filled up my Nalgene water bottle, and this would prove to be crucial.

The drizzle became steadier as I pushed on, determined. The trail, which had been almost teeming the first few days, was abandoned; I was to see no other hiker the rest of the day. I kept looking for this old forest service road Beeker had mentioned, but had trouble making anything out in the increasingly dense fog. Meanwhile, the trail was winding up and down, but with the elevations increasing for each peak.

On a nine-mile stretch I would normally take at least a couple breaks. But I was reluctant to do so here because of the time constraint and the worsening weather conditions. I did, however, keep swallowing water and chewing on GORP (Good Ol' Raisins and Peanuts). Meanwhile, I was becoming concerned because I was stopping quite often to urinate, even though my mouth felt dry. My assumption had been that I didn't need to bring a lot of water out of Low Gap Shelter, which had a stream, because I would be able to find water easily on such a rainy day. However, the water spewing from the rock was the only drinking water I would see, and I was steadily drinking it down. As I later learned, this was misguided, because higher elevations often lack any water sources at all.

I had belatedly put on a rain jacket, when I realized just how drenched and cold I was from the steadily increasing downpour. But now that I had begun chilling it was tough to warm up again — a classic rookie mistake. But what was even more unnerving was that I had started feeling lightheaded, which could have been caused by my having walked as hard and as fast as possible with very few breaks for about seven hours. Or maybe it had something to do with waking up at four o'clock. Or maybe it was all a figment of my imagination.

However, I wasn't hallucinating about the fundamentals: It was cold and getting colder; I was soaked; the trail was getting muddier by the minute; the visibility was poor and getting worse the higher I climbed; my water supply was running low; the howling winds were adding to my paranoia; and nobody else was on this trail as night approached.

Finally, I saw a wooden post that I hoped would be for Blue Mountain Shelter. But instead it read Brass Town Bald, a name every Georgia school boy knows because it is the highest point in Georgia. This fact contributed to the forbidding feeling that I really was stuck in the mountains, and that I was totally reliant on the remaining energy in my legs to get me out of there in one piece. One of the scant comforts I could honestly conjure up was that I had made out my will before starting the AT.

I kept straining to hear the sound of cars from the road, down at the bottom of the mountain. But every time my hopes were lifted by what seemed like a whirring sound, I would look over to my left and realize that it was just another powerful wind gust sweeping over the mountain. Trees swayed as if they were going to bend in half. I began to wonder if I would ever see another human being.

As I cleared the next rise in the fog, the trail began to flatten. *It's the summit.* I looked ahead expectantly for a descent that would lead straight to the road. Instead, it was a false summit and the outlines of yet another mountain appeared in front of me. I was exhausted and felt unable to continue.

A friend back home with hiking experience had told me that if immobilized and faced with high winds and rain, I should just take out my tarp and wrap it around me like a burrito. I pulled out my tarp, wrapped it around me, and lay in the middle of the AT. I attempted to relax and breathe deeply, only to be buffeted by cold, slanting, merciless sheets of rain. This wasn't working. Now all the concerns and paranoia of the last few hours morphed into a full-fledged fear for my life. As cold and soaked as I was, I didn't think I could survive the night exposed to these elements.

I began envisioning my funeral. In a perverted way I even felt "embarrassed" for my family, that I had so ceremoniously undertaken this long journey only to die the first time the weather turned sour. I had to get out of there quickly and decided to do something that had been at the back of my mind the last couple hours. I would abandon my backpack. I rushed it over to a clump of trees, quickly gulped down some Tylenol from the first aid kit, and grabbed the remaining quarter-liter of water. Then I urinated again for approximately the tenth time since Low Gap Shelter three hours before — a telltale sign of *hypothermia*.

Then, deciding I was in a dead-even situation and that this was my best chance, I took a deep swallow of my precious remaining water, said a quick prayer for faith, and resolved to walk very slowly up the mountain. Concentrating on each step, I felt a tangible difference without a backpack. This was a relief. Within about 200 or 300 hundred yards I began to make out through the fog yet again what looked like a summit. As it flattened at the top I wondered if I was in for yet another false summit. But then the trail seemed to be descending, and finally it started down steeply. The distant noise of cars from the road 1.4 miles away was now unmistakable. Yes, I considered turning around to retrieve my backpack, but after hours of nagging doubt, followed by fifteen minutes in which I thought I was looking death straight in the eye, I was happy to be apparently out of danger and decided to continue descending to the road. A half hour later, I arrived at Unicoi Gap and Ga. Hwy. 75. The rain had almost stopped and the visibility was much better, but I consoled myself that I had made the right decision to abandon my backpack. The weather was probably still diabolical up on the mountaintop.

It was getting dark and it was a ten-mile hitch east to Helen, Georgia. Furthermore, not many cars were passing. After a few failed thumbs, the thought occurred that, without a backpack, I looked more like a bum than a hiker. With no sleeping bag, shelter, or dry clothes and the nearest town ten miles away, I could be facing a long night. Finally, another car rounded the hill, and I threw up my hands as if in prayer. A thirty-ish, rotund fellow stopped and agreed to take me to Helen. Despite the odd circumstance of my backpack being on the mountain I was positively giddy and had him drop me at the first motel we saw.

That night my relief turned to worry, as I lay awake wondering if a bear or rodents were tearing through my backpack, which contained not only a food bag, but thousands of dollars of equipment as well. At first light I got up and caught a taxi back up the mountain to Unicoi Gap, hoping to retrieve my backpack.

The first thing I saw heading up the trail's steep ascent was my light blue balaklava, which had obviously fallen out of my rain jacket on the descent. The climb up was steeper than I had remembered, probably because I'd had so much adrenaline pumping the previous day. Finally, I got back up to the summit of Blue Mountain and hurried down southward, remembering that my backpack should be only a few hundred yards down and just off the trail to the left, in the bushes. I spotted it and anxiously checked to see if the contents were intact. They were. That probably wouldn't have been the case in high summer, but bears weren't hanging out at the higher elevations yet because the forest was still dormant.

I was jubilant. Justin had said yesterday afternoon at Low Gap Shelter that he might go to Blue Mountain Shelter, which was only about a half mile south of where my backpack had been, so I decided to continue south and check on him. When I got there he was the only person in the shelter, still bundled in his sleeping bag.

"Man, what in the world are you doing here?" he asked. After I filled him in on my mishap, he said, "Wow, that sounds like more than your average hiker bitch. You weren't lying when you said how new you are at this."

But then he said, "You might have done the smart thing, not stopping here. I froze my ass off. I don't know why they built this shelter completely exposed to the wind from the north."

When I hoisted my backpack to head back down the trail he perked up from his sleeping bag, and called out, "I hope you're not gonna' quit."

Looking back, I said, "No way, man." As fate would have it this was to be the last time I ever saw him.

***

One doesn't just skate away from a "day from hell." I may well not have been in as much danger as I had feared at the time. I honestly don't know. But for days I would feel a deep down-to-the-bone weariness and nagging anxiety in the wake of the incident. And wild rumors of my having been carried off the mountain and revived in a hypothermia ward would proliferate among hikers.

Two days later I arrived at Dick's Creek Gap and hitchhiked easily into Hiawassee, the northernmost town in Georgia. This picturesque mountain village had an indefinable, mysterious quality. One guidebook described it as a place where "everybody is very white, very heavy, and very slow." Indeed, I didn't see a single black person in the entire town. This was especially noteworthy in a state in which African-Americans constitute 30 percent of the population.

"What did you guys do around here?" the ever garrulous Vertical Jerry, a real-estate broker from New Jersey kept badgering me. "Did you kill all the blacks?" In fact — being hemmed in on all sides by mountains — little assimilation had taken place, thus occasioning the stereotype of the underbred hillfolk.

Vertical Jerry, Linebacker, and I opted for the local buffet that night. "Skywalker," Vertical Jerry said, "is there some reason all the locals have a stricken look when you walk by?"

"Yes," I replied, "they can sense my parents married outside the immediate family."

Continuing on his theme of southern provincialism, Vertical Jerry announced to nobody in particular, "Ladies and gentlemen, the Deliverance factor is alive and well in this town. Make sure all doors are latched and bolted this evening."

He, of course, was referring to the infamous movie, *Deliverance*, in which some north Georgia backwoodsmen rampage on some visiting urbanites to the point of their humiliation and doom. The good news is that over the course of traveling fourteen states from south to north many stereotypes would be exploded as hikers entered regions previously unknown to them.

Linebacker continued being very quiet, especially to me. The previous day I had, with the best intentions, goaded him into attempting to make it over Kelly's Knob and all the way into Hiawassee.

"It shouldn't be that difficult to make good miles tomorrow," I said. "The weather forecast is good."

"You didn't know what you were talking about yesterday," he shot back. He then solemnly recounted how after going all out the entire day it had taken him three hours to cover the last two miles in the dark. Apparently, he viewed it all as *his* "day from hell."

"The car noise from the highway saved me," he succinctly noted.

"How much do you weigh, man?" Vertical Jerry brazenly asked.

"Three-twenty," Linebacker stated flatly.

Good gosh, I thought. *If I had known that I wouldn't have recommended he try that yesterday.*

Vertical Jerry suggested that the three of us meet out front at seven forty-five in the morning. to catch a ride back to the trail. "Count me in," Linebacker said. But Linebacker didn't show up, and we never saw him again. From what I later heard he apparently never made it out of Hiawassee.

Chapter 3

At the end of World War I millions of American soldiers poured back into the country. Two trends — urbanization and mass industrialization — dominated the American landscape. However the trauma of the war — *116,000 Americans were killed in one year of fighting while European losses were much worse* — had created a contrarian intellectual philosophy.

One prominent adherent to this contrarian ideology was Benton MacKaye, a patrician New Englander who had received a Master's in forestry from Harvard. He plainly did not like the way America was moving and saw rapid mechanization and urbanization as hurting mankind. He even spoke of American cities' tendency to "over-civilize."

In April of 1921, MacKaye's wife, a prominent women's suffragist, hurled herself off a bridge into New York's East River. Soon after a friend noted that he seemed depressed, and invited him to his estate in the New Jersey Highlands. MacKaye accepted, and it was there he wrote the essay *An Appalachian Trail.*

The customary approach to the problem of living relates to work rather than play," MacKaye wrote. "Can we increase the efficiency of our working time? The new approach," MacKaye asserted, "reverses this mental process. Can we increase the efficiency of our spare time? Here is an enormous undeveloped power — the spare time of our population."

MacKaye mentioned the great public service that the national parks in the West (Yellowstone, Yosemite, and the Grand Canyon) had provided. However, he said, "For camping grounds to be of most use to the people they should be as near as possible to the population centers. And this is the East." MacKaye noted the happy coincidence that throughout the most densely populated portions of the United States lie a fairly continuous belt of under-developed lands and ranges which form the Appalachian chain of mountains. Better yet, within these ranges lie "secluded forests and water courses which could be made to serve as the breath of real life for the toilers in the 'beehive' cities along the Atlantic seaboard."

The net result of all this, according to MacKaye, would be to reverse the migration from the cities back to the countryside.

The Appalachian mountain chain actually runs from northern Alabama all the way up to Nova Scotia and Newfoundland. MacKaye originally proposed a 1,700-mile trail that connected the various mountain ranges from north Georgia to Mount Washington in New Hampshire. About a third of this proposed trail, according to his estimates, already was in existence, mostly in the Northeast. MacKaye rallied his network of mostly New England friends behind the idea, and the first AT Conference was held in Washington D.C. in 1925.

The idea of a linked trail running almost the length of the Appalachian mountain chain had wide appeal. "The Appalachian Trail is to the Appalachian region what the Pacific Railway was to the Far West — a means of opening up the country," MacKaye told an enthusiastic conference.

MacKaye also advised that the path of the trailway should be "... as pathless as possible. It should be a minimum path consistent with practical accessibility." The idea was to disrupt nature as little as possible. True to this, the trail today is on average about two or three feet wide throughout its impressive length.

The timing of MacKaye's AT proposal was auspicious because a new bridge had just been built across the Hudson River in New York. This was to provide the critical link between the New England and Mid-Atlantic States.

***

It was at this point in the late 1920s that the other seminal figure in AT history entered the picture. Myron Avery was born and raised on Maine's majestic eastern coast. But oddly enough, he preferred the mountains on the western side of the state. Upon graduating from Harvard Law School Avery threw himself into the half-built AT project. He successfully lobbied to have the northern terminus located not at Mount Washington in New Hampshire, as MacKaye had envisioned, but all the way up at Mount Katahdin in north central Maine (Many a thru-hiker has regretted this decision!). This assured that the trail's length would be greater than 2,000 miles.

Avery also noted that the AT in its initial stages had been a mostly northeastern project, and he endeavored to change that. With fierce determination he rallied volunteers and helped form trail clubs in the southern Appalachians to sign on. He personally hiked through rugged, isolated backcountry areas in North Carolina and Tennessee (the Smokies) to try to find the best route for the trail to Georgia. Also, he oversaw the cutting of 265 miles of trail from central Pennsylvania to northern Virginia with used hand tools. And he became president of the ATC (the AT's governing body) in 1931 for the next twenty-one years. He was a born leader, and an endearing set of old photos invariably show a man of action directing trail construction in the wilderness.

Finally, on August 14, 1937, in rural Maine a six-man CCC (Civilian Conservation Corps) crew completed the final link to make it the AT continuous footpath. It originally measured 2,025 miles and had taken sixteen years from the time Benton MacKaye had envisioned it in 1921 to its final completion. Myron Avery himself became the first person ever to hike every step of the trail, done in sections over a period of fifteen years.

MacKaye and Avery were both Harvard men; without MacKaye the trail might never have been envisioned, while without Avery the trail might never have been built. So presumably they got on swimmingly, right? In fact they got along like a dog and a cat.

For starters MacKaye took the community planning features (food farms, community camps, etc.) of his proposal with the utmost seriousness. He looked upon it as a higher human evolution, while others considered them socialist and utopian. For Avery a trail was simply a trail. He spent his every day strenuously trying to find a way to overcome the numerous obstacles to a continuous footpath throughout the Appalachian mountain range.

***

In 1948 a World War II veteran from Pennsylvania named Earl Shaffer became the first person to thru-hike the AT. During the war Shaffer had spent four years in gruesome conditions in the Pacific, building landing strips and radar stations. A loner by nature, Shaffer's only true friend had been gunned down on the beach at Iwo Jima. Depressed, he set off alone on the AT in the spring of 1948. "Much of it was very rough," he reported, "with thousands of downed logs across it, and some areas so overgrown that finding the trail was practically impossible. Marking often was faint or even totally lacking."

Nonetheless, Shaffer completed the trail in fewer than five months to become the first thru-hiker. One reason is that the trail was not as difficult then. The AT Shaffer hiked had many logging roads and livestock pastures. Volunteers have since relocated stretches to more scenic, rugged mountain stretches. The irony is that during Shaffer's initial thru-hike the ATC in its annual meeting had discussed the seeming impossibility of a thru-hike. Gene Espy of Macon, Georgia, became the second thru-hiker in 1951. "Earl was glad I did it," Espy recalled. "Some people had questioned whether he really had done the whole thing."

The first and oldest woman ever to hike the trail was the renowned Grandma Gatewood. Emma Gatewood was a sixty-six-year-old great grandmother from Gallipolis, Ohio, when she set off from Mount Katahdin in 1954 for a southbound thru-hike. She had read about Earl Shaffer in *National Geographic* "… and immediately knew this was something I wanted to do. I got lost right off the bat," she recounted.

For three days and two nights she searched for the trail in the 100 Mile Wilderness, even setting signal flares to alert search planes. Finally, four rangers found her just as she was running out of food. "Go home," they told her, and she did.

But the next year she headed south to Georgia to hike northbound, carrying only eighteen pounds of essential items in a duffel bag. Her bare-bones luggage included a light blanket, a shower curtain, a lumberman's jacket, and a Swiss Army knife. She ate almost all cold food.

"I'm not afraid of anything in the mountains," she had stoutly asserted at the outset. "And as long as I can still chop wood I'm not too old to hike." As she entered the home stretch in Maine, *Sports Illustrated* started covering her trip. Maine's rangers also picked up on her trip and rowed her across Maine's streams. On a cold, windy September day in 1955 she summited Mount Katahdin and sang "America the Beautiful." She had lost twenty-nine pounds, and her foot size had swollen two sizes. During the trip she wore out four pairs of shoes, and four raincoats.

And she had some strong words about the trail: "This is not a trail. This is a nightmare. For some fool reason they always lead you right up over the biggest rock to the top of the biggest mountain they can find. I would never have started the trip if I had known how tough it was, but I couldn't and I wouldn't quit."

But, amazingly, she came back two years later and did the whole trail again.

There have been other notorious female hikers as well. The Barefoot Sisters of Maine set off sans shoes (sandals for the very rockiest areas) from their home state in 2001 and managed to make it all the way to Georgia. The very next year

Six married, middle-aged mothers, known as the Mountain Marchin' Mamas, set off in 1978 to hike the Appalachian Trail in sections. Twenty-one years later in 1999, five of the six arrived on the summit of Mount Katahdin in Maine.

they turned around and hiked northbound from Georgia back to Maine.

The Mountain Marchin' Mamas were six middle-aged women from Sarasota, Florida, who set off on the AT in 1978. Their goal was to hike 100 miles a year. In 1999, five of the six — the other dropped out in the fifteenth year due to injury — completed their marathon section hike. They were so gratified by the experience that they funded the construction of the Roaring Fork Shelter in North Carolina and started a still very active local AT Club in their hometown.

***

The AT has had a steadily upward trajectory in terms of popularity and participation. By 2005 the annual hiker population had reached an estimated four million. Its thirty-one trail-maintaining clubs boast a combined membership of more than a hundred thousand people. One could credibly say it has worked out almost perfectly. It's well within modest driving distance for many of the nation's eastern population centers. It winds through the wildest and most mountainous areas in the eastern United States, including two of its greatest national parks. Its topography and terrain are extraordinarily varied, from gentle wooded walkways to bogs, streams, and steeply inclined rock scales. The plants and fauna are of the widest variety, and supplemented by a plethora of water sources. And the trail ends with that jewel of a state, Maine.

With such a storied history it's easy to fall into the trap of thinking it would have happened one way or another, regardless of particular individuals or events. But a close look at its storied history reveals that in fact a linked trail running almost the length of the country so near major population centers was anything but a foregone conclusion. After all, the other large countries, Russia, Canada, and China, have no footpaths even approaching the AT in terms of geographic diversity or popularity. But from its inception the AT has been a model public-private partnership. The Appalachian Trail is an American success story.

Chapter 4

One of the more embarrassing scenarios for a thru-hiker is to set off for Maine, but not even make it out of Georgia. Apparently, 20 or 25 percent of wanna-be thru-hikers suffer just such a fate. Tales are legion ("Nobody ever told me about all these mountains out here") of just such mishaps. Thus, I derived a small measure of solace upon crossing the North Carolina border, although I still felt unsettled from the abandoned backpack incident and it was going to be several days before arriving in town to re-supply.

I climbed steadily to the Muskrat Creek Shelter, which at 4,600 feet, is one of the most elevated shelters on the AT. I was delighted to see Seth and amazed to see Study Break on hand. "You're the most improved hiker on the trail," I noted to Study Break.

"I've already dropped twenty pounds," he cheerfully noted, "and am picking up speed."

Despite the beautiful weather, I was having trouble staying warm as the cool late afternoon wind wafted over the mountain. Further, the shelter's open side was exposed to a stiff late-afternoon breeze. And Warren Doyle's axiom that a thru-hiker should hike long hours on nice days still infected me. Thus, I decided to assert my independence and move on from where everybody else was going to stay. Before leaving, the conversation at the shelter turned to wild boars. "They're nocturnal animals," Seth said, "and can be quite mean." With that soothing thought in mind I headed out from the shelter alone, at dusk.

My goal was to find a lower elevation to set up my tarp and stay warm, but no appreciable descent presented itself. After a couple miles I came to an old jeep road called "Chunky Gal Trail" which looked like it had some spots flat enough to string the tarp to some trees.

After setting up "camp" and climbing into my sleeping bag it became clear the terrain wasn't as flat as I'd originally thought. Getting out of my bag to make some tarp adjustments in the dark, I was amazed at how cold it had gotten. Not only had the temperature dropped precipitously, but the wind was roaring. I was to be continuously amazed in the early going at how powerfully, almost overwhelmingly, the wind blows at night in the mountains, even after calm, nice days. Channels of wind could be heard originating from seemingly miles away as it thrashed through the forest toward me with gathering intensity.

I put on every ounce of clothing I had, which was six layers in all, including two sets of long johns. Over the next couple hours I tried every position I knew to get warm, but nothing succeeded. Compounding my misery were the menacing creatures I imagined in every shadow and sound in the black as pitch night. My food bag was in my backpack, right next to my legs, which could be inviting to a bear. Then there was my new bogeyman to worry about, wild boars. *What in the hell am I doing out here*?

I finally remembered that in my backpack was an item I picked up as an afterthought at REI. It was an emergency space blanket that weighs only four ounces. The package showed a shivering, desperate-looking man out in the woods with this blanket wrapped around him. It had seemed like a pretty good bet for four ounces. Lyle Wilson, the outfitter back at Neel's Gap, had urged me to throw it out, but I uncharacteristically asserted that I would keep it as an ace-in-the hole for the worst conditions. So, here deep in the mountains, in a state of great distress, I finally pulled it out of the box and slipped between the aluminum foil layers. The idea is that the aluminum foil traps the body heat, and indeed it seemed to be working. It helped turn a disastrous night into merely a bad one as I was able to relax my muscles and even sleep some.

***

A sign on the bulletin board read:

CAREFUL!

*BLACK BEAR SEEN BETWEEN HERE
AND SILER BALD SHELTER
STOLE A HIKER'S BACKPACK
SHOWS NO SIGN OF FEAR OF HUMANS*

As I started the climb out of the gap and up Indian Mountain along came Seth from behind after another early start. "Really comforting sign back there, huh" he said, "and we have to worry about that bear for the next twenty-six miles until Siler's Bald."

I climbed to the top of Indian Mountain and saw an overall-clad sixty-ish fellow, called Billy Goat. Listless from such a poor night's sleep and overwhelmed by the nighttime cold in the mountains, I sat there in the shelter sullenly chatting with this stranger. Morale was running dangerously low. My fitness for the entire enterprise was being called into question. Soon, it became clear that it was time for a bowel movement. This was one of the few shelters on the trail without a privy — the small outhouses built by the local trail clubs. After fumbling through my backpack I pulled out some "Wipes" and asked Billy Goat if he was familiar with them.

Sensing that I was a bit uneasy with the task ahead he lit up and said, "Yes, they're great." I nodded dutifully, when he added, "You can wash your face, your hands, and your rear end with one wipe. The *order* is what's important."

Never was any advice more appreciated.

After sixteen miles for the day I arrived at USFS 67 and looked around for the trail. It appeared that it might go up the dirt forest road when I spotted a blaze on the steep embankment in front of me. This was Albert Mountain. In a preview of New Hampshire's White Mountains, I started scrambling up the boulders using all fours. Lucky breaks have a way of evening out; this could have been outright dangerous on a bad-weather day. In fact there had to be hikers who flat out wouldn't be able to make it up this single section.

Soon I was at Big Spring Shelter, and was reunited with several friendly faces, including Scottie Too Lite. After being deep in the dumps so early on in the day, my spirits immediately soared. I was even considering trying to sleep in the shelter for the first time, despite ample warnings about mice. "What's the status on these shelters?" I asked.

"Expect something between a Swiss chalet and an outhouse," Scottie Too Lite replied.

The AT shelters are decidedly rough-hewn, three-sided structures that are open on the front side. Their wooden sleeping platforms sleep anywhere from four to twenty-five, and availability is on a first-come basis. They are quite popular, especially with thru-hikers, despite the hazard of serial mice-infestation. They run on average about every ten miles. Many hikers religiously planned their hiking schedules to arrive at a shelter late in the day, and the spirit of camaraderie tended to be high as everybody recounted their day's toils.

"This is the area where Eric Rudolph hid from police for years after bombing the Atlanta Olympics," Pockets said. "He was even on the Appalachian Trail some of the time."

"How the hell could you ever catch somebody in mountains like this, anyway?" I remarked.

"But remember the main reason they couldn't find him," Scottie Too Lite interjected. "He was a hero to all the hillfolk around here. Everybody helped him hide."

"Hey now, we've come a ways since John Wilkes Booth was given safe harbor after shooting Lincoln," I protested.

"We're sure glad to finally hear it," Scottie smiled. Fortunately, the stereotype of the backwoods, armed, militia-prone crackpot was not in much evidence on the AT.

Sure enough, when darkness fell I heard the pitter-patter of tiny feet seemingly doing gymnastics all over the rafters and under the sleeping platform. However, none of the creepy scenarios of mice on the forehead, or even worse, materialized. The shelter kept me shielded from the wind despite being open on one side, and I resolved to sleep in them more often.

***

At Winding Stair Gap a mother and father were having an emotional farewell with their daughter, Tigress. They had planned to try to thru-hike with her, but the mother had been shocked by the mountainous terrain and dropped off after thirty-one miles at Neel's Gap. Tigress had continued on with some others until meeting up with her family here at Winding Stair Gap on U.S. 64. Her mother was now making a final plea for her daughter to get off the trail, but her daughter was determined to continue. Tigress was a brown-haired, freckled, young woman in her mid-twenties with a distinctively innocent look about her. After chatting with them a bit she said emphatically, "Skywalker, will you please tell my parents I'll be okay?"

"She looks like a lot safer bet than me," I said. "Have you hiked much, Tigress?"

"Yes," she emphasized. "I'm a wilderness therapist. I lead groups of recovering drug addicts on outdoor trips." Her mother didn't look convinced, but they had a tearful departure and Tigress headed off north alone.

I ran into Tigress again a night later at Cold Spring Shelter after trooping all day alone. Far from looking threatened or out of sorts, Tigress seemed to be having the time of her life in the company of her all-male retinue.

A jolly, confident, healthy-looking fella' in his mid-twenties from Montana named Rooney was entertaining everyone at the shelter with his stories about his thru-hike the previous year.

"Skywalker, the shelter only holds six," Rooney said when he saw me looking around for an open spot to put my sleeping bag. "You can have my spot."

"That's all right," I responded, "I'll just sleep at a right angle to all of you at the entrance to the shelter." This was a group of folks I liked.

The humor took a turn to the bawdy side. I told an obligatory southern incest joke, and there was demand for more. The entertainer in me won out. *What the hell. We were in the middle of nowhere, and they seemed to love them.*

Captain Hook asked, "Is it really true, Skywalker, that they eat their young in the South?"

"Only when we run out of possum pie and squirrel innards," I responded.

Then, out of nowhere, Rooney lit up with a spate of racist jokes. It came as a surprise to everyone; he seemed to be too upbeat and bright to wallow in such filth.

"You can't really be a racist, Rooney," Tigress protested. "You have a full set of teeth."

***

It was a three thousand-foot, sharp drop-off from Wesser Bald to the Nantahala River. Even traversing the switchbacks, it was a rugged descent. Fortunately, I was part of a big group traveling down together. Hiking was often fulfilling, but a big, chatty group like this also made it fun.

Scottie Too Lite and I shared a cabin at the Nantahala Outdoor Club and allowed Captain Hook to sleep in the loft. Hook was an eighteenyear–old, just out of high school who had been accepted to Harvard, but was delaying it for a semester to thru-hike the AT.

"How in the world could you pass up Harvard for the AT?" Scottie Too Lite wanted to know.

"Everybody said I would learn more on the AT than in my first semester of college," Captain Hook replied.

Scottie Too Lite wowed several of us at dinner with details of his meticulous planning for the AT. He was optimistic at all times and equally voluble. One female hiker named Scholar claimed that one day she had been listening to him talk non-stop about every bit of trail minutiae to the point that she couldn't take it anymore. She began to run from him. She swore that as she fled he ran after her talking nonstop.

Scottie went to the pay phone at about nine o'clock to call his wife. Forty-five minutes later he came back ashen-faced.

"Hey man," Captain Hook said, "what happened?"

Uncharacteristically terse, Scottie said, "My daughter in France."

"Oh no," I said alarmed.

"Well, she's okay right this minute," he said, "but I have to get off the trail."

Scottie was kept off the trail for more than a month, but didn't give up. He got back on the trail and began racing all-out every day. But, on October 7 torrential rains made the trail impassable in Massachusetts and he spent several days waiting to cross a swollen, impassable stream. Finally, he had no choice but to give up on his dream. He's now back in the computer business and wondering if he will ever get another shot at a thru-hike.

***

We had been warned that the pull out of Nantahala would be the most difficult thus far. That alert, combined with a dire weather forecast, had me tense. Unfortunately, most of the group I had traveled with the previous day had dispersed.

The first eight miles up to Cheoah Bald offered a net ascent of 3,300 feet. Almost immediately upon embarking, thunder began rattling in the distance and my gut tightened. The tendency in such situations is to hurry, which I tried to resist. Attempting to sprint up a mountain that long and steep was a hopeless enterprise.

Big, cold rain drops began to pelt me, and the sky became a veritable pyrotechnics show. The conditions steadily worsened with the elevation. I saw a tarp set up very low to the ground, right in the middle of the trail. Squatting down I yelled inside, "Hello, dry person."

"Skywalker, is that you?" Seth's voice came from parallel to the ground. "With your height you might want to look for somewhere to hide," he yelled out.

"I'll see you at the shelter," I said and hurried off.

I had never thought my height made me much more vulnerable to lightning, despite many jokes over the years. But someone at the Appalachian Trail headquarters had told me that lightning (which travels at a decidedly brisk two hundred seventy thousand miles per hour and has the width of a pencil) was an underrated source of danger. I would later meet a hiker named Lightning Rod, who had twice been indirectly struck by lightning in previous years on the AT.

But the one thing my height did make me vulnerable to was getting "clothes-lined." In the rain I would wear my baseball cap with the bill pulled low and the hood of the marmot jacket pulled to my eyebrows. This reduced my line of vision to just a few feet. Many times in the rain I would be walking along, only to have my head ram into some low-lying limb. Every time it rained I worked on my technique to avoid such headers, but never completely solved the problem.

As for trying to stay dry — forget it. All that expensive equipment we had purchased, with expert advice about how this or that piece would keep you from getting wet, ran into overwhelming reality on days like this. A hiker just had to become resigned to listening to the staccato patter of rain drops bouncing off synthetic equipment as your backpack, clothing, and persona became ever more water-logged.

A couple hundred yards farther up the mountain someone called out, "Skywalker."

It was Tigress, hiding under some thick rhododendron bushes that lined the trail. Joining her, I asked "Do you think we should head back down the mountain? We're heading to exposed areas."

"No, that's not a good idea," she said calmly. The minute there was a letup in the intensity of the rain we hightailed it to the Sassafras Gap Shelter and settled in for what would be a long, miserable afternoon.

As the afternoon progressed, the shelter filled up, and the conversation was lively. One couple, Greenpeace and Greenleaf, were doing their doctoral theses in environmental science and couldn't wait to get to the Smokies to view all the rare plant species there. Indeed, the southern Appalachians in Georgia, North Carolina, and Tennessee are said to boast greater biodiversity than any deciduous forests in the world.

"We're from Asheville," Greenpeace said. "It's the San Francisco of the South." The counterculture element on the trail was strong.

Normally quite social, I sat curled up in the corner of the shelter, in a sullen mood. I have always been cold-natured, due to my tall, thin frame. Nonetheless, I had lived through ten Chicago winters. But the stark difference was that on frigid days there I always went inside at the end of the day. Out here I was stuck outside with neither the prospect of warmth, nor a good night's sleep.

As things stood I had only done 5.9 miles for the day, which was not a pace that would get me to Maine before winter.

∗∗∗

The next day was to be the coldest single day I experienced on the AT. It was a sharp climb to Cheoah Bald, and the visibility steadily worsened. The one thing I could see was a tarp set up right at the top of the bald, just ten feet from a steep dropoff! *Is this person crazy or am I just a wimp?*

I practically ran to get off the exposed bald, but then it began to sleet. This brought out my worst phobias, and I hurried to catch up with Seth. Not having expected weather quite this bad, I had taken off my long johns before hiking, and didn't want to slow down to put them on. This was a mistake; the same one I had made on Blue Mountain in Georgia.

"The nice thing about sleet," Seth said, "is that you don't get wet." The guidebook was wrong. The topography in this section was ferocious and made all the more difficult by the high winds buffeting us. Once again I was urinating every fifteen minutes. "Looks like you're hypothermic again," Seth noted in half droll, half-serious fashion.

We finally descended steeply into Steccoah Gap. But the powerful wind howling through the gap made it impossible to take the usual break before beginning the climb out of the gap.

The ATC guidebook didn't even mention a climb out of Steccoah Gap, which was a grievous oversight. Had I known what lay immediately ahead I might have tried to hitchhike somewhere on the highway that runs through the gap. The trail ran straight up the mountain, with the wind tearing at me from the west. It was impossible to keep up with Seth as he galloped ahead. That was a bad sign for the simple reason that I had usually outpaced him during the first couple weeks on the trail.

On the steep ascent I ran into Ken and Ruth, a middle-aged couple from Michigan. Ruth was reed-thin and diminutive, while Ken had a strong, ruddy complexion and a powerful gait. As I passed by he was cheerleading her with the likes of, "Yes, honey. You're the one. This is your trail." Ruth, meanwhile, had a stricken, exasperated look. She also appeared to be the only person on the trail colder than I was.

Coming the opposite direction, down the mountain, I made out the face of Uncle Charlie. He had passed by the shelter the previous day and then announced in his salt-and-vinegar style that he was going to continue despite the weather.

"Uncle Charlie," I called out as he approached, "looks like you've found the best direction to hike this bloody mountain."

After letting out a blue streak of expletives, he said defiantly, "Fuck this. I'm going back to Florida."

As he quickly disappeared into the fog I began to wonder if I shouldn't at least follow him down to the road. Instead, I stopped to quickly eat a Pop Tart. Ken and Ruth trudged past, and I handed them each a piece as they grunted thanks between gasps of breath.

After nine miles I finally arrived at Brown Fork Gap Shelter, which had been my intended destination the previous day. It was sleeting again and Seth was lying there in his sleeping bag. I quickly pulled mine out and jumped in to preserve my body temperature, but the shelter was exposed to the cutting wind. It was useless. The discussion all around was whether to risk going, but staying there in that kind of cold also seemed like a risk to me. I was seriously considering retracing the 2.5 miles I had just climbed to get back to the road.

Ken was urging Ruth to continue. She looked as enthusiastic about heading out as she would have over the prospect of contracting leprosy. Her hands were so cold, even wearing mittens, that Ken had to buckle up her backpack. "We'll be okay, honey," he said as he literally physically aided her forward progress back to the trail. (Their game effort lasted another 150 miles).

One way or another I had to get out of there as well. Bidding Seth goodbye, I retraced the side trail on which the shelter lay to get back to the AT. Up to within five feet of arriving at the AT I honestly didn't know whether I was going to take a left to go back down the mountain I had just climbed or take a right and go forward.

I turned right and continued north, but once again I wondered if my life was at risk from exposure. It's unnatural to do any strenuous physical activity without breathing through your mouth. However, the one useful thing I had taken away from two years as a feckless kung-fu student back in Chicago was how much energy a person can save by breathing through the nose. It helps relax the muscles and regulates the energy flow. As I bore into the howling winds and sleet, focusing on this efficient breathing technique helped relieve my anxiety, despite the trail being abandoned. After several miles of roller-coaster terrain I was elated to come across Yellow Creek Mountain Road.

I walked three miles down it without seeing a soul, until the well-known Hike Inn came into view. Jeff and Nancy Hoch offered me a room and a ride into town to resupply.

Out in the parking lot to my surprise were Tigress, Greenpeace, and Greenleaf. They had gotten off back at Steccoah Gap and hitchhiked here. That was ironic considering that I had been treated at the shelter the previous evening as some sort of hypothermic freak show, but lasted longer in the diabolical weather today than they had. That evening I savored one glass of ice water after another without ever urinating — a sure sign of deep dehydration.

I awoke buoyant at the Hike Inn, after my first good night's sleep on the trail. Yesterday's gruesome-but-successful march in adverse conditions seemed like a big step forward mentally. Jeff drove me back to the trailhead to hike the remaining seven miles to Fontana Dam.

I came upon Seth and Rooney in the Cable Gap Shelter after less than a mile. Both had the grizzled look of having been in the woods; they were poorly fed, cold, wet, and were moaning about everything. I, on the other hand, was clean, well-shaven, well-fed, warm, and upbeat. The tables had been turned on them, and in unison they exclaimed, "Asshole," when I walked up. We started hiking, and I noticed I had regained my speed.

At the top of the mountain Fontana Dam came into full focus. Built by the TVA during the Depression, it is the largest dam east of the Mississippi, and the view is spectacular.

When we got to the dam there was a booth set up to get a free permit to enter Great Smoky Mountain National Park.

Chapter 5

Smoky Mountain National Park, which is spaced out on both sides of the North Carolina-Tennessee border, is the most visited national park (ten million annual visitors) in the United States. The Smokies are labeled the second wettest place in America, and are especially renowned among AT thru-hikers because this is where the trail passes through its very highest elevations. Due to the sudden upward thrust in elevation out of the Tennessee Valley the weather here in April is utterly unpredictable — *in the spring it rains twenty out of thirty days in these parts.* Many experts suggest hikers carefully plan their entrance into the Smokies — the same advice given for the White Mountains in New Hampshire.

Sal Paradise and Scavenger arrived at the Fontana Dam Shelter — affectionately known as the Fontana Hilton — and immediately began marveling at this piece of trail handiwork which includes a heated shower among its amenities. Sal, a lanky 6'5" Wisconsinite, was making his second attempt at a thru-hike after being injured in Virginia the previous year. He was being sponsored on the trail by his hometown Lutheran Church. We wandered down to the Fontana Dam Visitor's Center, where a bulletin board had the weather forecast.

"Rain," Sal said calmly upon returning. "I'm taking today off."

"I'll second that," his hiking partner, Scavenger, replied.

"I'll never make it to Maine at this rate," I said in anguish.

"Don't worry about miles at this stage," Sal intervened. "Virginia's a twenty-mile superhighway." I was modestly assuaged, although it was worth noting the irony that he had dropped off in Virginia the previous year.

At 11:30 that morning Sal and I went up to the bridge of Fontana Dam, which the trail runs right over. I spent the next two hours in Hamlet mode over whether to head into the Smokies.

I still didn't think I was going to head in this afternoon, until Sal noted an area of blue sky poking through the clouds. This was like a shot of adrenaline, and I jumped up to go retrieve my backpack. "Come on, Sal," I said with sudden urgency. "We can make Mollie's Ridge Shelter before dark."

But Sal replied, "You never know if it's one of those sucker blue spots. I'm waiting for tomorrow."

So off I went, alone and uncertain, into the Smokies.

It was a three thousand-foot climb and 12.4 miles to Mollie's Ridge Shelter. My work was cut out for me.

Further, to be perfectly honest, I was worried about bears. Except for a brief respite in southern Pennsylvania the possibility of bear encounters extends throughout the entire AT. But Smoky Mountain National Park, along with Shenandoah National Park and New Jersey, is one of three places on the AT with the highest concentration of bears. Practically everybody who has ever hiked in the Smokies seemed to have some story of a bear encounter to relate. I had discreetly questioned everyone I could about bears and the responses ran the gamut from "Don't worry. All you will ever see is the back of them as they are running away," to "You just don't really know what the hell a bear is gonna do."

On the way up Shuckstack Mountain I heard thunder, and immediately the old phobias surfaced again. Then, it began to drizzle. Rain changes everything, especially at high elevations. I could have been back at Fontana Dam, warm and dry, waiting for tomorrow, when the weather report looked much more favorable. Instead, I was unnecessarily headed out into cold, rain, and misery. Such are the maudlin sentiments of the novice hiker.

The rain worsened. As I stopped to add another layer of clothing before summitting Shuckstack Mountain, a couple middle-aged section hikers passed headed toward Fontana Dam. "How far away is the top of Shuckstack?" I asked.

"It's only about a mile, but pretty steep," he half-shouted through the wind and rain. Then, he added, "The weather is kinda' nasty up there."

"I believe it," I replied. "You've got a solid-downhill cakewalk back to Fontana Dam."

"Music to our ears," one replied, and they hustled on eagerly. I looked back at them enviously and started to trudge on. Then, reasoning that the absolutely single biggest problem I had faced thus far was clearing mountaintops in heavy wind and rain, I made a split-second decision to cut my losses. Hurrying back down the mountain I caught up with the trailing hiker. After a bit of chatter I asked if they could give me a ride into Fontana Village when they reached the bottom of the mountain. They readily agreed, and as we continued down

The fullness of my face at the outset of the journey was pretty much gone by the time I hit the Mid-Atlantic States.

the mountain I tallied my losses. I had climbed about four miles, and thus was going to have walked eight miles at the end of the day with no forward progress to show for it. My equipment and clothes would be soaked, and it was another blow to my confidence.

They dropped me off in Fontana Village, which was a summer resort with a deep discount on off-season rooms. After a warm shower I entered the dining room and saw Sal Paradise and Scavenger enjoying a buffet dinner. "Have you decided to turn around and hike back home to Georgia?" Sal asked incredulously

The nice thing about having come to long-distance hiking so late in life is that I had no hiker ego. So I proceeded to describe my latest mishap.

"Skywalker, just stay with us; we'll get you through the Smokies in one piece" Scavenger said with a confidence belying his mere nineteen years.

"And the weather is supposed to be good the next few days," Sal added.

***

So off I went the next day into the Great Smoky Mountains for a second time — and alone again because Sal Paradise and Scavenger had evacuated the Fontana Hilton when I passed by. The weather was pretty good at the outset, but, once again, the higher I went the worse it looked. The trail climbed steadily for miles to reach Doe Knob and the crest of the Smokies. At this point the AT maintains high elevations for the next sixty miles. And this was where the wind picked up and sleet began pelting me. I had turned around the previous day hoping for good weather this day. More regrets.

When I finally arrived at Mollies Ridge Shelter on my second attempt to reach it, Sal Paradise, Scavenger, and others were starting a fire, even though it was only about two in the afternoon. "Sal, it doesn't appear that you have a career as a weather forecaster," I needled him.

Scavenger, jumping into the fray, retorted, "You could have turned around and gone back to Fontana Dam again." TouchŽ for Scavenger.

"Ya'll aren't stopping here, are ya'?" I asked.

"No," Sal assured me. "We're just warming up."

But an hour later the wind and sleet had become predominant, and there was no sign of progress on anybody's part. The shelter was beginning to fill up, and it seemed prudent to claim a spot. Because of heavy use the shelters in the Smokies are made of concrete, rather than the typical rickety wooden structures. This shelter had an upper and lower deck and given my longstanding habit of nocturnal urinations, the lower deck seemed a better choice. But even that would be problematic because the upper deck is only about three feet above the lower-deck floor.

Once again, the biggest problem would be staying warm. Scavenger, appropriately, was in charge of scavenging for wood to build a fire. The bigger logs were wet, rendering them useless unless someone could break them apart. "Hey, SkyWalker," somebody called out. "This shouldn't be any problem for you with that wide arc."

I put on my mittens and started heaving wet logs away against a stump.

"Skywalker is from the South," someone commented. "Surely he's lifted many a bale of cotton."

"Then why aren't those logs cracking apart crisply," Scavenger asked skeptically.

Right then a rambunctious thru-hiking foursome arrived at the shelter and immediately one of the two males ran over and started flailing logs wildly at the stump. Everybody was shouting, "Come on, Joe, you're the man." Finally, he achieved a breakthrough, to great applause.

Joe was from Ireland, and he was hiking with another Irishman, Guiness. Two girls were with them. One was O'Connor, a short, leggy speedster and former New York state junior tennis champion who had her head shaved like the singer Sinead O'Connor. The other was Thumper, a muscular New Hampshirite who had worked as a cook at the international station in Antarctica the previous year.

I gloomily sat in the corner, munching on cold bagels and peanut butter as everybody else enthusiastically went about cooking with their stoves. Once again it seemed I had on more clothes than anybody, but was colder than everybody. It was beginning to dawn on me just what a long, difficult slog the Smokies were going to be.

By nightfall the shelter, with a capacity of sixteen, held at least twenty. Items from backpacks to wet clothes were hung out to dry all over the shelter. A quiet-spoken couple on their honeymoon broke an impasse over the last couple possible spots by volunteering to camp outside.

My sleeping bag and pad were sandwiched between Sal Paradise and the wall, and I warned him I wouldn't be able to sleep through the night in this cold weather.

"What's your sleeping bag rated?" Sal wanted to know.

"Fifteen degrees," I answered. Everybody was constantly touting their sleeping bag ratings. But after shivering through so many nights I had come to the conclusion that the rating is the temperature up to which the bag will keep you alive, not the temperature at which you can sleep.

With six layers up top and two sets of long-johns for my lower body, I was warm in my down sleeping bag. But when I woke up to visit the bushes the wind was howling overwhelmingly through the mountain passes. *The power of nature both awed and terrified me.* Even though the shelter was frigid at least it provided protection from the wind, and I honestly wondered if I could make it through a night like this without a spot in there.

I was damn glad to see the first shade of light and quickly packed up and headed out on the trail. The sun was beginning to appear over the horizon, so it looked like a chance to make a lot of miles after the previous day's weather-shortened hike. Russell Field Shelter was only a few miles up the trail. When I arrived a couple of the inhabitants from the previous evening were still there.

"Hey," I said. "Did ya'll have a full house last night?"

"No," one hiker wearily replied. "But that didn't keep a black bear standing on her hind legs from clawing at the grilled fence during the night." It occurred to me, not for the first or last time, that I could have run into either this or some other bear during a midnight urination.

Animal life in the Smokies is a rich topic. After being almost exterminated early in the last century bears have made a stunning comeback. It's estimated that more than a thousand bears currently live and eat in the park. They are so numerous that park officials have constructed grilled fences on the shelters to keep them out.

Unlike the bear population, the wolf population in the park was completely exterminated by hunters early last century. With this top predator eliminated, small and medium-sized animals, ranging from deer to raccoon to mice, now saturate the park.

Another shock to the ecosystem occurred in the 1920s, when hunting clubs released Russian wild boars, weighing up to four hundred pounds, into the southern Appalachians. This was the sport of European royalty and attracted throngs of hunters from across the Atlantic.

But soon after the hunting clubs introduced the boars, the National Park Service realized they had badly miscalculated. Boars feed voraciously on the native vegetation, and most of their diet consists of things they have to dig up. They use their enormous power to rototill the forest floor, thus wreaking havoc on the food supply of other animals.

Park officials set out to remedy their blunder by hunting the wild boar population in the southern Appalachians to extinction. However, they quickly realized the enormity of the original error. Wild boars are the most prolific mammal in North America. They start breeding at seven or eight months and often have litters of four or five. *Park officials now estimate that they have to kill half the existing population annually in order to just maintain a stable boar population.* One ranger told us he goes out several nights a week hunting wild boars, and that a group of bears often follows him to feast on his kills.

Meanwhile, in the 1990s Smoky Mountain National Park introduced the red wolf to the region to try to counter the overpopulation of deer, raccoons, skunks, rabbits, mice, etc. The locals in the surrounding valleys were extremely skittish about this idea. But so far, the results have been encouraging. The wolves have preferred feasting on medium-sized animals with little damage to livestock in the pastures below. Better yet, wolves, the very best hunters in the entire animal kingdom, have shown no interest whatsoever in smelly hikers!

***

About midday the sky surprisingly started to darken again, but I counseled calm, to myself, as well as to Sal Paradise and Scavenger. "Don't worry; they're probably just localized clouds," I said. "I saw the weather forecast last thing before leaving Fontana Dam yesterday and it's supposed to be perfect today." The wind then picked up, it got colder and started to sleet.

"Skywalker," Scavenger said. "Let us know about any other pearls of wisdom, okay?"

"Welcome to the Smokies, boys," Sal said. "Everybody who came through last year put up with the same crap."

Despite it being late April, most of the trees were bare due to the high elevations. In fact it still looked like the dead of winter.

I arrived at Derrick Knob Shelter at 1:30 in a grim mood, as the sleet was now coming down steadily. The speed team of the two Irishmen, O'Connor, and Thumper were eating lunch. Are ya'll planning on going on?" I asked. "You know the next shelter at Siler's Bald is at 5,500 feet."

Soon most of the others from the previous night's shelter arrived, and it became clear that everybody was stalled out. For the second straight afternoon we were all stuck in a shelter having hiked an unsatisfying 11.7 miles. I was fatigued by the cold and my poor night's sleep. I was going to be miserable and unable to relax.

Misery loves company, of course, and I found some grim satisfaction that Sal Paradise and Scavenger seemed humbled by the elements as well. A month earlier park rangers had airlifted four college students by helicopter out of this exact shelter due to hypothermia. It was almost twenty miles to the lone road crossing in the Smokies. Between here and there lay Clingman's Dome, the highest point on the entire Appalachian Trail. Thus, it was quite probable that the same joyless scene was going to be repeated at some shelter the next evening, only the elevation would be even greater and the weather even colder. But then I had an idea.

***

"Hey, I've got it," I said to Sal and Scavenger. "The guidebook says there's an observatory for sightseeing at Clingman's Dome."

"So," Scavenger replied.

"Well, according to this, a half-mile down a side trail from the observatory is a public bathroom."

"And…" Scavenger said, slightly annoyed.

"We can hike ten miles to there tomorrow," I replied, "and spend the night in the bathroom. It might even be heated. Anything will be better than freezing our asses off another night in a crowded shelter."

Sal had a Ward Cleaver-like reasonable-man persona. But as he considered the idea a smile began to purse his lips. "I'm sick of this whole scene," he said to Scavenger. Looking outside at the diabolical weather he added, "And the bathroom back at Fontana Dam wasn't that bad."

Looking skeptically through his wire-rimmed glasses Scavenger intoned, "It's a totally fucked-up idea. But given the alternatives it has some logic. What's it going to smell like in there?"

"A lot like us," Sal replied.

Looking around at everybody crammed into this shelter I excitedly whispered, "Hey, there is sure as hell not room for everybody else in here to do it also unless people are sleeping on top of toilets. Let's keep it to ourselves."

My morale had been given a sharp boost by the prospect of being out of this cold within the next twenty four hours. Better yet, I, *Mr. Incompetent and Helpless in the Woods*, had hatched this brilliant plot all by myself. A flourish of pride swept over me.

Scavenger still seemed dubious about the whole enterprise and a little later in the maelstrom of the shelter I heard him calmly tell the person to his left, "We're going to spend the night in a bathroom tomorrow night and take shits all night."

As the seemingly interminable afternoon and evening wore on, the same group of five that had seemed so cliquish the previous evening was continually howling with laughter among themselves. But the worst part was they were making jokes about sleeping in the bathroom.

"Skywalker," Sal asked me. "Do we have a claim on the bathroom if it was our idea first?"

"At that altitude I'm not being denied," I declared.

Stories abounded on the trail of shelters so densely packed that everybody has to sleep sideways. When somebody needs to shift sides, there is a countdown, one-two-three, and all twenty or thirty bodies shift in unison. I never got in one that completely crowded, but this evening was the closest thing to it. We looked like circus clowns we were so packed in, with the hoods of our sleeping bags cinched in the cold.

Derrick Knob Shelter —mile 191

4-28-05: Muslims kneel with their heads on the ground pointed towards Mecca. We hikers should do the same for several hours per day, but with our heads aimed at Mount Katahdin. — SkyWalker

Again, I was up at first light. But there was more company this morning because with the higher elevation it had been even colder than the previous evening. And unlike the previous day, this day didn't even start out nice as the wind, fog, and periodic sleet predominated.

The worrisome thing was that the group that had been joking about sleeping in the bathroom was preparing to leave with uncharacteristic dispatch. When they filed out of the shelter and disappeared into the fog Sal, Scavenger, and I looked at each other thinking the same thing.

"Bastards," Scavenger yelled in their direction.

***

The trail was a quagmire from the steady precipitation and heavy use. Whereas I had only fallen once in the first two hundred miles, my legs came out from under me several times in the next ten miles. Inevitably, many hikers, including me, tried walking off to the side of the trail or even to straddle it.

When Sal, Scavenger, and I got to Siler's Bald Shelter at 5,460 feet the drizzle had turned into a steady rain and the visibility was now reduced to about fifty feet. We were getting ready to head up to Clingman's Dome, the highest point on the AT, where things could only be worse.

Renewing my concerns about hypothermia, I was reduced to muttering, "God, all that physical conditioning and weight-gaining I did for months to get ready for the AT and it all goes out the window in nineteen days. I can feel myself hemorrhaging weight. And that makes you more vulnerable to hypothermia. I'm back to pissing a lot. It all weakens you."

"Skywalker, you exaggerate," Scavenger jumped in, protesting. "We're all in the same damn situation; cold as shit. You don't look like you're about to die and you're keeping up with us."

Scavenger was iconoclastic, but not egocentric. So despite the irony of a nineteen-year old lecturing a forty-four-year-old, I said, "I apologize. And you can bet your bottom dollar when the weather finally turns warm, you won't hear a single word of bitching out of me." It was a promise I was to keep.

I pulled out my sleeping bag and lay inside it to retain body heat, with my backpack as a pillow. An air of indecisiveness pervaded the shelter. Finally, Sal Paradise got up very purposefully, strapped on his backpack, said, "Love it or leave it," and disappeared up the mountain and into the fog. I got up and followed him by a few minutes.

I continued trying to straddle and walk to the side of the trail in order to avoid wallowing or falling in the mud. Sal and I were turning one corner and I took an especially wide turn away from the muddy trail when I heard somebody screaming at me from the opposite direction. "You're not hiking on the Appalachian Trail," the voice berated me. "I don't know what trail it is, but it's not the Appalachian Trail."

A late twenty-ish fellow with a patch on his jacket that said "Ridge Runner" came right up to me and yelled, "Why are you off the trail?" I filibustered a bit that I was falling a lot and the trail was dysfunctional. Sal looked on amused. He had been doing the same thing, if not in the serial fashion I was. But a tongue lashing was the least of my concerns; being cold was the foremost.

"Is there a public bathroom at Clingman's Dome?" I asked him.

"Yes, but don't sleep in there," he immediately shot back. "A group ahead of you just asked me the same thing." Sal and I looked knowingly at each other (*"those slimebags."*)

When I started to head off he renewed his magisterial tone, "Now let me see you stay on the trail."

"But look at the damn trail," I said, exasperated.

"That's what you bought those expensive boots for," he answered with certainty. "Plant them in the mud and put one foot after another. That way you will avoid a two-hudred-dollar citation."

The part about one foot in front of another proved prophetic. The trail soon turned up a narrow ledge that didn't allow any more lateral dodges. Two guys who had been at the shelter the previous evening came up and I ended up between them, silently marching one foot after another in the mountain's deep mud. I felt like a pack mule.

We were nearing the highest point on the AT, as evidenced by the falling temperature. The high altitude and Fraser fir trees lent the area an alpine setting belying its comparatively southern geographical location. It was a pristine setting and gave impetus for a tired person to keep on humping.

Finally, the sign appeared pointing to Clingman's Dome Observatory Tower. Sal was waiting there, and Scavenger soon arrived from behind. We were now at the highest point on the entire Appalachian Trail and very close to the highest point in the eastern United States.

A U.S. Senator from Tennessee, named Clingman, had maintained a long-running dispute with a professor from North Carolina, named Mitchell, over which state had the highest peak. Finally, both mountains were surveyed and the mountain in North Carolina was forty feet higher than Clingman's Dome. So Professor Mitchell had won, but, lo and behold, fell to his death from a cliff on the mountain bearing his name.

***

Desperate is desperate. We started the half-mile trek to the Clingman's Dome bathroom. All along the way we engaged in false bravado about what we'd do if we arrived and the group from last night's shelter already had it fully occupied. "With ten million visitors per year in this park they ought to have a half-decent place to take a crap," I said hopefully.

"The women's bathroom might make more sense from the standpoint of hygiene," Sal noted dryly.

"No, let's do this right, dammit," I said insistently.

Suddenly, two barracks-like buildings appeared out of the fog to the left. We entered the bathroom which was empty, but the first impression was uninviting. It was dingy and somewhat cramped quarters. The ceiling was low, and it would be a stretch to fit three people unless one of us slept with his head under a urinal. Worse yet, the floor was covered with a cleaning solution that would get our sleeping bags wet.

"Skywalker," Scavenger said loudly, "I can see my breath. It's cold as shit in here."

"Well, it's warmer than a damn shelter," I said defensively

"Look at all this steam rising off my urine," Sal exclaimed. "What temperature is it in here?"

Irked, I said, "Well, let's see what the women's restroom is like." But a quick tour revealed that the fundamentals were essentially the same. We had to decide what to do, and quickly.

We were on a ridge, well above six thousand feet, and exposed to howling winds. Downhill from the bathrooms was a parking lot for the Clingman's

Dome Observatory. Not surprisingly, it was practically abandoned. Further, it was twenty-two miles down winding mountain roads to the resort town of Gatlinburg. It was obvious we couldn't stay out here exposed for long.

Another hiker we recognized from the previous night's shelter, Snackman, appeared in the distance.

"There's a couple without a backpack behind me," he reported.

Presuming they owned one of the three remaining vehicles in the lot, I said, "Sal, use your diplomatic skills on them." Sal walked over to them and, after a quiet conversation, he came back and flashed the thumbs-up sign.

We loaded up our backpacks and started down the cold, windy trek down a snake of a road. Then suddenly I screamed to Sal, "Where the hell is Scavenger?"

He looked around alarmed. Three of us were in the back of the pickup truck. But Snack Man, the new arrival, was the third.

"Oh, my God! What should I do?" Sal panicked. He started beating on the window at the driver and signaling back up the mountain, but to no avail.

"We've been together since the second day on the trail," he moaned disconsolately.

***

The steep road to Gatlinburg offered some of the finest scenery I've ever witnessed. Lush green forests, sharp, jagged mountains, and rushing water abounded. The temperature and visibility increased steadily as we descended. By the time the driver dropped us off in Gatlinburg I was in disbelief.

"It's twenty or thirty degrees warmer down here than up on the mountain," I said exuberantly.

"Oh yeah," Sal said. "Weather forecasts in town are utterly useless to hikers."

I was even more cheerful as we checked in at the one motel in town, which was known as "hiker friendly." Some didn't even allow such vermin on their grounds. While I sat there savoring the comforts of this downmarket motel, Sal said, "I've got to go back out and see if I can't find Scavenger."

An hour later, Scavenger and Sal walked in and Scavenger yelled out, "Bastards."

After some heated explaining on our part he lashed out again. "None of those assholes in their fancy cars would pick me up once I got to the main road. Finally, some hippies came along in an old car and were decent enough to give me a lift."

I had known Sal Paradise and Scavenger for six days and Snack Man for two hours, but we laughed and clowned it up that night at dinner as if we were all best friends. The grim conditions of the past three days had given us that elusive sense of shared ordeal. All things considered I couldn't think of anywhere I'd rather be, or anything I'd rather be doing. Not even a phone call to my mother dampened my mood. She expressed disbelief that I had made just fifty miles of forward progress in the last week. "Bill, you had better start thinking of making it to New Jersey," she advised.

Chapter 6

The Appalachians have had a tremendous effect on the country's development. It's a 2,500-mile chain of more or less continuous mountain ridges and valleys. They span three hundred to 350 miles in width in the southern Appalachians, and eighty to one hundred miles of width in the northern regions, and are consistently more steeply inclined and jagged than the Rockies and Sierras. In fact, this inhospitable terrain had the effect of restricting the British settlement of the Americas to thirteen seaside colonies. And to this day there are still only a handful of roads that pierce the hills to link the east coast with the heartland.

Looking over the craggy, rugged landscape, another thought occurred as well: No wonder people living in terrain like this tend to be more provincial and less cosmopolitan than somebody living in Manhattan or Boston. These two seaboard cities have easy waterway access to ships from all over the world. What's more, as major entry ports for immigrants, they're regularly exposed to diverse cultures and ideas. Compare that to people living in these parts. It was often said they live so far in the "hollers" they have to pipe in the daylight. Of course, in popular culture this has all spawned multitudes of yarns about incestuous hillbillies.

But the hardworking, pleasant nature of the denizens of these parts has won over many an unsuspecting soul from other parts. Thomas Jefferson, a Virginian, believed virtue and character came directly from rootedness and attachment to the land. This set him in direct opposition to rival Alexander Hamilton, a New York central banker, who extolled the virtues of large cities. Needless to say, the AT is an overwhelmingly Jeffersonian experience.

***

Miraculously, the weather had cleared and we were afforded some of the breathtaking views the Smokies are known for. We passed an area known as "Charlie's Bunion," a rocky outcropping that stuck out like a bunion on a hiker's foot. Then the trail traipsed a chillingly narrow shelf called "the Sawteeth," which features steep cliffs on both sides, poised above scenes of incredible mountain grandeur. This exposed ridge would have been nigh impossible to do in the wet, windy weather of a few days before. But despite the often miserable weather and rugged terrain the Smokies are a must-see destination.

Finally, the trail finally left the ridgeline and descended several miles into a forest bursting with spring flowers and watery coves. The northeastern boundary of Smoky Mountain National Park is at Davenport Gap. Standing Bear, a new hostel, had just opened near there. The owner, Curtis, showed me around his newly constructed bunk house, but as usual, the bunks weren't nearly long enough. He asked if I minded sharing the guesthouse with another hiker.

The hiker, named "Drama," was doing "work for stay," an arrangement in which a hiker does various tasks around the hostel in return for free stay. It wasn't clear whether Drama was male or female, a mystery that created a stir among other hikers. When Curtis noted my apparent reluctance he said, "What have you got to lose if it's a he-she or she-he? You've got a bed to sleep in." His reasoning was ineluctable, and I nodded my assent.

Around the campfire that night Drama regaled us with her trials and tribulations. "I was a sex worker for several years," Drama intoned. "I specialized in S&M."

"What is S&M?" I meekly asked. It must have been a stupid question the way everyone looked at me — not Drama — strangely.

"Sado-masochism," Drama solemnly said. "I was a dominatrix in several films."

"I'm sorry," I again interrupted reluctantly. "I've heard the word 'dominatrix,' but could you define it for me."

"Sure," Drama replied helpfully. "A dominatrix is someone who takes the upper hand over a man during sex, usually with a combination of toys and weapons." Again *I* seemed to be the person getting the most odd looks and finally decided to go to bed.

When I pulled my clothing bag out I looked all around for both sets of longs johns. Thrashing around frantically everywhere in the backpack it soon became obvious they weren't there. The thought immediately occurred that perhaps Drama thought some XXL long-johns might jazz up her wardrobe in her other career. But the more likely explanation was that while shivering this morning at six thousand feet — as I hurriedly packed up in the maze of clothing and equipment hanging off various hooks in the Tri-Corner Knob Shelter — I hadn't packed them.

Without long-johns I shivered, tossed, and turned again for the second straight night, and wondered if I hadn't spent more energy trying to stay warm that night than in the day's hike. Also, I had gone to bed wondering when Drama was going to return to the room we were sharing, and whether I needed to be on alert. But Drama never arrived, and in the morning I noticed Drama had tented out. Perhaps Drama was just as afraid of me as I was of Drama. If so, that was a well-needed ego boost for an insecure, rookie hiker!

...

It is often a great relief to emerge from extended deep immersion in the woods and confront civilization. And it's especially cool in a town like Hot Springs where hikers follow the white AT blazes on the telephone poles right down the main street. This town's mineral baths had so mesmerized German prisoners of war during World War II that many chose to stay there. One of its main industries now is hikers, and a center of hiker activity is Elmer Hall's Sunnybank Inn.

Elmer had hiked about eighty percent of the trail in 1976. He was so captivated by the experience that he purchased a two-story Victorian edifice in Hot Springs — that is a state historical site — to put up hikers. When I entered he made it clear this was no ordinary business. "You are a guest in my house," he plainly stated. "You are expected to follow my guidelines." He handed me a rules sheet.

"For sure," I replied and ambled upstairs with my backpack.

I wandered down the main street where hikers were making rounds of the usual places (outfitter, grocery store, Laundromat, Post Office).

I passed a motel where a tall, leggy brunette was pulling something out of a red Volkswagen. Our eyes met and she came over to ask, "We saw you walking into town and were making bets. Just how tall do you happen to be anyway?"

"Almost as tall as my little sister," I replied to her horror. (My sister is actually 5'10").

"Are you a hiker?" I wanted to know.

"Not only am I a hiker," she replied, "but I hiked the entire *width* of the Appalachian Trail just today." This seemed like a pretty good line, but it unfortunately ended up being the first of approximately sixty-three times I would hear it from her over the next several hours.

"Do you want to see my home?" she asked. "My name is Tanya, by the way." No other hiker, or any female on the trail, had invited me to see her home, so I readily accepted.

When we got over to the red Volkswagen, brimming to the top with clothes, she cheerfully said, "Welcome to my home."

"Do you sleep at this motel?" I asked.

"Sure," she replied, "and I've got a big king-size bed you could probably fit in. Come take a look." Entranced, I dutifully followed her as she pulled out the key to her "big" private room.

Upon entering the room she said, "Look at this bed." She jumped into it and lay down as if exhibiting a toy, as I looked on in amazement. "Here, try it," she slapped on the mattress right next to her. "If you have to, you can lie diagonally." This was surreal on the face of it. But there was something about this girl's modus operandi that said she wasn't the genie out of a bottle that she might seem on the surface.

I went to the post office to check on the long-johns I had ordered. When I returned to Tanya's hotel she was engaged in an animated discussion outside her "room" with G.I. Joe, a big, red-headed hiker of about thirty. He trained his total attention on her to the exclusion of me, and I didn't feel compelled or able to outlast him. I moved off to the grocery store to re-supply.

But upon leaving the grocery store I looked across the street and, to my surprise, GI Joe was gone. I would soon find out why. She saw me and yelled out, "Hey, you're not getting away so easy."

Dutifully, I walked back over and into her room. She posed sassily and said, "So what are you afraid of?"

"How much did this big suite cost you?" I asked. It was an obvious question to someone whose home was her car. An awkward look came over her face.

"Have you seen the Indian guy who owns this place?" she asked.

"Can't say that I have," I replied.

"Good," she said. "He might be a little jealous because he has, you know, a thing for me."

Not shocking news. I nodded, "So the price is right, huh?"

"Yeah," she said wearily, "but there is just one catch." I listened in rapt attention. "This guy's weird," she said intently. "I mean really weird. The deal is, and this is the third time I've stayed here, but, he gets to feel my breast for five minutes. And, God, I never knew five minutes could seem so long until

I met this guy."

I was unable to find the appropriate reply, so she continued. "And listen to this," she said in an amazed tone. "The last time when I was staying here I turned to him in the middle of the five minutes and said, 'Can I ask you a question? Are you dehydrated?' He looked confused," she continued, "and said, 'No, why?'"

"*Because your hands are so cold*," she said cracking up.

***

We entered the Bridge Street Cafe to a virtual standing ovation from the tables full of hikers. Sal Paradise and Scavenger were joyfully feasting at the next table after completing a night-time, twenty-two-mile hike into Hot Springs. Scavenger called over, "Skywalker, you're my hero. How do you do it?"

But then Tanya stood up on her chair and announced at the top of her lungs, "I hiked the width of the Appalachian Trail three times today."

Cheers rained out in her direction, which encouraged her to ramp it up. "Fellow hikers," she called out. "After dinner I'm leading a group of any and all takers to the world famous Hot Springs Spa."

She finally sat down, but then her eccentricities began to morph into lunacies. After hugging the blushing waitress several times and aggressively questioning her about her various proclivities toward both the male and female genders she took to her feet on the chair again. "Ladies and gentlemen," she shouted out. "Silence, silence," she barked at an inattentive hiker. "I have a question," she said firmly when all had been hushed. "Does anybody know the difference between a female thru-hiker and a possum?"

"There is no difference" a stray male voice in the back blurted out.

Tanya, luxuriating in her starring role, shouted down all murmurs and blurted out, "The difference is, you *might* consider eating a *possum!*"
The uproar was deafening as the males let out sounds of ecstasy, while the females looked at each other ashen-faced.

"But ladies, ladies, shut up everybody. ... Ladies," Tanya shouted. This was beginning to look like her fifteen minutes of fame. "Raise your hands, raise them high, like this, yeah," she demanded, "if you are a member of the Lorena Bobbit Fan Club."

"Remember our motto, male hikers," she threatened, "*if you abuse it, you lose it!*"

Shouts of pandemonium erupted from all quarters of the restaurant, and Sal and Scavenger screamed over, "Skywalker, watch out tonight."

Finally, to my great relief, the manager came over to diplomatically inform Tanya she would have to depart. I jumped up apologetically and tried escorting Tanya out as boos rang out over our ejection. At the door she gave a curtain call, screaming out, "Happy hiking," at which point a voice in the back shot back, "Happy humping, Skywalker."

When we finally got outside I immediately announced, "I'm headed back to Elmer's."

"I've been to Elmer's," she said. "Do you mind if I tag along with you?"

We got to Elmer's and I began to introduce Tanya to some guests Elmer was entertaining. She dove into conversation ("I hiked the width of the AT three times") as I sat over in a corner. Finally, I went upstairs to bed.

***

An organic breakfast is served at eight o'clock sharp every morning at Elmer's. I got down about fifteen minutes late, grabbed the far chair at the end of the crowded table of hikers, and busied myself eating. A few minutes later everybody cleared out, except Elmer.

"I want you to know," Elmer opened his speech, "that in the thirty years I've been living here and putting up hikers, last night was the single most unpleasant experience I've ever had here." Gnashing his teeth he asked, "What were you thinking? I don't understand such a thought process; bringing somebody over and letting her run amok."

I was hoping to take a "zero (rest) day" and stay another night, and it was quite clear a half-hearted apology wouldn't suffice. "I completely blew it," I said plainly. "I'm embarrassed by the whole thing and apologize."

This seemed to soften him up a bit because he said, "I guess naivete is no crime." But then he added, "This woman is a terrible human being. She offered to have sex with one guest, accused a woman of having fake breasts, and called a close friend of mine a pipsqueak." Finally, his diatribe ended, but it didn't leave me resentful. He was right, and I was damn lucky he didn't chuck me out.

When I walked onto the main street, where hikers were already roaming, I ran into Sal Paradise and Scavenger. "Skywalker," Scavenger knowingly said. "Congratulations."

Sal added: "That girl from last night is looking all over and asking about you."

My stomach sank and I mildly replied, "You guys are giving me more credit than I deserve."

Scavenger would have none of it. "Skywalker," he said wryly, "You're a sandbagger. You always say you can't handle the cold weather, and the other night you claimed to have no interest in getting laid on the trail. Now here you are — the toast of the town."

"Jesus Christ," I muttered as I went off to find this nut case and try to muzzle her.

Bear Can ambled up and said, "Skywalker, that girl from the restaurant last night just asked us where you are." *Oh great.* Bear Can was on anybody's list of most attractive females and popular people on the trail.

Finally, I ran into Tanya near the motel where this whole misadventure had begun. She was standing on a wall wearing a green Mao cap and looking like a street agitator. "Where the heck have you been," she immediately barked out. "Have you made up your mind whether you want to go to the mineral baths?"

I filibustered and headed on, deciding to cut my losses. A while later I passed by and her Volkswagen was gone. I never saw her again. Perhaps the poor owner of the motel had experienced a sudden epiphany. Or maybe he was suffering again from hypothermia in his extremities!

At the beginning of the Appalachian Trail trek the weather in the north Georgia mountains was mountain springtime cool and the forest was still dormant. I signed the register for thru-hikers and was number 1,093.

Chapter 7

It was overdue time for me to mature as a hiker and leave the crises of the first few weeks behind — the unseasonably cold springtime weather had wracked me. And there was another imperative: I had to start covering more miles. It's a sixty-eight-mile hike over consistently mountainous terrain from Hot Springs, North Carolina to Erwin, Tennessee, the next trail town with few road crossings along the way.

I was looking left at the mountains when I exited town and was surprised how long I had to remain on the main road because the AT rarely runs on major roads for any appreciable length. After about fifteen minutes of going straight up the highway and not seeing the trail to the left I flagged down a car and asked, "Is this the AT I'm on?"

"Yeah, yeah, straight up the highway to the bridge," came the friendly reply.

I kept on trooping and even began thinking that the rectangular white reflector plates on the guard rails off to the side of the highway were blazes. After all, they were white and rectangular. But after another mile of walking straight uphill into the sun it just didn't seem possible that this was the trail. So I flagged down another car and sure enough it stopped immediately. "Excuse me, can you tell me if this is the AT?" I pleaded.

"Yes, yes, just go up to the bridge. It's another mile or so." Finally, after hiking uphill another mile, a bridge came into view. I had been walking straight up this highway for about four miles. At the bridge I finally saw a painted white blaze. My attitude was that whatever the hell had happened, and I honestly didn't know, I was at least on the trail now and had a long hike ahead.

I greatly preferred company on the trail, but didn't have any today. I walked all the way up to the Rich Mountain Fire Tower before noticing there weren't any blazes, and had to worriedly retrace my steps back down to find where I had missed a turn. At Allen Gap, the fifteen-mile mark for the day, I finally saw another hiker and began chatting with him. He told me about a hostel on a dirt road about one and a half miles up the trail.

This lifted my somewhat fragile morale, and I bounded on, planning to stay there. After about a mile I began looking; after one and a half miles I became worried; and after two miles I assumed I had missed it. This kind of thing was disheartening and it contributed to my lingering concerns that I was still somewhat illegitimate as a hiker, with little orientation toward critical aspects of the outdoor lifestyle. But the one thing I did pretty well was walk, and the Little Laurel Shelter finally came into view, 19.6 miles from where I had started.

Gus, a nice fellow with a handlebar mustache, was there. I had last seen him three nights before at the Roaring Fork Shelter when he offered me some noodles, and he did so again.

"Boy, Hot Springs is a fabulous trail town, isn't it?" I remarked.

"I don't like towns," he responded to my surprise. "I stopped at the grocery store passing through town and headed on."

"You're a real hiker, Gus," I responded. "The rest of us are just pretenders."

But actually, my true feelings were different. The AT is well developed at this point, with hiker hostels, re-supply points, and hiker-friendly rural towns, all of which facilitated making friends and finding hiking partners. It is now normal to start off alone with the idea of meeting people along the way. And I knew very few hikers who didn't look forward — sometimes to the point of craving — to arriving in one of these backwater trail towns after several days out in the wilderness. The current balance seems just right.

***

G.I. Joe rolled in at dusk. He, of course, had been an early contender in the Tanya sweepstakes before mysteriously disappearing, either from discouragement or good judgment. "You were wise to cut your losses with that girl the other day," I ventured. "She ended up being a bad bet."

"Oh, I never had the least interest in her," he said reflexively.

I didn't know him well enough to kid him (and he was kind of big), but it sure hadn't looked that way at the time.

"Did you go to Iraq?" I asked.

"Yeah, I just got back," he replied. "I'm out here getting back on my feet."

"By the way," I said chattily, "the first few miles up that highway today were a nightmare. I didn't think the AT had any three- or four-mile roadwalks."

"What are you talking about?" G.I. Joe asked. "You didn't walk for miles straight up the highway to get to that bridge?" I asked.

"No way," he said. "The trail turned right on the outskirts of Hot Springs and followed the ridgeline for five miles." Then in disbelief he asked, "You walked up the road?"

I defensively recounted what had happened.

"That's an amazing story," he said.

I sat there, glumly trying to decide if this blunder marred my whole dream of being a thru-hiker. However, I had made good mileage that day in spite of getting lost and, for once, didn't lie shivering throughout the night. I even got something approaching a real night's sleep.

It was a good thing I did because the next day I hiked alone from dawn until dusk. The trail ran for a half mile over Blackstack Cliffs, a jagged boulder field along a ridgeline. It was the first "rock scrambling" (having to move on all fours) for a prolonged period of time. All day I had debated whether I could make it to Hogback Ridge Shelter — a hike that included a two thousand-foot climb late in the day. Needless to say, I was elated when the shelter finally came into view. It was a twenty-one and three-tenths-mile day, the longest yet.

G.I. Joe had arrived there ahead of me and was reunited with three of the people who had tried to purloin our bathroom plan back in the Smokies. On the face of it the four of them were polite, but their body language told a different story. "Well, Skywalker," G.I. Joe wanted to know, "did you find any more roads to take today." The others laughed knowingly; it was quite clear the group had been fully briefed on my previous day's mishap.

Then more pointedly he asked, "What did you think of Blackstack Cliffs?" His tone was subtly insinuating, and it occurred to me that maybe he had been telling the others that I had "blue-blazed." Blue-blazing refers to someone who took a blue-blazed side trail around a difficult part. Indeed, Blackstack Cliffs has a bad weather trail to avoid having to scramble over the exposed rocks in high winds and rain. But, I hadn't taken it, and it bothered me not a little that he might have told the others I had. That might sound like false pride, but it struck straight at the heart of what being a thru-hiker is all about. I resolved then and there that if I managed to make it all the way to Mount Katahdin in northern Maine I would go back to Hot Springs and walk that five-mile section I had inadvertently missed yesterday.

I was determined to make the paces with this group the next day to show I wasn't a fraud. It again entailed a dawn-to-dusk hike, and the trail went over Big Bald Mountain at 5,500 feet. The weather was gorgeous for the third straight day, but I was to see this can be a two-edged sword. For the first time on the AT water became an issue. As important as food is to a hiker, water is even more important.

***

Everybody was asking about water on this hot, sunny day. But there weren't any springs or high-altitude sources of water which thru-hikers often drink straight up. We were forced to draw from the least desirable source of water — streams running at the bottom of mountains in the "gaps" or "notches." This water can be contaminated by either human activity or animal feces. Unlucky users can contract giardia, an intestinal infection that is the bane of long-distance hikers. Stories abounded of hikers sidelined by this malady.

At the last minute, before beginning in April, I had cast aside my newly purchased filter, which is considered the safest option, in favor of chemical tablets. It saved me one pound. Again, the Warren Doyle influence was at work. Warren, after all, doesn't use tablets or a filter. But in his class he admitted that he had once contracted giardia, and it had taken him *seven years* to get rid of it!

The rule of thumb was that a hiker should leave a water source with two full liters, and to be on high alert anytime you fall below one liter. For the first time since that godawful fourth day on the trail I fell below one liter. I was hot and thirsty, and water dominated my thoughts. I kept crossing dried up streams that showed up in the data book as a water source.

I passed a man and woman of approximately sixty-five and thirty-five years old, respectively. He had an erect, martial bearing, and trim physique, while she was rather scantily clad. "Have you seen any water?" she gasped.

"Not hardly," I said dispirited. "And I've been looking."

She quickly turned away in disgust before I could elaborate, while the man stood by stoically. I soon learned the man was Seiko, and this was his new girlfriend. Seiko was known for having hiked anywhere from 10,000 to 30,000 miles on the AT, depending on who you talked to. Some even said he lived on the trail.

"I passed by you at two o'clock asleep in the shelter last night," he said to my surprise.

"You've got to be kidding," I said incredulously. "How did you decide to do that?"

"With the heat and lack of water yesterday night-hiking was a no-brainer," he responded.

It was no surprise that somebody with twenty thousand miles under his belt had a few arrows in his quiver the rest of us didn't have. It also was worth noting his graceful, confident stride despite his relatively advanced age.

Finally, the trail dropped down steeply to Spivey Gap, which U.S. Highway 19W ran through. A stream flowed, albeit slowly. I gulped down the remaining half-liter of the water I previously had, and scooped two cloudy liters of water out of this stream. If nothing else appeared I would have to treat this water with chemicals and drink it. But sure enough, up the next mountain was a stream with white rapids tumbling over rocks. I poured out the two cloudy liters and filled up with this presumably higher-quality water.

The miles weren't coming easily on this day, and I was tired. On a good day I would stop once every three miles, but on a day like this I found myself stopping every mile for a quick swallow of water and a handful of GORP. Finally, I came up on No Business Knob Shelter which made 61.5 miles in three days. *I'm doing better.*

An attractive blondish, reed-thin woman in her late forties was there setting up camp. "Hey, I'm Wrongway Grace," she said. "I'm directionally challenged."

"What is directionally challenged?" I wondered.

"I have a history of hiking the wrong way," she said plainly. Her self-deprecating tone made for delightful company, especially after feeling like the odd man out in the previous night's shelter. Wrongway Grace was about ten years into what was shaping up to be a twenty-year AT section hike. She would have nothing to do with shelters because of an abhorrence of mice and other rodents, and dutifully set up her tent each night. This was in spite of her section hike the previous year when, in Shenandoah National Park, a bear had entered the far end of her tent and snatched her food bag out her backpack. "It was scary," she said.

"No kidding," I replied.

Minnie, a nurse from Michigan who had been with the group the previous evening, arrived soon after I did. "Those three guys are such wimps," she said scornfully. "They didn't want to do this last climb and are going to sleep down by the road."

"Without you around, Minnie," I said delightedly, "who can police them so they don't blue blaze or yellow blaze (take the highway)."

The strings — with cans halfway down — hanging from the shelter roofs are supposed to keep mice from crawling into your food bag. As Minnie and I lay in our sleeping bags she said, "Hey, what's that?"

Jumping up, I yelled "How the hell did that mouse get to my food bag?" The mouse's head was burrowing into the food bag. I grabbed my hiking pole and swatted the back end of the mouse a good fifteen feet in the air. I often heard stories of hikers killing mice and even rattlesnakes and copperheads with their hiking sticks, but this was my best effort. Minnie laughed hysterically. I was in a light mood as well, and would look back on this rugged three-day, sixty-one-mile hike as the turning point for me.

Chapter 8

The fifty-mile stretch from the gorge of the Nolichucky River through the mountains in northwestern North Carolina and northeastern Tennesee is probably the class of the trail before New Hampshire and Maine. It is gorgeous and very difficult. The trail climbs three thousand feet to a big, grassy area aptly known as Beauty Spot. Springtime's blushing beauty was at last revealing itself at these higher elevations. WrongWay Grace only slightly diminished the grandeur of it all by remarking, "If only my boyfriend were here."

When we descended to Beauty Spot Gap where several people were camping for the evening, including sixty-eight-year-old Steady Eddy from Minnesota, Grace said, "This looks like a nice spot for the evening." I looked over and saw what appeared to be the rare perfect spot in a grassy meadow between two trees the right distance apart for a tarp. But it was only five thirty.

"Grace," I said, "we can make it up Unaka Mountain to the Cherry Gap Shelter before dark. It's about five miles."

"I'm quite comfortable right here, thank you," she replied securely.

She had done eleven miles for the day, mostly uphill, which is quite respectable for a section-hiker. But as a thru-hiker I had to be loyal to my miles more than even an enjoyable hiking partner. Thus, WrongWay Grace, Steady Eddie and I said our goodbyes. I didn't see her again and missed her company. I also didn't expect to see Steady Eddie again as he lay there smiling in his sleeping bag after a day of climbing. But that would prove to be a very bad underestimation.

···

AT thru-hikers come together suddenly and spontaneously. Hiking groups just form based on necessity. I had to leave behind some people I enjoyed, and others left me behind based on a survival of the fittest mentality — a kind of "enjoyed it, but we aren't waiting."

When the Cherry Gap Shelter came into view at dusk, the shelter was packed and I immediately went to work looking for a place to set up my tarp. I struggled with various formations, but succeeded in none of them. After cursing myself for switching a tent out for this tarp I finally just threw my sleeping bag down on the ground to attempt sleeping "cowboy style."

A young couple I hadn't yet seen was watching me flail around. He looked to be in his early thirties, short and rather stocky. With his square cut jaw and dark, brown beard he even resembled a younger version of Ulysses S. Grant. She appeared a good bit younger, and with her athletic physique and doe eyes, was extremely attractive. "May I assist you with that tarp?" he asked in his soft-spoken, working-man's style.

"No," I answered, slightly embarrassed. "It's not supposed to rain."

He introduced himself as Whitewater (he's an expert kayaker). The girl, his wife, had the trail name of Nurse Ratchet.

"Now there was a hell-bent lady named Nurse Ratchet in the book One Flew Over the Cuckoo's Nest," I said, "but surely that's not a proper characterization of you," I stated.

"Well, wait til' you get to know me better," she replied.

Indeed I would get to know them quite well, and we would end up hiking together a good part of the next 1,200 miles. And when we did get to know each other better Nurse Ratchet admitted that on this first night when she saw me helplessly attempting to set up my tarp she didn't give me a snowball's chance in hell of making it all the way to Maine.

***

I slept like crap, and decided in the future I should leave sleeping cowboy style to cowboys. I was up and off at first light. One problem with beating everybody on the trail in the morning is that you get plastered with spider webs, although I had this problem practically every day due to my height. This particular day was to be a tremendous challenge in topography and miles. After 7.6 miles I stopped for a break at the Clyde Smith Shelter. Nickie NOBO (Northbound), foul mouth and all, rolled in with a couple other guys and immediately his testosterone started acting up again.

"I'm going to beat the *bleep* out of this Crocker asshole that keeps carving, 'One step at a time — Crocker,' in every shelter," he threatened. Then looking around he raged, "Holy *bleep*, it's *bleeping* hot out here, today. It feels like a *bleeping* inferno."

Mark, a mild-mannered Indiana biologist, whispered, "This guy has a five-word vocabulary and three of the words are fuck."

The hot topic along the trail was strategies for dealing with hot weather. The consensus was you needed to take a few hours off in the middle of the day and double or triple your water intake. I noted the irony that now everyone seemed to be obsessing with hot weather the way I had obsessed with cold weather the first month. With that I jumped up and headed off, leaving these "*hyperthermia* freaks" to vent themselves.

From here, the trail dropped off one thousand feet to Hughes Gap and then ascended 2,300 feet up Roan Mountain. It was an interesting progression from typical hardwood southern forest up to balsam-fir "Christmas tree" forest, and proved to be an early taste of alpine hiking in New Hampshire and Maine. The climb was steep to the summit, one of the high points in the southern Appalachians. Occasionally, it required moving on all fours, and it was times like this that some hikers, including me on this occasion, question their fitness and capacity for the entire enterprise. But whether it was the Almighty's intelligent design or prescient planning by the trail designers, the AT often seemed to let up at just the point when it began to feel impossible to continue.

Finally, the trail topped out at Roan High Bluff, an open, windswept meadow with a Scottish Highlands feel. Then it winds around the shoulder of the mountain and finally comes up on the Roan High Knob Shelter. At six thousand two hundred eighty-five feet it is the most elevated shelter on the entire AT.

This was my original destination for the evening. But when I opened the door and poked my head in it became clear that at this elevation, even this rare four-sided shelter would be cold. I resolved to move on to a lower elevation.

I had thought it was straight down to the next shelter, but couldn't have been more mistaken. The AT crosses five summits greater than fifty-four hundred feet over the next dozen miles. It traverses open, grassy balds offering spectacular views in all directions. Of course, in foul weather it would have been outright treacherous. Damn, North Carolina (and parts of Tennessee) was tough as hell.

***

My heart was set on reaching the Yellow OverMountain Shelter, a converted farmhouse. The sun had dropped behind the mountains, and I was running on fumes when I finally saw the sign to the OverMountain Shelter, which was three-tenths miles off the trail. It was my single-best effort as a hiker. I had literally hiked the entire day. I wondered if the two-story farmhouse/shelter would be empty. Nobody from the previous night's shelter was likely to have traveled the 21.1 miles over this steep topography. Upon turning the corner I saw the lone figure of Seth sitting there on the first deck. My mood jumped from good to great.

"Skywalker," he said merrily. "I saw Justin today and we wondered whether you were still out here."

"And what was the verdict?" I responded.

"Well, we didn't know how far you'd go after the abandoned backpack incident," he said diplomatically.

"How is Justin?" I asked.

"Did you hear he got bluff-charged by a bear?" Seth said.

"What the hell is a bluff-charge?" I quickly asked.

"The bear charges you, but pulls up short."

"And what are you supposed to do?"

"Hold your ground," Seth said smiling.

"I'm kinda' disappointed I haven't seen a bear yet," Seth added sincerely.

"That makes one of us," I retorted.

The view out into the valley at sunset was gorgeous, and we sat there taking it in. Bill Bryson had written about the *low-level ecstasy* that hiking the AT affords, but which is so lacking in America's sensationalistic, hyper-materialistic culture. Indeed, after hiking all day I was in a good mood almost every night, as long as I could get warm. It was that priceless feeling of having done a good day's work. "Man, this whole AT is great, isn't it?" I said.

"Yeah," Seth sighed. "But I'm actually thinking about getting off in Damascus."

"Aw come on, Seth" I responded. "You were the closest thing to a sure bet that I saw in Georgia. And I remember how disappointed you were about not going all the way last year."

"I get bored and depressed out here," he said quietly. "And wait 'til Virginia. It goes on forever."

"I honestly look at it as an once-in-a-lifetime opportunity," I said. "This is the kind of thing you'll be reminiscing fondly about when you're ninety years old in a wheelchair in a nursing home while crapping all over yourself."

***

"Hikers are demanding," one hostel owner told me. "They have to be

Whitewater and Nurse Ratchet were good hikers and even better hiking partners. Nurse Ratchet was hospitalized for kidney stones in Virginia, but showed her strong character in getting back on the trail and gutting it out.

taken to the grocery store, the post office, the Laundromat, everywhere. And most of them are half-broke. To top it off they eat like cannibals and smell like rendered cats."

The owner of the Mountain View Hostel took me to the grocery store to re-supply. When we returned, Whitewater, Nurse Ratchet, their hiking companion Mark, and Air Puppy were waiting on the front lawn. Air Puppy, an early twenty-ish, innocent-looking hiker from New Hampshire, approached the owner in what I would soon learn was his trademark helpless manner and asked, "Would you mind if I did work for stay?"

The owner agreed and sent him over to work on trimming the bushes. A few minutes later Air Puppy approached the owner again with a pitiful look on his face and said, "I'm sorry. I'm allergic to poison ivy."
The owner grunted and looked around for something else for Air Puppy to do. But Air Puppy just went inside the hostel and proceeded to take over the sofa, the television, the radio, and just about everything else inside.

I wandered outside to get away from him when Flying Pig, a burly, soft-spoken math teacher from Pennsylvania, approached me. "I don't know if you're aware," he said in a hushed voice, "but there have been some rumors that this Air Puppy guy might have stolen some things from other hikers. It all came to a head at Miss Janet's hostel back in Erwin. She actually had to hold some guys off from beating the hell out of him."

"Yeah, I heard about that, but didn't know who it was," I said alarmed.

I went to bed that night bothered by Air Puppy and worried about the ski pole (used for balance) I had left in Outrider's truck. I had chosen a spot up in the loft, in order to maximize the distance between Air Puppy and me. Then, suddenly, I heard some quiet steps coming up the ladder to the second floor loft. "Jesus Christ," I thought. *Is this guy really that brazen?*

But it wasn't Air Puppy. It was Outrider. "Skywalker, you left your ski pole in the back of my trunk," he said.

"Yeah," I responded. "But when did you realize it?"

"When I got to Damascus and unloaded Seth's backpack."

"Well, for Godsakes, I hope you didn't come all the way back from Damascus just to deliver this," I said amazed.

He mumbled an answer that made me think he had done just that. I went to sleep, swept up with gratitude.

***

"Boy, I've been waiting for this opportunity," Mark, a biologist from Indiana who couldn't stand Air Puppy, said eagerly. "I've tried speeding up, slowing down, even taking a day off, and still haven't been able to shake him. But today I'm gonna' haul ass and lose him for all time." We had all been packing up to go back to the trail after a hiker-sized breakfast when the owner had diplomatically asked Air Puppy to stay behind and help clean up.

So off we galloped, Mark, Nurse Ratchet, Whitewater, and I, all hoping to do big miles and lose Air Puppy. Nurse Ratchet chided her husband, "Adam (Whitewater), you're the reason he's still with us. You always fall for his sob story and give him money or food."

"Well, gee, when a man has four dollars to his name it's my custom to try and help him," Whitewater answered, obviously conflicted. "And to be honest, while he may be a thief, he's also a nice guy."

"Yeah, but it's not fair to the rest of us for him to be out here with no money," Mark interjected heatedly. "I've been saving up for this thru-hike for three years."

Our "escape" plan got more complicated when it began to rain cats and dogs. I was worried about getting a spot in the shelter at Moreland Gap, which was eighteen miles from where we had started the day. If not, I would be forced to try setting up the tarp in the rain. That line of thinking was a sure sign my lightweight tarp strategy had backfired.

My heart sank upon clearing the final hill and seeing the shelter in the distance. It was surrounded by what appeared to be a big group of Boy Scouts. It was a Saturday, which is when these groups tend to congregate. One veteran hiker had said, "Of all the cruel fates the hiking gods can play on you, a large, boisterous group of Boy Scouts is the worst."

But fortunately, the group had set up a big, sprawling tarp for all of them to sleep under.

The shelter filled up as usual on a rainy night and the Air Puppy jokes were merciless. As we all lay in our sleeping bags, with the rain pelting our shelter, Whitewater remarked, "This is the real sweet spot. You hike hard all day, get to the shelter, eat, arrange everything, and listen to the raindrops tumble down on the shelter roof. It makes it all worth it."

"Gee, Adam (Whitewater), I never knew you were such a romantic," Nurse Ratchet commented.

"And we're free of Air Puppy," Mark added.

Amid the laughter I heard steps fast approaching the shelter, and a silhouette appeared, followed by the disembodied voice of Air Puppy. "What the hell!" Air Puppy exclaimed. "Did you guys take a shortcut or something? I've been almost running all day to catch up with everybody."

Mark, lying right next to me whispered, "Am I having a nightmare?"

"He missed you, Mark," I consoled him.

According to the guidebook the Moreland Gap shelter holds eight, which is what we already had in there. But Air Puppy confidently said to two people on the far end, "Ha, just let me slide in there real quick." Now we had nine, although Mark briefly considered making it eight again.

As Air Puppy went about the usual campsite duties, he was in a chatty mood. "Did I ever tell you guys about how I hitchhiked all the way across Canada with no money?" He then let loose a veritable Niagara of tales, each one containing the theme of his brilliance and savvy triumphing against all odds, including hunger, sexual predators, and anti-narcotics laws. A common denominator among many thieves is their compulsion to feel they have outsmarted people, and that was evident here.

He spoke in rhapsodic tones of his lust for weed and other chemicals. "I've got two Mountain Houses (an expensive brand of dehydrated food he got from God knows where) in my backpack. I'd give both of 'em up right this minute for a joint."

At that, the leader of the group camped out under the tarp next to the shelter rushed in.

"Hey, man," he said anxiously. "This is a group of recovering drug addicts out here for wilderness therapy. Can't you find something else to talk about?"

Air Puppy, feeling himself in a commanding position as he was safely ensconced in a packed shelter, shot back, "I'll talk about whatever the hell I want. You got a joint, man?"

"My God," the wilderness therapist said as he walked out in disgust.

***

It was great being with Whitewater and Nurse Ratchet. They seemed to go almost exactly my speed and shared my task-oriented philosophy. This was a once-in-a-lifetime chance that needed to be treated like a job much of the time.

We were deluged with rain again near the top of White Rocks Mountain, and as we started down the mountain I was traversing a big, slanted rock. Just like that my feet went straight out from under me. I hit the rock hard on my left side and my AT dream flashed before my eyes. Whitewater rushed to help me, and I quickly started flexing my left leg to be sure it wasn't broken. I had already fallen several times, like most hikers, but this was by far the worst. I had a deep bruise for three weeks.

Falls were one of the more prominent hazards of the trail, and have ruined many a thru-hiker's dream. They tended to come in three situations:
- When it was wet.
- Late in the day, when you're tired.
- When you're in a hurry.

We ended the day at Watauga Dam Shelter, right by the second largest dam in the east. Pioneers Daniel Boone and Davy Crocket had once lived and hunted in this valley, which is now often flooded by the dam.

***

Two days later, I was psyched to make the twenty-five and nine-tenths-mile hike into Damascus, widely advertised as the "friendliest town on the AT." I got off to an early start and it was the easiest terrain yet on the AT. Two miles before Damascus the trail crossed into Virginia, the fourth state.

After eleven hours and 25.9 miles, I descended into Damascus and followed the blazes right through the main street. My mood was ebullient, and not just because of the day's high mileage. I had always figured that making it to Virginia would mean at least partial success.

Walking through the streets of Damascus were bikers speaking many different languages.

The coast-to-coast National Bike Trail runs through Damascus. It was hard not to notice how much less famished they looked than the hikers strolling around. After all, while they traveled considerably greater distances on their bicycles every day, they usually slept in motels and ate real food.

Just three days before there had been upwards of *ten thousand hikers and ex-hikers* celebrating "Trail Days" in this tiny little town with a population of one thousand. Most had camped out in a field known as "Tent City." Events ranged from a parade down the main street, to a best-ass contest among female hikers in a section known as "Assville," to a speech by Warren Doyle.

The Place is a well-known Methodist Church hostel, with the sole purpose of putting up hikers. The four-dollar-per-night suggested payment was on the honor system. I had run into a healthy-looking, brunette named Lizard on the main street on the way into town. Surprisingly, Lizard, who was in her late-twenties swung by The Place to see if I wanted to eat, which added to my sky-high morale. In disbelief Nurse Ratchet asked, "Did you ask her on a date?"

"In fact I did," I responded, "and she said that with extensive plastic surgery it's not at all out of the question."

At dinner Lizard appeared to be in just the opposite spirits as me. "I've been with a great hiking group, but we all got separated and some quit. I've considered getting off the trail myself."

"My big problem is I'm hemorrhaging weight," I said.

"You want to know something funny," she laughed. "Almost every guy out here has lost at least twenty pounds, but I don't know a single girl who has lost over ten pounds. I've actually *gained* six pounds."

"Get outta' here," I said in disbelief. "We're expending five-to-six thousand calories per day. You can't carry that much food."

"Oh, but we're different animals from you males; I'm telling you," she said. This sounded amazing so I listened intently. "Even thin women have lots of fat reserves for child-bearing, breast-feeding and so forth," she continued. "And when you do this much exercise those fat reserves turn into muscle, which weighs more than fat. So we get thinner out here, but we don't lose as much weight and get stronger."

"Well I hear you and believe you," I said taking in all this. "But short of a sex change I've got to figure out a survival strategy for the next seventeen hundred miles. At the rate I'm losing weight I won't make it."

*The terrain early in the hike was nothing compared to what I would find in the later going. The aggregate amount of elevation gain and loss on the Appalachian Trail is equivalent to climbing up and down Mount Everest **sixteen**times.*

Chapter 9

Of all the creatures on earth, humans are the only true walkers. Various creatures crawl, climb, swim, or even fly. Others hop and gallop. Many run very fast. Humans walk. Scientists have noted that the human bone structure is ideal for walking. We are embarrassingly slow runners compared to other mammals. For sitting we are especially poorly constructed, and not much better for standing. But the human bipedal mode of walking is unrivaled.

One would reasonably think that a book on the seemingly mundane subject of walking would be quite tedious, to say the least. But Rebecca Solnit in her marvelously researched *Wanderlust: A History of Walking*, actually brings the topic to life.

Various intellectuals have even been attracted to this subject. "Of all the exercises, walking is the best," wrote President, architect, author, and walker, Thomas Jefferson. Jean Jacques Rousseau was the writer who wrote the most of walking. "Never have I realized my own existence so much, never have I been so much alive," he wrote rhapsodically, "than when walking."

The champion walkers are the British. A greater cultural value is attached to walking there than anywhere else. On weekends eighteen million Brits head for the countryside and walk for recreation. Private property rights are much less absolute in Britain than in the U.S., and they readily tramp all over fields and pastures owned by others. "There are no barriers on the moors and you say hello to everyone and overcome our damn British reserve," says British outdoor writer Roly Smith. "Walking is classless, one of the few sports that is classless." And it presumably is no coincidence that the average British life is several years longer than the average American life, and the rates of obesity and other pathologies are sharply reduced from our levels.

Dramatic historical events have often centered around walking. President Carter recounts in his memoirs how he broke the deadlock in the Camp David talks by shepherding the Israeli and Egyptian leaders away from their advisors for a walk around the wooded compound. President

Reagan and Mikhail Gorbachev reported the same phenomenon at their first summit when they headed off along Lake Geneva with only one interpreter present. And Martin Luther King's marches were pivotal in the civil rights movement. One Buddhist magazine even made the extravagant claim that all the world's problems would be solved if only the leaders would walk!

Unfortunately, the golden age of walking has passed. The 1970 U.S. Census showed, for the first time in the history of any nation, that the majority of Americans were suburbanites. This suburbanization has radically changed daily life, usually in ways averse to traveling on foot. Of course, suburban areas aren't designed for walking at all, but for driving. A recent study contained the eye-opening statistic that more than 20 percent of Americans are now obese — not to be confused with merely overweight or fat. Do the math. The nation's population just hit three hundred million which means we have *sixty million* obese people — equal to the entire population of Great Britain. This is a national tragedy. Of course, many of the greatest fortunes in history — Ford, Firestone, Rockefeller — have been reaped by those who made it easier to travel sitting on one's bum. But the great irony is that speed has made travel not more interesting, but more boring. Just compare the palpably buoyant mood of someone who has completed a long day's hike with the nauseous mood of a jet-lagged traveler.

"I have two doctors — my left leg and my right," wrote George Trevelyan. That is a simple, but profound, truth.

***

The AT covers more miles in Virginia than any other state — more than five hundred from Damascus in the southwest corner all the way up until crossing into West Virginia at Harper's Ferry, north of Washington D.C. All during the tough, jagged mountains of North Carolina I kept hearing, "Just wait for Virginia. It's a flat speedway." But Warren Doyle had said, "Watch out for Virginia. It may not be as difficult as Georgia and North Carolina, but it's tough. A lot of people drop out here." Thus was coined the term "Virginia Blues."

Two days out from Damascus I arrived at Mount Rogers, the highest point in Virginia. It was a bit of a surprise that the trail did not go over the summit because it's often said the AT leaves no summits uncovered. The trail then enters Grayson Highlands State Park, a marquee point on the AT.

Several miles are exposed, without tree cover in rocky meadows. Wild, feral ponies roam throughout the park. A frequently heard hiker complaint is that in the summer the trail becomes one long green canopy or tunnel so it was nice to get some broad, open vistas. But it also entailed straining to follow blazes painted on rocks for miles.

At the Hurricane Mountain Shelter that night I ran into Lizard again. Her spirits seemed greatly lifted because she had been reunited with her hiking partner, Fork Man.

"Dude, how tall are you?" Fork Man opened up our relationship. After I mumbled an unenthusiastic response he followed with my next least favorite question, "Do you play basketball?"

"No," I responded, "the money is much better in hiking than professional basketball."

"Wow, you must be the fastest hiker on the trail," Fork Man exclaimed. This renewed the running debate I had been engaged in off and on since the very beginning about whether height is an advantage or disadvantage. I always took the latter position, and lost track of the number of times that much shorter hikers buzzed past me on the trail with the observation, "God, if only I had your height." Once when I was panting up a mountain a little roadrunner named Stewy Boy shot past me and said, "No fair. Give me some of that height." I quickly yelled forward to him, "But, if I had *your* height I'd already be in Maine." He quickly shot back at me a look of utter bewilderment.

Fork Man himself was about 6'2", and solidly built. He was in his early thirties and had apparently been a successful government contractor. But based on the earring through each nipple and large amount of marijuana he smoked on a daily basis, he appeared to have "gone counterculture."

I asked Fork Man, "Are you going to try to make it to Pearisburg in two days? It's forty-two miles."

"Sure, just stay with me," he said boldly. "We'll make it there in two days."

"But the next shelter is twenty-six and three-tenths miles away," I said concerned. "That's one-tenth mile longer than a marathon."

"Be somebody, Skywalker."

***

I was dubious about meeting Fork Man's challenge, but we set off in a drizzle together. Fork Man soon disappeared into the distance, despite my best efforts to keep up with him. Fortunately, the sun soon came out brilliantly, making it a good day to max out. When I got to the Jenny Knob Shelter, 12.1 miles out, Fork Man was just finishing lunch.

"Bad news," he said. "There's no water in the creek down there."

I had started with two liters and had judiciously drunk just one, hoping to fill up somewhere along the way. But the area was in the midst of a drought.

Appearing slightly embarrassed, Fork Man said, "The data book lists a water source at this shelter." Then the normally commanding Fork Man meekly asked, "Do you have any extra water I could have?'

I pulled up my liter bottle and carefully said, "A bit," and threw it to him.

"I'll just take a little bit," he promised.

"Take a third of it," I suggested. The fact of his drinking water I had been toting all morning clouded the situation.

I looked at the data book and it showed no more water sources for seven more miles. "It is awful dangerous to run out of water out here," I said.

Fork Man nodded dutifully.

I had gone day hiking a few years before in Chilean Patagonia and ended up with a group of Israelis. I only had brought a half-liter for the day. They all gave me a stern lecture from their military training about the absolute necessity of always staying well-hydrated. But they also had insisted on sharing their water.

Fork Man then finished the bowl of marijuana he was smoking and headed off. A half-hour later I finished lunch and headed off again, focused on hunting for water. A mile later the trail descended steeply to Lickskillet Hollow. The most reliable water sources were usually at bottoms, such as this. But my search turned up nothing. There was nothing to do but move on. I slowly climbed the mountain out of Lickskillet Hollow with the grim knowledge that at higher elevations I was less likely to come across running water. It was a sunny, windless day.

Suddenly, I heard something very heavy about forty yards to the right on the other side of the ridge. A quick look revealed a very heavy, jet-black animal tearing down the other side. Although I didn't see the face, my first thought was that it might have been a wild boar because I didn't think bears were so black. However, that night I learned that bears are, indeed, just that black, whereas wild boars are a lighter shade. Thus, I had in all probability had my first spotting of ursus Americanus, the American black bear. Besides its color, this creature had other notable characteristics. Its size and strength were awesome, its speed was blinding, and, it had an apparent total fear of me.

Several miles later, with my water level reaching an alarming stage, the trail crossed Kimberling Creek. When I dipped my Nalgene bottle into this "creek," the water was so cloudy I could see only the top of the bottle. I dumped it. Fortunately, a couple miles later at the point of maximum concern, I came upon a gushing stream, and it gave me a second wind. The sun had disappeared behind the hills, and I was still loping along a stream at my maximum speed of about three miles per hour. Finally, I heard voices, and Fork Man yelled out, "Skywalker, you're a marathon man. I knew you could do it." We had hiked 26.3 miles.

Night Owl and his son, Quick Quiet, were there at the Waipiti Shelter as well. Night Owl was a mystery man on the trail. Various theories had been expounded on who he was. For starters he was always dressed to the eights and nines, while the rest of us were dressed like tramps. Then, there was the strange fact that he and Quick Quiet had passed me on a half-dozen occasions and were destined to pass me several more times. How could that be? He had tried thru-hiking with his teenage daughter the previous year, but she had become disillusioned over the lack of telephone contact with her friends back home and they had dropped out in Virginia. But this year Night Owl was back thru-hiking not only with his son Quick Quiet, and had his other son, Outrider, driving a van to meet them at various road crossings. Not only were they well dressed, but they always looked well fed. In fact, on this occasion he pulled out a spare corned-beef sandwich that Outrider had just this day purchased for them and offered it to me — which only added to my giddy mood.

Night Owl and Quick Quiet pulled razors out of their backpacks and headed over to the nearby stream to bathe and shave. When they got back to the shelter Night Owl was polished to a fine sheen.

"It is incumbent on me to provide a bit of history of this shelter," Night Owl said. "Two women were murdered at this shelter about ten years back."

"Get outta' here," Fork Man rejoined.

"Scouts honor," Night Owl said. "Apparently, they were literally in the act of a homosexual liason when some hillbilly kook came up and shot them."

"I hope nobody spots us and gets suspicious that there happen to be four males in this shelter tonight," I half-joked. "Let's try to space out as much as possible."

It ended up that the impeccable Night Owl for once had his facts wrong. Two lesbians were murdered during lovemaking in Pennsylvania. However, two people had been killed on a separate occasion at this particular shelter. So perhaps that huge, furry animal I had seen tearing down a hill earlier in the day wasn't the animal I needed to worry about most. Maybe it was those animals they let loose out there called *humans* that represent the greater threat.

***

"Are you going to be stopping in Pearisburg?" I asked Fork Man before he pulled out of camp.

"No way, man," he said firmly. "I'm going to get a quick bite to eat and head out of town."

The relatively flat terrain of the previous day was short-lived as the trail gave way to a much more angular and jagged topography. At the Doc's Knob Shelter at the eight-mile mark I wrote in the register:

Doc's Knob Shelter — mile 610

5-29-05: Ladies and gentlemen, fellow hikers, fellow Americans: It is my high honor and great privilege to inform you that Pearisburg, which lies just eight miles ahead, is the most underrated town on the trail. The citizens even genuflect when smelly hikers pass by. Take extra long strides to get there as soon as possible. — **SkyWalker**

There was a steep descent into Pearisburg where the trail emptied out of the woods with a motel just across the street. Better yet, the parking lot was bustling with hikers.

In the parking lot it became clear that the group of about ten hikers all knew each other well, as they tossed the Frisbee around. A quite attractive brunette in her late twenties wearing a University of Michigan cap was sitting out taking it all in.

"Are you all hiking together?" I asked her.

"It's ended up that way, yeah," she said. "My name is Vogue, by the way."

"I'm Skywalker," I replied.

"Hi, Skywalker," she replied.

"Did you all start together at Springer or meet on the trail?" I asked.

"We met and formed a group of five the first night on the trail, and have been together ever since," she replied. "Then, we hooked up with another group of five. The ten of us have been together ever since."

"Wow, everybody must be on their best behavior to hang together like that," I said, amazed.

"We've had some colorful arguments, to be sure," she replied, "but it's been to everyone's advantage to hang together."

Given Vogue's grace and seemliness she seemed like an unlikely candidate for all the controversy she would soon find herself in.

**

Hot weather was finally setting in after a cooler-than-average spring, and I seemed to be almost the only person on the trail happy about it. Fork Man, Lizard, and Mark, the biologist from Indiana, all became exhausted and bored, and dropped out in the middle of the 500-mile stretch known as Virginia. Like Seth before them, these were all strong, fast hikers. But they were classic victims of that congenital trail condition veteran hikers had warned about: "The Virginia Blues."

After the trail crosses the New River outside Pearisburg it climbs twenty-eight hundred feet to Rice Field, an exposed, grassy expanse. With the mid-day sun beating down directly on me I hurried through the wide-open field. Suddenly, I heard a sharp, hissing sound. About ten feet in front of me was a coiled rattlesnake. I had seen snakes ("no shoulders" one hiker memorably described them) almost every day up to this point, most of which didn't appear to be terribly dangerous. But I had wondered if I would even recognize a rattlesnake when I finally saw one. Yet the way this tanned, diamond-exterior reptile in front of me rattled, it left no doubt.

I stepped back about twenty feet, but the snake didn't move. The way it was so tightly coiled I wondered just how far and how quickly it could uncoil and strike. A friend who is an avid hunter later told me they have the capacity to uncoil about half their length to strike. Finally, I grabbed a rock and threw it at the snake as I ran by about twenty feet to its left.

About a quarter mile later I came upon another hiker stopped in the middle of the trail. "Excuse me," he said somewhat sheepishly. "There is a rattlesnake in the middle of the trail here. Do you happen to know the best way to deal with these types of situations?"

"Yeah," I said breezily. "Just give it a wide berth and run around it." Then without slowing down I proceeded to "bushwhack" about twenty feet to my left and ran around both the hiker and the rattlesnake. When I was about twenty yards past the snake and back on the AT I looked back; the man had a confused look on his face as he grudgingly edged over into the bushes to get around the snake.

Those were the first, but not last, rattlesnakes I saw. Almost invariably when I came across one it would be in hot, muggy conditions in an area blocked off from any breeze. Given the menacing, poised-to-strike posture they adopt, it is easy to see why some people feared them more than bears. Indeed, statistics showed that hikers are more likely to die or suffer serious injury from a rattlesnake than from a bear. But I never worried about them as much as bears. And Shenandoah National Park, with its renowned dense bear population, lay ahead.

***

On May 16, 2006, David Sharp lay with his life in danger at twenty-nine thousand feet in the infamous "Zone of Death" on Mount Everest. It isn't clear what ailed Sharp. Some say he had used all his oxygen, while others say he was suffering from standard altitude sickness.

As Sharp lay fighting for his life it is said that no less than forty-two people passed by him. Many of those forty-two passed by twice — on the way up and down. What was their response? In most cases they did nothing.

One of those who passed by Sharp was Mark Inglis, a forty-seven-year-old New Zealander. Inglis had already lost both legs to frostbite on Mount Cook, New Zealand's highest peak. Now he was gaining national attention for his attempt to summit Mount Everest with two prostheses.

Interviewed about the episode, Inglis said, "We talked for quite a while and it was a very hard decision." They radioed down to their expedition leader who said the situation sounded hopeless. With that, they did what everybody else did. They left Sharp to die.

This incident stirred an international debate about outdoor and mountaineering ethics. Edmund Hilary, the legendary New Zealander who was the first person ever to summit Mount Everest was outraged. "The people just want to get to the top," Hilary fumed. "They don't give a damn about anybody else. I think it was the responsibility of every human on that mountain to try to save his life, even if that means they don't get to the top of the mountain."

***

The second night out from Pearisburg I got to Laurel Creek Shelter and ran into Nurse Ratchet and Whitewater. Also, on hand was a married couple from California. Both were doctors.

That evening, I kept hearing muffled conversations on the other side of the shelter between Whitewater and Nurse Ratchet. "Is there a problem?" I asked.

"Erin's (Nurse Ratchet) hurting," Whitewater said softly about his wife.

"Is there anything I can help with," I asked. But, of course, there wasn't. I tried with little success to get back to sleep.

I was up at first light because my goal for the day was to hike 22.8 miles over mountainous terrain and get to the Pickle Branch Shelter. I went through the usual, glum morning routine of eating cold food, visiting the privy, retrieving water, and packing. My goal was to be off by seven o'clock. I was ready five minutes ahead of that.

But while I had been putting the finishing touch on things I heard increasing moans and anguished discussions from Nurse Ratchet's corner of the shelter.

"Are you all right?" I asked.

"She's hurting again," Whitewater said glumly. "It's coming from her stomach or kidneys."

"You know, that couple out back are both doctors," I mentioned. "They're stirring around. Let's ask them." I went over to them and mentioned what was happening. They walked dutifully, if warily, toward Nurse Ratchet.

The wife, who was the spunkier one, asked, "Would you like me to get involved?"

"We would appreciate that greatly," Whitewater said meaningfully. Then addressing the obvious question, he said, "And there isn't a one in ten billion chance we'd ever sue you."

The female doctor then jumped into the shelter with Nurse Ratchet and did what appeared to be a routine checkup, sans instruments. Finally, she said to Nurse Ratchet, "It could be that you're pregnant, or it could be kidney stones. But I highly advise you to get it checked out soon."

Her husband, who as fate would have it was a urologist, said, "I can pretty well assure you it isn't kidney stones."

But his wife quickly interjected, "You need to have it looked at."

I was sitting there quietly digesting this, wondering whether to head off as planned, or what. I looked at the data book and saw that the trail crossed Virginia Highway 30 in four miles. I suggested, "I can carry your backpack down to the road and ya'll can hitchhike from there."

Finally, Nurse Ratchet unconvincingly said, "I'm feeling a little better. Don't worry about me."

I asked a couple more times if there was anything I could do and again offered to carry her backpack, but Nurse Ratchet quietly said, "No, go ahead, Skywalker." She had a fiercely competitive side that hated to see a peer like me get ahead of her. For my part I reasoned that she had her husband and two doctors there, and there was nothing I could possibly do other than carry her backpack four miles to the road (which wouldn't have been easy). I needed to leave to have any chance of making 22.8 miles in undulating topography. So, off I went.

My conscience gnawed at me all morning. I got down to the road, which was paved, but there weren't any cars. *Hitchhiking could be a problem for them.*

***

At this point there was nothing to do but continue hiking and try to forget it. We were now in the Blue Ridge Mountains and the trail went steadily up and down. I hadn't heard a weather report in a few days so I asked the first southbounder that looked like a day hiker if he had any updated weather information. "Oh, boy," he sighed. "Done heard dis' mornin' there is a big weather system comin." The early morning sun had indeed given way to an overcast sky with high-hanging clouds. I subconsciously quickened my pace and was glad to see the Niday Shelter, which marked twelve miles for the day.

The ten hikers from the motel parking in Pearisburg were there. They were all having a laugh at the shelter register. The entry that garnered their attention was from a hiker provocatively named Hump Master. He was apparently quite infatuated with Vogue, the girl in the white University of Michigan hat.

I told them about Nurse Ratchet and what I had done (and not done), looking for some comfort.

"Well you offered to help, and they said no. What else can you do?" Vogue responded.

"Yeah, I guess so." (Over the next few weeks I repeatedly asked people for information about Nurse Ratchet but got only vague reports.)

This group gave off good vibes so I hurried lunch and caught up with them. Frugal, a squirrelly, blonde-headed twenty-one-year-old male seemed to be involved in much of the group revelry. On the subject of the Boy Scouts Frugal said, "Ninety-nine percent of my bad habits, I learned from the Boy Scouts."

"Don't worry, Frugal," Mother quickly replied, "it's still not too late for you to become a heterosexual."

The group was close knit, but finally they spilled one of their group secrets to me. "Did you ever meet a hiker named Drama?" Mother asked me.

"Yes," I replied, raising my eyebrows at the mention of the "S&M" dominatrix.

"Back in Franklin, Drama took Frugal into a motel room for a 'spanking,'" Mother recounted deliciously. "I guarantee you Frugal was a changed man from the time he went in there to when he walked out fifteen minutes later."

***

The weather forecast was beginning to look on target as a slow-but-steady drizzle set in. Something about the absence of visible clouds in combination with a darkening sky said this storm was for real.

When the group stopped to look at the Audie Murphy memorial, I half-apologetically responded, "I'm trying to get to the shelter before getting too soaked." But I had an embarrassing and selfish reason to hurry to the shelter: I still had no confidence in my ability to set up my tarp on a rainy night, and wanted to secure a shelter spot. This was my Achilles Heel — one of them.

So I got to the shelter after 22.8 miles of rugged terrain, some of it in bad weather. Had I stuck around longer and waited on Nurse Ratchet that morning I likely would have had to stop 10 miles back. Had I made the right decision or did I make a Faustian bargain?

Looking back on it, my conscience dictates I should have stuck around. Whitewater and Nurse Ratchet were my best friends on the trail, and a better sense of outdoor ethics dictates that I should have hung around, even if it wasn't clear what I would have done. No, the case isn't in league with that of David Sharp on Mount Everest, but it conceivably could have been.

Chapter 10

Once safely ensconced in the shelter it was a pleasure listening to the rain pounding on the metal roof after having hiked for more than twelve hours. The sound of pounding rain continued all evening. The only disturbance came in the middle of the night as Frugal, snoring away lustily, was interrupted by a rodent visiting his forehead. He awoke in horror and screamed at the top of his lungs, "Holy fuck! What the hell is that?" This sent a shelter full of hikers in the middle of nowhere on a rainy night into uncontrollable spasms of laughter.

The reverie of the evening rain gave way the next morning to the reality of some truly nasty hiking conditions. The rain was steady, the wind was whipping, the trail would be muddy, and there wasn't another place to seek shelter for fourteen miles. I briefly considered taking a zero day in the shelter, but figured I would get cold — not to mention bored — lying around in there all day long.

Finally, after exhausting all other options, including reading the trail register from cover to cover, I departed mid-morning. Within a half-hour I was soaked through and my mood was grim.

Warren Doyle had described this stretch as particularly steep and rugged. The trail ascended Cove Mountain before reaching an infamous section called "Dragon's Tooth." It was slick, rocky, and had a steep drop-off. Throw in the nasty weather and being alone, and it was quickly becoming a nightmare.

At the top of Cove Mountain the trail cut sharply to the left and went down the mountain. I could only see twenty yards ahead, but what I did see looked like a sick joke. It wasn't clear where the trail went, but there were metal rungs going down what looked like a cliff off the mountainside. I took to all fours and slowly lowered myself in the whipping wind and pouring rain. *Is this hiking or is it mountain climbing?*

After slowly descending the steepest part I finally saw a blaze, which, always an affirmation, was especially so here. And once again, I noticed that characteristic I mentioned before. Just when the trail appeared to be getting beyond the average person's capacity, it eased.

At the bottom of the mountain the trail crossed a state road, and I considered bailing out right there, but God knows where to. Another state road crossed the trail in six miles. The more detailed "Wingfoot" (seven-time thru-hiker) data book didn't list any significant climbs between here and there.

So, soaked to the bone, I bounded up an open field the trail ran through, waiting for it to flatten as sheets of rain deluged me. Finally, the trail leveled out and started downhill. At this point I figured it would be an easy glide to the next road. But then the trail started climbing again and continued climbing some unlisted mountain. I was exhausted and hadn't taken a break in eight miles of rough hiking. Wingfoot's data book had become the source of great controversy on the trail — as well as occasional angry promises by cuckolded hikers to put him out of business with a more accurate data book. For starters, he reportedly hadn't hiked the AT in thirteen years, and there had been changes in the trail he simply wasn't familiar with. This must have been one of them.

Finally, I dropped my pack in exhaustion halfway up a hillside and sought some bushes for cover while gobbling some GORP. It was impossible to relax long while being pelted by the cold rain, so I got back up and started climbing the mountain again. In these conditions, I always feared losing the trail. It would be difficult to relocate it with such poor visibility. On another seemingly endless climb I noticed that I didn't seem to be on a clear path. I panicked and turned around and ran back in the direction I had come from. A hundred yards down the mountain I finally located the AT and resumed climbing.

Almost all road crossings come after descents. This thought deepened my paranoia because I was still climbing, which meant the road must not be close. Then suddenly the road appeared *after a climb*, a rare event. Better yet, an elderly lady in the trail parking lot rolled down her window and asked, "Would you like a ride to the restaurant in Catawba? It's the best on the entire AT." I stuffed my wet belongings and my wet self into her car and off we went.

Within five minutes she had dropped me off in front of a big, white house with two gazebos in front. After effusively thanking this trail angel, I walked into "the best restaurant on the trail" where some members of the Gang of 10 were already present. Tables groaned with enough food to feed not only every hiker in Virginia, but half the bears as well. Things had gone from very grim — bordering on dangerous — to perfect, just like that.

**

One way or another, the big investment of time and money — along with the huge energy and emotional investment — makes an AT thru-hike attempt a big part of anybody's life. When I chatted with another Gang of 10 member, Pumpkin, she mentioned she was getting married on August 14.

"Oh really," I responded. "You must not be planning on thru-hiking."

"To the contrary," she said firmly. "The wedding is in Vermont. I should be somewhere near there at that point. After a few days' honeymoon I'm going to return to wherever I got off the trail."

"With your husband?" I presumed.

"No, alone," she said in a logical tone. "This might be my last chance ever to thru-hike."

Even though I was only a peripheral member of the Gang of 10, I started hiking with them the following day. After the previous day's grueling hike we were braced for the worst going up McAfee's Knob, which is advertised as the best view in Virginia.

McAfee's Knob is a ledge running several hundred yards, with a steep drop and a clear, open view to the mountains to the west. It ended up being a surprisingly easy hike, and soon the entire group hovered over the steep ledges in rapt contemplation of the gorgeous landscape. It became clear that the Gang of 10 had a more leisurely approach to hiking, frequently stopping for photographs along the way. Having focused so intently on mileage for so far, a change of pace was nice.

"Are ya'll aware of the rumors flying around the trail about the 'Gang of 10'?"

"No, what are people saying?" Vogue asked.

"Oh, where do I begin?" I responded. "The general story is of a cult-like secrecy, Omerta code, group chants on the march, a secret handshake, and much more."

Vogue laughed and said, "That had better not be true."

I soon learned one reason the gang wasn't hurrying was that none of them wanted to catch up with the "Sleazebags." The Sleazebags were a group of nine males, each in their early to mid-twenties. One member of the Gang of 10 described the Sleazebags as "testosterone-laden, to the point of steroids."

In the Catawba Mountain Shelter register Hump Master, a Sleazebag, had written a long reverie of Vogue as Princess Leia to his Hans Solo.

Vogue had read it first and responded, "Man, what is this guy's problem? That's why I don't want to speed up; so I don't run into him."

After reading it myself I asked her, "Do you know him?"

"I've talked to him a couple times in passing at shelters," she replied.

"Well what did you do," I asked, "quote Romeo and Juliet?"

"No, I talked to him about my boyfriend," she said intently. "But he just kept chain smoking and giving me this cool-hand-Luke look."

Pumpkin then entered the conversation in a slightly spooked tone. "I had no idea before coming out here," she paused with a slightly haunted gaze, "that almost every guy hits on every girl almost every time. I'm blown away by the whole thing. From here on out I'm going to view men in a different light." A dark side of male human sexuality had apparently been revealed to her.

Mother, perhaps feeling the burden of defending the entire male gender calmly said, "Back when we were cavemen, we wore skin suits and carried clubs. Nowadays, we at least make a pretense of being civilized." "Barely," Pumpkin muttered.

One thing that seemed to magnify the differences between the genders in the wilderness is that male's appearances, hygiene, and body shape, seemed to go into a freefall. Females, meanwhile, often became fitter and more shapely. One hiker, Knees, had adamantly said, "I haven't seen many ugly women on the AT." He had a point.

It was a pretty interesting discussion, but I made a mental note to be careful while around hikers of the female persuasion, and Vogue, especially. I hadn't exactly been hitting on her, but I wasn't blind. She was quite pleasing to the eye, and I may have been paying her undue attention. And it's embarrassing to admit this, even now, but I was a bit jealous of this Hump Master fella' who was so keen on her.

***

After a couple more days of this leisurely stroll in increasingly hot weather we came to Daleville, Virginia. A Howard Johnson's was fifty yards to the right of where the trail ran, so I went over and checked in. This central Virginia town of perhaps eight thousand people was the biggest borough we had seen since embarking from Springer Mountain.

After eating ravenously with the Gang of 10 I went to the grocery store. There I ran into the renowned *Sweet Sixteen*. Her tantalizing trail name had, according to trail gossip, inspired all kinds of night hiking and "pinkblazing." Pink-blazing refers to a hiker altering his or her hiking schedule to connect with a member of the opposite sex. Turbo Joe had reportedly become so obsessed from reading Sweet Sixteen's journal entries in shelter registers, that he went into a three–day, souped-up frenzy of day and night pink-blazing to reach her. Upon finally arriving and greeting this matronly figure of no more than sixty-four or sixty-five years young, he had become so disillusioned that he quit the AT. Another hiker named Saxy Lady (saxophone player) reported a similar phenomenon of panting, sweating hikers arriving at campsites after dark, and discreetly inquiring if Saxy Lady was on hand.

"What is the key to your success out here?" I asked Sweet Sixteen.

"Opposites attract," she said, "and I've found lots of opposites to hike with." Indeed she was with a group of middle-aged males who seemed to enjoy her personality for no other reward than that. Pumpkin would have been shocked!

"Are you planning to go the distance?" I asked her.

"I negotiated six weeks on the trail with my husband before beginning," she said. "At the end of that I negotiated a second six weeks. That's on the verge of expiring and now I'm contemplating my negotiating strategy for a third six weeks." She added, "One bargaining point in my favor is that I spend less money out here than at home."

I wished her the best and never saw her again. Apparently, she was out about another month and finally got off with plans to do the second half of the AT the following year, perhaps as Sweet Seventeen.

***

I got my first really good night's sleep since Fontana Dam, five hundred miles back. It was a hot, humid day, and the Gang of 10 was nowhere to be found. I had felt like an addendum to their group to begin with and was especially sensitive about becoming another unwanted presence to Vogue. So off I went, solo. It felt especially lonely at first, perhaps because I had been surrounded by so many friendly people lately.

The trail was surrounded by thick, tall grass on each side, which effectively blocked out all breeze. Even for a hot weather aficionado such as myself it was very unpleasant. The romantic haze that gives the Blue

Ridge its name is the product of plant transpiration and great humidity. But on this Sunday morning, as the trail began to ascend into the Blue Ridge Mountains, I was soon enveloped by a fresh mountain breeze that made for a perfect day to hike.

Three miles later I ran into the Blue Ridge Parkway for the first time. The AT used to be exactly where the Parkway now runs, but after great debate and a power struggle the AT was expropriated to build it. The current AT runs up and down ridges, with frequent crossings of the Parkway. It is 469 miles long, bookended by Great Smoky Mountain National Park on the southern end and Shenandoah National Park on the northern end, and covers some of the east's highest peaks. A total of twenty-six tunnels were blasted through hills and mountains to construct the parkway during the Great Depression. But the effort was worth it because its pristine condition is striking — trucks are not allowed on it — and with its many overlooks it's one of the few roads worth driving purely for pleasure.

***

I hadn't seen any water in thirteen miles, when I took the steep drop-off from the AT to get to the Bobblet's Gap Shelter. I got down to the shelter expectantly listening for the steady hum of flowing water. A mid-fifty-ish couple was there, and I said, "Please tell me there is some water."

"Well, you might be able to filter some out of a pool of water right behind us," the lady said sympathetically in a rich, New England accent. "Otherwise, you're going to have to go aways."

I went aways, bushwhacking farther and farther downstream, trusting I'd find my way back. I was sensitized for the sound of any trickle. Finally, after about a quarter mile of slashing through bushes and trees I finally found a little falloff to put my Nalgene bottle under and fill up. The upside of this kind of activity was that it actually made me feel a bit more like a real outdoorsman.

The couple at the shelter were Buffet and Goat, from New Hampshire. They had been planning their thru-hike to the most-minute detail for two years. Further, they seemed totally disciplined and intent on executing their plan flawlessly.

"What is it," I wanted to know "that makes every single New Hampshirite such a good hiker?"

"Take a look at a map." Goat said chuckling.

Goat was in trim form, but that night he exploded my theory that snoring was the exclusive domain of overweight people, as he practically blew the roof off the shelter. Not surprisingly, he and Buffet were up and out by 7 o'clock. That beat me by over an hour because once again I had to go slashing down the creek bed, even farther than the previous evening, in pursuit of water.

At midday I stopped at the Cove Mountain Shelter and read Hump Master's latest entry to Vogue. In it he worried that she was holding back and mused about the possibility of reverse-hiking to find her. I still hadn't met him, but began to conjure up images of Robert DeNiro playing a deranged villain in Cape Fear.

Cove Mountain Shelter — mile 734

6-8-05: *Vogue, Hump Master's latest entry conjures up the dreadful possibility that he is morphing from a pink-blazer into an all-out stalker. Thus, it might be prudent for the Gang of 10 to consider altering their renowned single-file trail-marching formation in favor of a more protective, circular formation, with you in the middle.* — **Skywalker**

It had been so nice the last few days that at the first sound of distant rumbling I thought it was an airplane or even firecrackers. However, it soon became apparent that it was thunder and there was a twenty-two hundred foot climb ahead. Even though I was tired and the sky looked ominous I felt a compulsion to continue and reach my goal for the day, which was five more miles. I was in a *Virginia mindset*, feeling the need to go to full capacity each day for maximum miles. The idea was to give myself a cushion to avoid getting caught by early winter in New Hampshire and Maine.

Thus, I started the long climb up Floyd Mountain and immediately the pyrotechnics started. I cursed myself for being so "mileage greedy." Soon it began to pour and I took refuge under some bushes. But it turned out to be just the basic run-of-the-mill afternoon thunderstorm. These afternoon cloudbursts and electrical shows would be part of life over the next two or three months as heat and humidity reigned. And unlike the miserable early experiences in the southern Appalachians, it would now be possible to get warm and dry afterward.

Just before dark Buffet and Goat trudged in, wet and weary, but happy.

Since I considered myself a close call to make it all the way I figured their game effort would fall somewhere shy of the mark. Upon bidding them farewell the next morning I said, "See you down the road."

Buffet responded, "At the rate you're going, probably not."

I demurred, but secretly agreed with them. But we were both wrong. The two denizens of the Granite State were tough as granite, and I would see them again, well up the road, when I least expected it.

***

When I arrived at the bottom of Apple Orchard Mountain (forty-two hundred feet), the highest point on the AT between central Virginia and Massachusetts, a girl in her early twenties was sitting on the ground having lunch.

Knowing the Sleazebags were somewhere up ahead, I asked, "Are you with that group of guys ahead?"

She looked slightly scared, even hunted, and said, unconvincingly, "Oh, yes."

I remembered that the AT guidebook had suggested telling suspicious hikers you were with a group just ahead or just behind. Apparently, suspicious was the category into which I fell, and she wanted to avoid any betrayal of vulnerability. I had planned to take a break right there as well, but decided to hike on a mile or so to alleviate her concerns.

Central Virginia was proving much more rugged than everybody had anticipated, with rocks and steady ups-and-downs day after day. Like many other hikers, my feet were throbbing from the daily pounding. As the trail wound down the mountain along a stream toward the James River, I decided to try soaking them in the cold, running water. The numbing effect was as magical as several hikers had promised. Unfortunately, another black snake appeared after a few minutes and my comfort level plummeted. Nonetheless, the frigid torrents had numbed and freshened my feet and the effect lasted for hours.

The quiet, apprehensive girl I had passed a few miles back wandered up while I was taking a break. "For once the data book is right," she said positively. "The water source mentioned in it actually contains water."

"Yeah," I replied, "I not only drank it, but soaked my feet in it. Fabulous therapy."

She seemed interested, then said, "We haven't met. My name is Seeker."

She had a demure, mild-mannered look, but I was just glad she seemed to no longer think I was a predator. After chatting amiably for a few minutes, I asked, "Are you going into Glasgow to re-supply?" But my question made her cagy again. I took that as my cue and headed on.

The trail wandered for miles in close, humid air along the historic James River. The James is notable to hikers because it flows east into the Atlantic. Every river and waterway south of it flows south and west to the Gulf of Mexico. I kept a close eye out for my new bogeyman — snakes — and was glad when a bridge crossing the James came into view. It is the longest foot-use-only bridge in the entire national park system.

A highway with a parking lot lies on the other side of the river. An elderly gentleman jumped out of his car as I approached and said cheerfully, "Would a cold soda do you any good on this hot day?"

"Mentally as much as physically," I replied lustily.

His eyes then lit up and he said, "I just witnessed the damndest thing. A big group of hikers (the Sleazebags, no doubt) was crossing the bridge, but guess what. One of them swam the whole way!"

"Well, I hope you were impressed," I laughed.

"I felt like asking him why he didn't walk across the water," he chortled.

"What in the world does it cost to build a bridge like that?" I wanted to know. "Two-hundred thousand?" "Try $1.25 million," he responded.

"Who paid for it," I asked, "the ATC?"

"A former thru-hiker named Happy Feet spent years arranging it with various agencies. It saves the hikers a 3.2-mile boring walk, much of which used to be on the highway."

He then shuttled me into Glasgow to re-supply. Summer was now evident enough that even a hypothermia freak like me felt secure enough to send my winter clothes home through the town post office.

Water was as precious as diamonds at some points during the journey. That often was coupled with bagels, peanut butter, raisins, and Snickers to form many a meal. Like many hikers, I vowed during the journey to never again eat another cold Pop-tart once I finished the trail.

Chapter 11

The skies had looked threatening all day, and within sixty seconds of reaching the Punch Bowl Shelter, the bottom dropped out in a full-fledged downpour. I counted my blessings that for once I had missed a rainstorm. I counted them even more thirty seconds later, when an attractive, middle-aged woman came running completely naked from the stream down below.

"Oh my God," she screamed when she saw me. "Somebody is in here. I'm so sorry."

She continued apologizing profusely ("No, no, really, it's okay") as she dressed behind me. Then a minute later a muscle-bound fellow in a pair of shorts came up much more calmly in the rain and said quietly, "We didn't know anybody was here. We were bathing in the stream."

He was Rambler, from New Hampshire, and she was just Doris, from Ohio. Despite the extremely fortuitous beginning at this shelter the night ended up being a nightmare. Bullfrogs from the pond, which lies just fifty yards away, croaked at the top of their lungs all night. That, along with insatiable mosquitoes, left everybody lying there in anger all night. It's the only place on the entire AT I would never, ever want to see again. There was nothing to do but get up blurry-eyed and get the *hell* out of there.

Rambler, Doris, and I crossed the Blue Ridge Parkway again that morning. A couple Gang of 10 members were standing next to a car doing "trail magic" (giving food, drinks, and rides to hikers). Not wanting to ask the obvious question, I politely accepted a cold drink out of the cooler in their trunk.

"We're down to less than one hundred dollars," Southpaw quietly said. "We can't make it to Maine on that."

"Well, you can feel good you're not doing what others have done — stay on the trail and welch off other hikers," I responded.

"We want to hike to Maine so bad," Nitmuck said poignantly.

All we could do was discreetly leave them a couple dollars in their car and slowly trudge off. They left the trail, went home and got jobs, and a couple months later they had saved enough money to get back on and do the tough northern New England states.

***

Finally, I came upon the infamous Sleazebags. They were milling around Brown Mountain Creek Shelter, girding for the climb that lay ahead. Sure enough there were nine males, just as advertised. They had picked up the Sleazebags moniker because of the extra-short shorts they wore and because of their cavalier attitude toward women. One trail wit had even described them as "a posse of hikers."

Bear, a rock solid early-twentyish hiker, started engaging me with standard hiker banter, and others joined in. While the language was coarse, with F-bombs dropping all around, it quickly became clear that most of them were pretty nice guys. Then I asked, "Which one is Hump Master?"

They pointed to a freckled, red-headed fella' sitting behind me, smoking a cigarette. I turned around and we looked at each other; it was a bit awkward. Neither of us said a word as he continued smoking.

We all departed, despite clouds welling up for what looked like a standard summer afternoon thunderstorm. A two thousand-foot climb lay ahead and the Sleazebags ardently denounced Virginia in a spate of three- and four-letter words.

When we crossed U.S. Highway 60 it had begun drizzling. Some of the Sleazebags decided to hitch ten miles down to a Subway restaurant in a small town to the west. Meanwhile, it started pouring steadily and Camel, a nice nineteen-year-old kid from Atlanta, set up his tarp right by the highway.

"Feel free to get under, Skywalker," he offered to me.

"Thanks," I said. But before I could get under there Hump Master quickly positioned himself right in the middle of the sheltered area and puffed away on his cigarettes while reading a paperback. I contorted my body to get it all under the tarp. But he didn't respond to my non-verbal communication by scooting over and the rain squall soaked my right side as his smoke wafted into my face.

The rain temporarily stopped and we got out from under the tarp, which Camel then pulled up. But a couple minutes later it started to downpour heavily and Camel quickly erected his tarp again. Hump Master once again beat me to spread-eagle himself in the center. And once again smoke hit me from the left side and rain from the right. I tried to rationalize it by thinking just how few truly annoying people I had met thus far on the trail. Finally, it quit raining again and the other Sleazebags arrived from the Subway.

Bounding out of the car, one Sleazebag shouted, "Dude, you completely fucking blew it. The chick at the Subway had a total knockout body. Better than that waitress in Hot Springs and a dead heat with the chick in Damascus."

But another Sleazebag dissented, "Yeah, but her face sucked."

"Fuck her face," the first Sleazebag countered. "Who gives a shit about a fucking face out here in the middle of nowhere?"

As they munched on their sandwiches, George and Ray, two nice section hikers I had chatted with earlier, were searching for their food box. These two were doing their annual two hundred-mile section hike. Their method is to bury food boxes in various places near roads to pick up when they pass by. That saves them re-supply trips into town and helps them maximize the distance they can cover in their annual two-week section hike.

One Sleazebag opined, "I saw those two guys earlier today and I guaran-fucking-tee you they're a bunch of faggots. They're probably just using looking for a food bag as an excuse to go wear each other out in the woods."

"Hell yeah," another Sleazebag responded. "Look at 'em out there with no fucking shirts on, preening around," ignoring the fact that most of the Sleazebags also were shirtless.

We all started the big climb up Bald Knob, and I chatted pleasantly with Sandy and Camel, between gasps. However, when we got to the top it started raining again·and everybody took the disheartening half-mile side trail to the Cow Gamp Shelter. I hurried to claim a spot in the shelter. But when the shelter filled up, lo and behold, Hump Man was right next to me. *Fuck*!

Then the skies opened up again and we were confined to the shelter. For the next two hours I raged within as Hump Master blithely smoked, with the prevailing wind blowing right into my face.

Hanging out with the Sleazebags was like a modern-day rendition of Hemingway's famous short stories, *Men Without Women*. All night I felt like I was in a junior high school locker room. Every girl on the trail was analyzed from head to toe. Speaking of one girl, Pocohantas — who had the courage to hike with them — Moonwalker said, "It's the strangest thing. The legs, the tits, the ass all look okay. But trust me, dude, the whole package together just doesn't work." Then he felt compelled to add, "Sometimes when

I see her early in the morning in a shelter I head straight to the privy."

Camel had the audacity to throw in some mild dissent saying, "Come on, now. Pocohantas is pretty cool." It was a good thing he mounted that minor defense because he and Pocohantas became an item for the last thousand miles on the trail. And unlike most trail romances, it apparently continued.

But there was one name that apparently was far too sacred to even mention: Vogue.

However, at nightfall as the rain slacked off, a former Sleazebag who had fallen behind arrived at the shelter with his headlight on. Immediately, he was debriefed on every detail of the Gang of 10 and specifically, Vogue. "They act like we (Sleazebags) are crazy," he said. "But, let me tell you, the minute they get to a shelter Vogue goes straight to your entries, Hump Master." This generated excitement all over the shelter. And Hump Man got up and walked around like a matinee idol as a knowing smile and "gotcha" look came across his face.

A half-hour later, as the noise lessened, George and Ray trudged through the mud and dark. They looked inside the shelter, saw it was full, and walked over to a clearing to set up their tent. This prompted a Sleazebag from the far corner of the shelter to remark, "Better put the earplugs in tonight."

"Earplugs, my ass," someone blurted from the middle of the shelter. "Remove butt plugs from backpacks and insert immediately!"

The shelter was full, as was often the case on rainy nights. Some contact and bumping was probably inevitable, but Hump Master had his legs draped over part of my sleeping bag. I got so distraught I tried switching from head-to-toe in the middle of the evening.

Overall, the evening was better than the previous evening with the bullfrogs, but not by much. I anxiously packed my bags in the morning and hurried out of there by 7 o'clock before the Sleazebags had even arisen. I didn't know about Hump Master, but most of them seemed like good guys. It was just too much testosterone gathered in one group for any sort of balance to prevail.

***

After thirteen miles I took a steep side trail to a hostel to escape the Sleazebags. I saw Ug there for the first time since Tennessee and with a full-flowing blonde beard and shoulder-length hair he looked like a true mountain man. But with his broad, easy smile he soon became my favorite trail hippie.

Ug (hippie, not caveman) and I took the big climb back to the trail where we ran into a stray member of the former Gang of 10. After several hundred miles of unity, their solidarity had cracked. "We've disbursed, and some have quit," he reported. "Vogue is in a hurry-up mode and is up ahead."

Now that news put a bounce back in my step after some initial apathy. But then I silently chided myself for the hypocrisy of criticizing Hump Master for aggressively pursuing Vogue, and here I was practically "pinkblazing" to catch her. Besides, she had shown no extraordinary interest in me.

But this wasn't a bad day to have a spring in one's step. The trail twice ascended above four thousand feet, including the Priest, which was a quasi-religious experience, with its majestic view of the very blue Blue Ridge Mountains. Then the trail quickly descended thirty-three hundred feet to the Tye River. The parking there in the George Washington National Forest was full on this hot, humid day. I had been thinking all the way down the mountain how heavenly some cold drinks and trail magic would be right here, but it wasn't to be.

Instead, another three thousand-foot climb presented itself. Starting up the mountain I ran into Grump, an elderly gentleman I seemingly passed every day. His signature characteristic was the behemoth pack strapped to his hunched back. "Did you hear the big news on the trail today?" he asked.

"No," I answered.

"There is a naked guy hiking around, scaring all the girls."

"Well, the way the mosquitoes are swarming, he's in a helluva' fix," I noted. Knowing Vogue was up ahead, and maybe the Sleazebags as well, I began to wonder if it wasn't Hump Master himself who had become completely unhinged!

"How do you do it, Grump?" I asked. "I've passed you four times. You must night hike every night to keep getting ahead of people."

"I hike til' these here legs won't go anymore, then I drop anchors," he said.

"Where did you sleep last night?" I asked. "It was raining."

"Oh, along about midnight," he replied, "I threw down my sleeping bag under some overhanging rock and passed out."

Now honing in on his backpack I said, "Grump, you're not in the army anymore. You ought to try some of this lightweight equipment."

Grump grunted.

"How much does that damn thing weigh, I've got to ask."

"Oh, in the neighborhood of seventy-five pounds," he answered.

"Jesus, Grump, you're not going to make it to Maine with that much weight," I lectured him. "Nobody could."

"Now don't worry about me," he said, "I'll be seeing you up there and I'll have enough stuff for both of us." I headed on up the mountain, never to see him again.

***

At the Harper's Creek Shelter a chatty middle-age guy exclaimed "A girl with a University of Michigan hat on just came through here. Good gosh, she was unbelievable." I had been thinking about calling it a day right there because of the big climb immediately ahead, but suddenly I felt a second-wind.

Harper's Creek Shelter — mile 816

6-11-05: *The people who said Virginia is flat are about as right as the people who said the earth is flat.* — **Vogue**

6-11-05: *I hike the AT because I can.* — **Knees**

The sun fell behind the mountains and I was urging myself on when I saw a familiar figure halfway up the mountain. We looked at each other for a second, then the person said, "Skywalker,"

"Ha, not since Hot Springs, right?" I said to Knees, a brainy twenty-nine-year-old computer consultant from Oshkosh, Wisconsin.

"Yeah," he said. "but I've been reading your journal entries in the registers." This was a double boost — to have some company to hike this tough section with and to hear that somebody was reading my journal entries.

Then he gave me a third boost. "Vogue is right ahead," he reported. "We were at the same shelter last night, but her hiking group is breaking up." Standard operating procedure was to take a Snickers break halfway up a large climb. But that news had me straining to keep up with Knees without a break. Finally, the sign for the shelter appeared.

Sitting on the picnic table in front of the shelter was Vogue, with her alluring combination of youth and maturity. She smiled as we walked up and I raised my hand for a high-five. However, she declined to reciprocate, saying, "I'm too tired."

"I heard the tragic news," I strained to gin up the atmosphere.

"What?" she said, semi-alarmed.

"That the famous 'Gang of 10' has officially disbanded."

"Oh, Yeah," she said matter-of-factly. "I was just being held up too much, and finally had to go ahead."

Knees moved off to set up his tent.

"*What a fool you are*," I thought to myself. This girl is very self-possessed and not vulnerable to theatrics. And she had obviously had enough male attention. I even noticed that unlike many females on the trail she didn't hike sleeveless or wear a halter-top. Rather, she wore a full short-sleeve shirt, probably to minimize gawkings. In a more low-key manner I asked, "The Sleazebags; are they ahead?"

With a roll of the eyes she pointed over to a group of tents in a clearing.

"I hiked with 'em a little bit a few days back and they seemed okay," I said. "All but your man, Hump Master."

"My man, Hump Master," she said disgusted.

I then pulled out my stove (alarmed at my plummeting weight, I had purchased it in Damascus) to try cooking. Remembering my previous ineptness she said, "Oh, we're going to try this again, are we?"

"Don't sell me short," I responded.

"Oh, this is the new and improved Skywalker, huh," she laughed.

"Actually, this is the Last Supper because I'm planning to send it home before Shenandoah National Park in order to not attract bears."

"Oh come on," she scoffed.

Blotter, one of the Sleazebags, came by and said to Vogue, "I'm going down to the stream to get water. Would you like some?"

"Oh, that would be nice, thanks," she said. "I'm exhausted."

Then starting down toward the stream Blotter stopped and said as an afterthought, "Would you like some too, Skywalker?"

But I quickly declined, realizing he was just trying to save face and not betray too much fondness toward Vogue. I don't know about all these other animals I was seeing out there in the wilderness, but we humans sure do have our weaknesses.

***

Summer was in full swing now, and like it or not, the woods were teeming with wildlife. When Knees, Ug, and I arrived at the Paul Wolf Shelter one hiker had just seen a bear running down the ridge from the shelter. And while we sat there eating, a big, black snake came out from under the shelter, showing its full seven-foot length. And Shenandoah National Park, with its famously abundant flora and fauna, lay just ahead.

We were planning to stay at this shelter, but the long-promised easier part of Virginia seemed to have finally materialized. We decided to hike the remaining five miles to Waynesboro and arrived at dusk.

When we exited the trail at Rockfish Gap we crossed the street into a big parking lot. A car pulled up with two girls in it. A college-age girl in a bathing suit got out and ran over with three slices of pizza on a small paper plate. "Welcome to Waynesboro," she said. "We love hikers."

"Can we get a ride into town?" I called out.

"We give out pizza, not rides," she shouted out the window as they sped off.

The townspeople in Waynesboro had been instructed to treat hikers well, as we were a source of revenue (which is a pretty fair working definition of a humble town indeed!). Thus, the minute we stuck out our thumbs, a pickup truck pulled over and carried us five miles to the Quality Inn in Waynesboro.

The Sleazebags were in evidence all over the place, from the swimming pool to the parking lot. Hump Master, in a last-ditch Hail Mary pass, had completely shaved his head. He then approached Vogue and apparently got right to the point. But Vogue responded negatively and brusquely headed to her room. Being an attractive girl on the AT has its advantages, but it apparently also has its disadvantages.

The next morning after being embroiled in a dispute over having too many people in our room — a common motel complaint against hikers — I called one of the many trail angels listed in the motel. Unfortunately, everybody seemed to have an excuse why they couldn't hike this day, but the real reason was the hot, humid weather. So a pleasant elderly man chauffeured me back up to the trailhead alone to begin the one hundred-plus-mile trek through Shenandoah National Park.

Chapter 12

On May 14, 2000, the remains of Claudia Bradley, a schoolteacher from Cosby, Tennessee, were found in Great Smoky Mountain National Park. She had been eaten by a bear.

This episode restored to focus a question that scientists, outdoor people, and others have puzzled over through the eons. That is, just why don't bears eat more humans? After all, they voraciously eat almost everything else, including deer, caribou, salmon, birds, ants, rats, wild berries, nuts, and an infinite variety of plants. Experts have noted significant behavioral differences in bears based on what they eat. Those that dine mostly on meat tend to exhibit significantly more aggressive traits than those whose primary diet is plant-based.

Of course, there have been other notable incidents. On April 13, 2006, Susan Cankus, from Ohio, and her two children were on a vacation in the Cherokee National Forest near Chattanooga, Tennessee. They were strategically located in a tourist spot below two waterfalls when a bear approached. They started yelling at it and clanking metal items together to scare it away, but the bear grabbed Mrs. Cankus' two-year-old son in its mouth. Mrs. Cankus frantically attacked the bear with sticks, rocks, and the like. While she ended up with eight puncture wounds in her neck and too many cuts and wounds to count, she successfully dislodged her son. Park rangers, alerted by the pandemonium, arrived and fired two thirty-eight caliber pistol shots into the bear's dense body. At that point the bear ran away. Unfortunately, Mrs. Cankus' six-year-old daughter had run into the woods. When the rangers pursued the bear into the woods they came upon the daughter's lifeless body. She had died from head wounds inflicted by the bear in its flight from camp.

But the fact remains, compared to hundreds of thousands, if not millions, of bear-human encounters yearly, the number of bear attacks is small. Do they respect us, do they fear us, or do they consider us irrelevant? Perhaps we humans smell so horrible and taste so bad that only the most decrepit bear, unable to chase down fleeter and tastier prey, would have the least bit of interest.

Would you believe that cubs only weigh from six to sixteen ounces at birth, and aren't much larger than your average mouse! It's conceptually difficult to reconcile with the enormous size and strength they later achieve? But consider just this one story. At a Philadelphia 76ers basketball game in 1979, a 105-pound, one-year-old *cub* earned a measure of notoriety by eating seventy-seven hot dogs, twenty-one pizzas, and nineteen Cokes just during halftime. Their appetites are truly awesome. Male bears, which are considerably larger than female bears, have even been known to put their lives at risk from irate females by eating their cubs. Bears spend their entire lives hunting for food — they prefer roaming in the daytime, but stories are legion amongst hikers of their moonlighting activities. And they are smart and fast — far faster than any human on the planet (up to thirty mph!), and they are famous for accelerating uphill.

The black bear was originally considered such a great threat to humans that, according to Charles Konopa, "Some Indians classified the bear with man on the hierarchical list; a few tribes thought it was superior." Konopa adds, "It was a ferocious brute. Unprovoked sorties against Indians and European settlers were common."

"I was wrathy to kill a bear," wrote Davy Crocket. He and other testosterone-laden woodsmen indiscriminately killed bears on the Appalachian frontier in the eighteenth and nineteenth century. Indeed, those legendary folk "heroes" were successful in virtually exterminating the black bear in parts of the American East.

Black bears survived by adapting to human behavior. After the advent of gunpowder and mechanized weapons, black bears greatly reduced their "unprovoked sorties" against humans. Instead, they became more cagy and calculating. It is now common for people to venture out into the woods unarmed without overwhelming concern about bears.

But there remain problems. Some, of course, can be chalked up to that old bugaboo — human stupidity. In one notorious case some loving parents poured honey on their young daughter's finger to feed to a bear. The bear liked it so much it helped itself to half of the girl's hand, too.

But another common source of bear-human problems is unavoidable and ultimately more problematic. Stories are legion of hikers ambling along only to see some rambunctious cubs darting around or climbing a tree. Moments later the mother arrives and finds a human with the inside position. There is no simple approach to defusing these potentially very dangerous situations. Ursine protocol calls for the hiker to back up and avoid eye contact with the bear. If the bear moves in your direction you are supposed to throw a stick in its direction. If this doesn't work you try to nail the bear with a rock, preferably in its very sensitive nose. After that, most guidebooks usually trail off with vague language that the hiker should then consider himself in quite a bit of danger (*Gee, thanks for the heads up*). Under no circumstances are you supposed to run, which triggers the bear's instinct to chase prey. Nor should a hiker lie down and play dead.

For the most part these enormous, furry animals are unchallenged in the wilderness with the exception of armed humans (which, incidentally, don't have a perfect record against bears). Black bears, ursus Americanus, have made an astounding comeback as hunting laws have become more restrictive. They now dot the Appalachian mountain range virtually from beginning to end, and chances of encountering one is not low at all. I was amazed to see monuments, drawings, and photographs of bears in almost every town along the Appalachian Mountain Range. Ancient cave paintings show the fascination and fear these enormously powerful creatures engendered, and there remains a general fascination here in the twenty-first century. And with human development encroaching on their habitat, the number of attacks is on the rise.

*

Shenandoah National Park ("the Shennies" in AT lore), which runs 104 miles from end-to-end, is considered one of the easiest parts of the AT. To be sure there are one thousand-foot climbs, but the trail is well-graded, and the inclines rarely more than ten or twelve degree angles. Indeed, I recommend the park as a good practice place for somebody trying to decide whether to attempt the AT.

Because it's a national park, hunting is not permitted. As a result, there's a prevalence of large animals, notably deer and bears — and they've largely lost their fear of humans. By some accounts there is a greater bear density in Shenandoah National Park than anywhere else on earth — more than one per square mile. And unlike in the Smokies, which we traversed at high elevations in the early spring, while the bears were still foraging at lower levels, we would be in "the Shennies" in high summer. Thus, when I entered the park it wasn't the usual things — weather and difficult terrain

— that occupied my attention. It was bears.

At the seven-mile mark I came across two hikers struggling to extract water from a grudging spring. "Any luck?" I asked, walking up on them.

"Barely," the barrel-chested Colonel Mustard replied.

His diminutive friend Pee Wee added, "There is a creek that runs pretty well a few hundred yards ahead."

I bolted ahead, and upon arriving at the creek looked around to make sure I wasn't invading the drinking space of any large animals. I heard a rustling sound on the other side, but it didn't distinguish itself from the hundreds of such sounds one hears here throughout the day. It never ceased to amaze me how much noise a mere squirrel could make. I took the bait every time I heard one.

After drawing some water I climbed out of the creek. Colonel Mustard and Pee Wee were passing by with wide-eyed looks on their faces. "Did you see that cub?" Pee Wee asked.

"No, where?" I asked.

"A minute after you passed us a cub ran down the hill between you and us."

"Did you see the mother anywhere?" I asked.

"No," he replied, "and we weren't about to wait for her either."

So now I had a one-second glimpse of what was apparently a large, but scared bear in southwest Virginia and a near miss of a cub here at the beginning of Shenandoah National Park. Everybody seemed to have great tales to tell on this entrancing subject except me. But I wasn't envious.

Camel and Bear came along while I was taking a break off one of the Skyline Drive crossings. They were two of the more likeable members of the Sleazebags and I was glad to have their company. As we sat there a car stopped and the driver opened his trunk to offer us a choice of soft drinks. Life wasn't bad.

We reached the Blackrock Hut at dusk, after what would be the first of a string of twenty-mile days. Because of an estimated six million annual visitors in the park I had perhaps expected something palatial. Instead, the shelters were modest abodes, but the sturdy native rock gave them their own distinction. It was classic CCC Depression-era stone work.

Over to the side were the bear poles we had heard about. After dinner I went over and used one of the heavy iron poles to hoist my food bag up onto one of the rungs, about twelve feet up.

"Quit staring up there, Skywalker," Bear said noticing my hesitation. "Not even Shaqille O' Neal or you could reach it; much less a bear."

***

But two days later I did find myself in a faceoff with a full-sized adult bear (mentioned earlier). It was the longest thirty seconds of my life. Finally, it slowly turned around and sauntered back up the trail in the direction it had disappeared before. This time I wasn't so calm and continued my mock two-person dialogue. Skyline Drive was only a few hundred yards away, and I pondered bushwhacking through the ferns to get there. But I would have had to walk right through the bushes where this bear had originally been to get there. Who was to say there weren't any more bears in there?

After waiting for someone else to come along in either direction, and maintaining the mock dialogue, I very tentatively started down the trail toward the bend where the bear had disappeared out of sight. Just before reaching the bend I stopped and threw some rocks in the direction the bear had gone to alert it that I was coming. Finally, I took a wide turn to get a better view of anything just beyond the bend. Nothing was there, so I hurried up the trail, scanning the shrubbery on both sides as I continued muttering.

Later, I talked to Bear and Camel who had passed this way soon after me. They had come across a bear at virtually this same point. The bear had stood in the middle of the trail on its hind legs, and the dense bushes on both sides of the trail blocked passage. They threw rocks near, but not at, the bear. The bear growled and continued blocking the trail. They then saw two cubs nearby so they realized it was a mother protecting her family. At that point they headed through the fern trees to Skyline Drive, just as I had previously contemplated doing. If you ask me it was rational behavior on the part of both the mama bear, and the two hikers.

I arrived in high spirits at the Hawksbill Mountain Shelter that third evening in "the Shennies" after having done 65.6 miles in three days, and reveled in telling the tale of "my" bear.

"The bear was probably trying to sucker you into dropping your food bag," Pee Wee said.

"I'll have to admit," I replied, "that while it didn't tear away or look scared, it didn't look aggressive either."

"Sounds like it was a good *starter* bear," Pee Wee said.

As I trooped through the lush foliage and gentle hills of Shenandoah

National Park, bears had now gone from something in the recesses of my mind to front and center. Two nights later I slept at the Gravel Springs Hut, and was stirring around early in the morning when a large black animal appeared climbing through the dense shrubbery in front of the shelter. At first I thought it was the black Labrador of one of the people tented out behind the shelter. But then I saw the prominent snout and wide face and realized it was not a canine, but something much larger. A bear emerged twenty yards in front of me.

Again, besides panic, I felt deceived. With a dog around bears were supposed to stay the hell away. Even though no dog is remotely a match for any half grown bear, the ancient enmity between bears and dogs is well known. And this bear looked in my direction, but it was the second bear in a row that didn't run or even look afraid of me. So there I was once more, carrying on this mock conversation and waving my hiking pole in the air at a nearby bear. Finally, it slowly turned away from the bear poles and moved back down through the shrubbery from where it had come.

One of the tenters then walked from the tent-sites past the bear poles. "A bear was standing there five minutes ago," I reported. He froze in his tracks and I quietly took pleasure in seeing another of these "don't ever worry about bears" hikers tense up when a bear was actually around.

I had been planning to hike out at first light that morning, but quickly changed plans to wait and hike out with the group camped behind the shelter. After being on hair-trigger alert at the mere sound of a pine cone being stepped on or a twig snapping the last few days I greatly enjoyed having company. But my companions took a side trail and I was alone again in Shenandoah National Park with only one mile left. Although I had hiked most of the park alone I became suddenly and irrationally paranoid about bears. The upshot was that I was hurrying, and when the trail went down a rock scale I tumbled headlong down the rocks. Luckily, I braked myself at the last minute to avoid serious injury, but my arms and knees suffered deep bruises.

When the AT exits the northern boundary of Shenandoah National Park it runs for a miserable mile on private property, with a fence along the left side, and dense, high grass on the right, blocking any breeze. All along the way I kept hearing gunshots in the distance. While the owners were probably none too happy to have hikers traipsing along their land I assumed it was probably bears rather than hikers they were shooting at. In a ghoulish way this made me feel more secure.

Ug and I were hiking along the next day and when we heard some heavy rustling in nearby bushes, he playfully said, "Heeeer, kitty, kitty, kitty."

"Wow, aren't you brave," I said impressed.

"No need to worry about these-here bears," Ug said confidently. "They've been hunted and will stay away."

***

Some thru-hikers went home for a vacation during the middle of their thru-hikes — often when the trail passed through their home states. But I didn't want to break the fluency of the journey north, so a two-day break at my sister's house in northern Virginia was going to be my AT "vacation."

Since none of our family or close friends had any experience in long-distance hiking, my sister examined me like a museum piece ("He doesn't smell quite as bad as we had thought.") while speaking on her cell-phone with my mother. I felt like an Apollo astronaut returning from the moon. She and my mother had decided on a quota of eight pounds for me to gain while at her house. This entailed virtual force-feeding to such an extent that twice I had to go to the bathroom to purge myself.

Of critical importance, my sister took me to the local REI to find a tent, but again I couldn't fit in any of the one-person tents. Finally, extremely disillusioned, I agreed to a two-person tent. It weighed almost five pounds, but I was desperate to get rid of my tarp. Amazingly, after *one thousand miles of use, REI gave me a full refund on my tarp.* This tent purchase would prove to be critical in liberating me from the shelters. And it fortified me that if I did make it all the way to northern New England in September, I might be able to handle the cold autumn better than I had the cold spring in the southern Appalachians.

Virginia's five hundred-mile trek finally ends in Harper's Ferry, West Virginia. I walked over the Shenandoah River Bridge on a brilliant summer day, looking down at the magnificent Shenandoah River flowing by. "The passage of the Patowmac through the Blue Ridge," Thomas Jefferson wrote, "is perhaps one of the most stupendous scenes in Nature." He added, "The scene is worth a dozen voyages across the Atlantic." It was all in stark contrast to my desperate hike down from the heights over Harper's Ferry in February with the dark closing in.

part III

"North the word had amplitude now.
North trumped all other places." — **William Fiennes**

Chapter 13

The AT headquarters in Harpers Ferry was surprisingly unimpressive. But my heart leapt when I walked in and saw Whitewater and Nurse Ratchet. I had repeatedly asked hikers for any information on her fate and had only gotten a vague trickle that they had left the trail due to her illness. "The rumors of my demise are greatly exaggerated," she exulted in quoting Mark Twain. They recounted how they had indeed gotten off at the road after the shelter where I had last seen them and hitched a ride to a hospital. She had been diagnosed with kidney stones, which the urologist back at the shelter that morning had said with certainty she didn't have. She was hospitalized for a couple days. Then they had gallantly headed back to the AT and made it all the way here to Harper's Ferry. Pretty damn impressive. It was that kind of spirit, and not a lush headquarters building, that makes the Appalachian Trail.

The ATC took a photo of everyone, along with the date passing through. I then went outside with Nurse Ratchet and Whitewater to reconstitute our hiking group.

The big news on the trail was of a gruesome raccoon attack on a hiker named Sleeveless at the Pine Knob Shelter in Maryland. She was a mid-fifty-ish New Hampshirite who always wore a sleeveless blouse. Well, that was unfortunate because just as she was finishing her camp chores at dusk a raccoon had suddenly lurched out of the shrubbery and attacked her in front of the shelter. At first she had thought it was a bear and screamed bloody murder. All hell broke loose as three hikers tried desperately to get the rabid raccoon off her. It kept latching itself onto different parts of her arm before somebody finally got it off. One of the other hikers then escorted her through the woods in the dark to the nearest road and there they were able to hitchhike to the hospital. The Pine Knob Shelter had been closed by the ATC because of the blood all over it. It gave me pause when I thought back just a few nights ago to a shelter in Virginia — also in front of dense foliage — that I had foolishly slept in despite warnings of raccoon infestation posted in the shelter.

***

The AT crosses a footbridge over the Potomac into Maryland and then ascends to Weverton Cliffs. I was halfway up in a hunched climbing position when I heard a familiar voice from the opposite direction say, "Skywalker." I looked up and saw Warren Doyle's beaming face.

Warren looked at least thirty pounds lighter than when I'd last seen him three months before on an awful evening on a mountain road in Virginia. This was no surprise given his famously horrific hiking diet (stretches of days eating nothing but Little Debbie cakes because of their high-calorie to low-weight ratio).

Better yet, he had a smiling, pleased look on his face and gave me an effusive, Indian-style handshake. "Hanging in there, are we?" he exclaimed.

"You said the trail was inherently difficult," I replied, "and you sure weren't lying."

"Just stay focused on completing each daily task," he advised, "and those distant peaks in New England will soon be right in front of your eyes."

I then introduced him to Whitewater and Nurse Ratchet. "Every time we go up a hill," Nurse Ratchet said, "Skywalker quotes you: 'You can never go too slowly up a hill.'"

"Sounds like you've learned a lot," Warren said approvingly.

"I couldn't have gotten any worse, if you'll remember," I said, and we both laughed.

"Warren, have you ever seen anybody hike that had kidney stones?" Whitewater asked.

"One time, about fifteen years ago, and it was one of the best hikes I ever saw," Warren said enthusiastically.

"My wife has them now," Whitewater said.

Furrowing his brow Warren replied, "I've rarely seen anyone hike the trail in its entire length without some severe pain at some point. But there is pleasure in pain." He turned to go and remembered to say, "Watch your zero days and stay focused on your daily task, Skywalker. Good luck."

And then he was off with his sideways waddle that has carried him thirty thousand miles on the Appalachian Trail.

***

The trail runs along Antietam Creek, scene of the historic Civil War battle. In fact, September 16, 1862, at Antietam was the single bloodiest day in American history. An estimated twenty-five thousand people were killed on just this one day, and that was when the country was only eleven percent of its current population.

Antietam was one of the two times — Gettysburg was the other — that Robert E. Lee's army crossed the Potomac to seize enemy territory. General George McClellan repulsed Lee's advance. But then McClellan inexplicably allowed Lee's army to slip back across the Potomac and regroup to fight other battles. President Lincoln was so aghast at McClellan's unwillingness to go on the offensive that he famously asked McClellan, "General, if you are not going to use your army, do you mind if I borrow it?" McClellan's response was unsatisfactory and Lincoln fired him a month later.

One-hundred-forty-three years later, walking through the shadow of history on this hot summer day in the midst of a drought, Antietam Creek was about the only source of running water.

We got to the shelter and anxiously asked about water. A hiker of ample girth named Not Guilty said, "There is a spring down that hill that is flowing very, very grudgingly." He was very, very correct. I pulled out my filter, which I had picked up at my sister's house, and thanked my lucky stars for having it. The spring just barely trickled into a modest-sized water puddle, with bugs dancing on top. Without a filter I would have dredged up a potion full of leaves, dirt, and bugs. As it was, after extensive pumping, I had a perfectly clear Nalgene bottle full of water.

We got back to the shelter and began chatting with Not Guilty. "I am a defense attorney in Alaska," he said. "I'm always pleading 'not guilty.'" Not Guilty was an ex-college football player, and had weighed almost four hundred pounds when he began his thru-hike in early March. He had lost almost one hundred pounds up to this point and was gaining speed every day as he regained his athletic form.

***

The Four-State Challenge requires hiking in four states in one twenyfour-hour period. Hikers start on the Virginia-West Virginia line at midnight. After covering five hundred miles in Virginia, The AT is in West Virginia for just 2.4 miles. The trail then enters Maryland for exactly 40.4 miles. Thus, to complete the Four-State Challenge a person must hike exactly 42.8 miles in one twenty-four-hour period.

Smiley and Crucible arrived at the shelter about eight o'clock that evening in their bid to meet the Four-State Challenge. He was a fit, twenty-six-year-old Texan, and she a thirty-one-year-old, ex-pro soccer player from New Jersey. Their body language bespoke two things. They were more than hiking partners, and they were exhausted. They had started hiking at midnight and done thirty-three miles so far. It was 9.2 miles to the Pennsylvania border to complete the challenge. They ate a quick snack and then as darkness closed in dutifully hoisted their packs to try to beat the midnight deadline. My heart went out to them.

"Goodbye," Not Guilty said. "At your pace we will never see you again."

"Oh yes you will," Crucible promised. "We're taking tomorrow off right where we finish at midnight tonight."

After nine miles the next day Whitewater, Nurse Ratchet, and I arrived at Penn-Mar Park, which delineates the border between the two states. "I'm surprised Smiley and Crucible aren't sprawled on the ground somewhere around here," I said.

"Didn't you see the no-camping sign?" Nurse Ratchet said.

Soon we were the ones sprawled out taking a break, but as usual Nurse Ratchet cracked the whip. "Pack up," she snapped. "Let's push on." And as usual she got off five minutes before I did. After two-tenths of a mile the trail crossed a train track that had a marker on the other side. It was the Mason-Dixon Line, an imaginary line that symbolizes passage from the South to the North or vice-versa. Mason and Dixon themselves were two surveyors who were contracted in 1763 to settle a border dispute between Pennsylvania and Maryland.

Less than a minute after passing the marker I heard a voice from behind some trees at the top of the hill call out, "Skywalker." Smiley opened his tent flap with a look that appeared flush with success.

"You made it," I said expectantly.

"Yeah, it was tough following the trail at night," he said. "That slowed us down and we didn't get here until 1:30, so I guess technically we didn't make it. But it was good enough for us."

"Congratulations, and to you as well, Crucible," I said.

"Thanks," she said demurely. Smiley was in a chatty, celebratory mood, asking where everybody was, etc., while Crucible looked like she didn't care if she hiked another single day on the AT in her life.

When I headed on and turned the corner Whitewater and Nurse Ratchet were having a good laugh. "Did you hear that couple in the tent up there?"

Nurse Ratchet asked giggling. "They must have been on their honeymoon."

"You're talking about Smiley and Crucible?" I asked.

"Is that who it was?" she exclaimed excitedly. "We were trying to guess. She was screaming at the top of her lungs."

"By the time I got there he called down to me and practically wouldn't let me leave," I reported. "She looked like she wanted to drop dead, though — after forty-two miles in one day and now Smiley rampaging."

And it was rich in irony. The Texan and the New-Jerseyite had chosen the Mason-Dixon Line to celebrate and consummate. The people from the two sides sure were getting along better than during the tumultuous events right in this area 143 years before. *Finally*!

Of course, it was no surprise that romances would be struck up in any endeavor as intense as an AT thru-hike. The same scene played itself out again a couple days later. Smiley had again called out to me from his tent in a chatty mood next to a supine Crucible. The sun and moon of sexual reassurance shone in his face. Fifteen minutes later I caught up with Mayfly, a prim and proper, lanky solo hiker from South Carolina. She had passed their tent, set up five yards off to the side of the AT, while the fireworks were in progress. She related in amazed tones what she had just walked past.

Don't ask me how, but Smiley and Crucible made it all the way through Pennsylvania. She then had to get off to return to her job as a school teacher, and, if what I heard was correct, her husband. As they say, the Appalachian Trail is the journey of a lifetime.

***

The AT runs 250 miles through Pennsylvania, third only to Virginia and Maine in length. The elevation is low throughout the Allegheny Range, but the footway is infamous. Seemingly endless broken-up boulder fields present themselves to the hiker. It is also reputed to have the meanest rattlesnakes on the trail. What's more, thru-hikers normally pass through Pennsylvania during high summer, when the bugs and heat are at their worst. Finally, the AT in Pennsylvania includes long stretches without any available water sources.

Given all that, it comes as no surprise that Pennsylvania is one of the least-favorite states for every thru-hiker. In fact, the two states after it, New York and New Jersey, are also rocky, hot and dry when thru-hikers pass in mid-summer. It all forms a sort of psychological test. And it's here in Pennsylvania that all the initial excitement and momentum from a long-planned hike completely ebbs and the adventure starts to feel like a real job. Depression sets in and people quit. I tried to look upon these down moments as existential to the entire endeavor.

The trail in Pennsylvania begins in the Michaux State Forest before emptying out onto checkerboard-like pastures of farmland. Arguably, the first one hundred miles in Pennsylvania are the very easiest on the entire trail.

Nurse Ratchet, Whitewater, and I, along with a young kid with an independent streak named Break Time, arrived at U.S. Highway 30 after a few days in Maryland and Pennsylvania. Nurse Ratchet had mentioned a particular "problem" that, if not attended to with a special product, would require her to get off the trail. The four of us hitched to the local grocery store to re-supply, but in keeping with most rural stores, its supplies were limited. While waiting in the checkout line I quietly asked a lady where to get this particular product around this area.

Looking at the four of us, she asked, "Are you hikers?"

"How did you ever guess?" I responded.

"I've always wanted to hike the AT," she bubbled. "Can I give you all a ride somewhere?" We jumped into the back of her pickup and she took us to a nearby pharmacy that had everything Nurse Ratchet required. She then took us to a local restaurant and we were obviously effusive in thanking her when she dropped us off.

As we were wrapping up our meal, Whitewater looked out and said, "Somebody must have left something. That lady is back." But we all quickly took stock of our backpacks, hiking poles, etc., and nothing was missing.

"I just got home," she said when arriving at our table, "and was bragging to my husband about these four AT hikers I met. He told me he wants to cook everybody some steaks and do your laundry." Even though we had just finished lunch we all looked at each other, laughed hysterically, and got up to put our backpacks back in her pickup.

Her husband, Mike, an ex-special-ops military guy was as down-to-earth and authentic a fellow as you could ever want to meet. So perhaps, along with rocks, snakes, humidity, and black flies, Pennsylvania turns out authentic people. All things considered, not a bad tradeoff!

Just as promised they did our laundry and cooked us a full steak dinner. Despite all his adventures overseas in the Special Forces, Mike was wide-eyed and wondrous as he asked one enthusiastic question after another about our journey. They even asked us to stay for the evening, but we were so self-centered we wanted to get back to the trail and eke out a few miles before dark.

When they dutifully dropped us back at the trailhead where we had gotten off earlier in that day, Mike said, "Could I just ask one thing of you?"

"Sure, sure," we all replied.

"Please," he pleaded, "just drop us a line when it's all over letting us know how it all came out," and handed us a piece of paper with an address.

"Not only will we do that," I said, "but we are going to be bragging to everybody about the best trail magic anyone has had so far."

We were certainly good for the latter promise (we bragged about it in the register at the Quarry Gap Shelter that night and to anybody within earshot for the next few days), but we weren't true to the former. We lost the address and never sent them a communique.

***

Hike Naked Day is a surprisingly non-controversial several-year-old tradition on the AT. Perhaps that is because it has been such a smashing success. "Nudity is a state of mind," one hiker infected with the counter-culture mindset stated plainly. In fact, political and social correctness has now set in to the point that many refer to it as "Clothing Optional Day."

The standard operating procedure in any male-female hiking tandem on Clothing Optional Day is for the males to hike boldly out front, with ladies meekly and furtively trailing far behind. One male hiker, Dasher, led a coterie of three women in a "clothing impermissible" jaunt through southern Pennsylvania. That night at a shelter he mocked them for self-consciously looking over their shoulders every few seconds. "Wait a minute," Cutie Pie (one of the three girls) said, "you promised you were going to do nothing but look ahead. How did you know we were looking around?"

"Because I have eyes in the back of my head," came back the predictable quip.

"How was the participation this year?" I asked Grandpa, a veteran trail wag.

"Better than ever," he enthused, "but a real gender gap is opening up. I don't know how we can improve female participation."

"Making blindfolds mandatory for males would be a start," Cutie Pie muttered.

For their part, Nurse Ratchet and Whitewater are God-fearing, teetotaling Baptists who don't smoke, drink, cuss, or hike naked. Nor did I participate. Given how much weight I had dropped, my 6'11" skeletal frame might have scared some unsuspecting hiker even more than a bear.

***

Pine Grove Furnace State Park marks the halfway point of an AT thru-hike. This was somewhat ironic to me because as a southerner I have most of my life thought of Pennsylvania as a northern state.

The long-running tradition among AT thru-hikers is to attempt at the halfway point to eat a half-gallon of ice cream in one hour. All day, as we raced at an accelerated pace to get there, the buzz on the trail was about who would attempt to do it. In the shelter register 3.7 miles shy of Pine Grove Furnace State Park appeared the following entries:

Tom's Run Shelters — mile 1,081

5-5-05: *To ice cream or not to ice cream. That is the question.* — **Paparazzi**

5-5-05: *Having skipped the Four-State Challenge, and even more inexcusably opted out of Hike Naked Day, I will not be denied the half-gallon challenge.* — **Skywalker**

A heavy thunderstorm delayed my progress, and upon finally arriving, fifteen or twenty hikers were gathered on the general store porch. As I approached people started shouting, "Skywalker, you're the man. Yeah, baby, you can do it!" I felt like a Roman Gladiator bracing to do battle. But being so soaked, I felt it necessary to dry myself off in the nearby bathroom. The crowd hissed when I announced this delay.

But ten minutes later I was back, determined to join the ranks of AT thru-hikers who have met the Half-Gallon Challenge. I put the half-gallon on the counter and paid the decidedly ambitious price of $5.95. No trail angel was this old tycoon. The rules of the Half-Gallon Challenge are that you are allowed an hour to consume the entire thing. After that, comes the tricky part. You had to hold it down for another hour before rushing to the conveniently located nearby bathroom.

Whitewater and Nurse Ratchet had both sailed through with flying colors earlier. Meanwhile, three hundred-plus-pound Not Guilty had proved to be no match for a half-gallon. After about a half-hour it became clear that my 6'11" frame, and now only 180 pounds, was no match either. Whitewater saw me slumped over the carton and said, "Skywalker, what's the matter?"

"The sugar's doing a number on me," I replied.

"Poor thing," Nurse Ratchet ridiculed.

When I went over to throw the rest of it away Nurse Ratchet said, "Skywalker, you are the biggest wimp in the world."

"No," I replied, "I'm the tallest wimp in the world." Then I moped over to the hiker register and wrote:

Pine Grove Furnace State Park — mile 1,087

5-5-05: *UNCLE — Skywalker*

***

Complaints were rampant as we traipsed through the Cumberland Valley grain fields in broiling sun. But, given my urban background, I found it pretty novel hiking through ripening corn and wheat fields. And there was another thing I liked about it. It was flat as a table top.

At several points the trail was a narrow corridor through high stalks of corn on both sides.

"Boy, those farmers sure have been generous to let the trail run straight through their crop like this," I remarked.

"Oh no, they hate hikers," the defense lawyer Not Guilty corrected me. "We're lucky if they don't shoot us. The ATC and the local trail maintenance clubs have fought many a legal battle to obtain the right of eminent domain for hikers to pass through here."

In fact he turned out to be correct. Originally, the trail ran over hundreds of miles of private property. Fortunately, the ATC and local trail clubs have been able to gin up enough money through private contributions, legislative grants, and the like to narrow to just twenty-nine miles the amount of private property through which the AT passes. And on those twenty-nine miles you have passages that have been carefully designed and negotiated through private farmland and the like.

After a couple more days the trail finally left the corn and wheat fields and entered the famous fields of Pennsylvania rocks. They aren't large boulders, but rather small, sharp stumble stones the size of bricks that keep your speed down as you pick from one to the next.

Whitewater was slightly faster than me, but in normal terrain I generally moved at a slightly quicker pace than Nurse Ratchet. However, in these rock fields, with my head down, I struggled to keep up with them. What's more, with my head constantly looking down at the rocks I was having trouble following the trail.

The trail went down Cove Mountain and then right through the streets of Duncannon, Pennsylvania. Once again Nurse Ratchet and Whitewater were ahead of me, and while descending Cove Mountain I wasn't seeing any blazes. Finally, instead of arriving in the center of town I arrived in what appeared to be the outskirts of the city. Spotting a fellow-human I said,

"Could you please tell me where the AT is?"

"You're on the old AT," he laughed good-naturedly. "The new AT runs through the downtown area." So, off I hiked a couple extra miles not so good-naturedly to the town center. I finally saw Whitewater and Nurse Ratchet waiting in front of the Doyle Hotel.

"Skywalker, did you get lost?" Nurse Ratchet asked.

"Somehow I ended up on the bloody *old* AT," I muttered.

She laughed and said, "When we took that left turn there on Cove Mountain we predicted you'd go straight."

Jesus Christ, I thought. Just when it looked like I was gaining some confidence as a hiker I had missed a critical turn in the trail. Worse yet, they had predicted it and turned out to be right! And to top it off, the well-known local trail angel Mary had been at the bottom of Cove Mountain to deliver trail magic to Whitewater and Nurse Ratchet.

If I made it all the way to Mount Katahdin I was planning to make up for my 5.5-mile blunder leaving Hot Springs, North Carolina. But I'd be damned if I was going to redo a mile I missed on the new section of the AT in Pennsylvania instead of the three miles I did on the old one.

Chapter 14

The Doyle Hotel looks like something out of the 19th century Wild West. It's one hundred years old and had been one of the original Anheuser-Busch hotels. You enter the hotel through a dilapidated saloon entrance, and make room arrangements with the bartender. The price had recently been raised to $17.50 for a single.

Walking through the streets of Duncannon, a fiftyish hiker named 49er observed, "This looks like another old company town that was devastated when the U.S. lost the steel business." Indeed, the main street along the train tracks had nothing much to offer in the way of thriving enterprises. Sadder still, many of the denizens looked as if they had taken to the bottle as consolation.

"It makes you wonder," I conceded. "I've always been an avid supporter of free trade, but this place shows the grotesque consequences." In fact, the last twenty years has seen an unprecedented reduction in poverty and hunger in the two largest countries in the world, China and India. But the hard-working members of communities like these in rural Pennsylvania, that had formed the backbone of the American middle-class, had borne the brunt of the pain.

I hiked out of Duncannon as quickly as possible the next morning after being kept awake by blaring music and revelry all evening. The trail runs for almost a mile on the bridge over the Susquehanna River. Normally, I was morose as the last vestiges of civilization disappeared behind me when leaving a trail town. But, on this occasion with huge trucks flying by on the left and a low rail on the right between me and the river, I was quite glad to arrive at the woods.

Pine Grove Furnace State Park, fifty miles back, is the official halfway point on the AT. However, Warren Doyle had said the Susquehanna is the real halfway point in terms of time and effort required for a thru-hike because of the greater difficulty in northern New England. Given that it was July 2, and I had started on April 10, I was on schedule to make it, though not with much time to spare.

The weather forecast was invariably the same on these high–summer days: hot, humid, and with a chance of thunderstorms. Whitewater,

Nurse Ratchet, and I often tried to predict whether it was going to rain on these days. My forecasting record was appalling, while theirs was merely bad. The irony was that each day we fervently hoped it wouldn't rain, but rain was absolutely essential.

Whitewater, Nurse Ratchet, 49er, and I climbed up Stony Mountain to make twenty-one miles for the day. Fortunately, I had carried almost two liters of water up the mountain from the creek below because it was dry as a bone at the top. Some hikers already camped out up there had walked a half mile down the side of the mountain looking for running water, but to no avail. Serendipity prevailed for Whitewater, who was dangerously low on water. A section hiker, who was headed back down the mountain, gave up most of his water to Whitewater. The next morning we all quickly packed up and moved on. The data book showed no water for eight miles, and not even that was a certainty.

The famous Pennsylvania black flies were beginning to reach full expression. Pesky bugs orbited our faces, and even running didn't seem to shake them. We were especially amazed at the way they dive-bombed our open eyes, presumably to get at the liquid inside them. Two hands were far too few for defense. Uncharacteristically agitated, Whitewater vented, "I can't believe it. The same bug has been stalking me for the last three days."

"But it wasn't in the tent with you last night, was it," I pointed out.

"No," he said, "he waits outside of it all night and jumps me first thing in the morning."

Nurse Ratchet and I laughed, but he sounded serious. I whispered to her, "He doesn't really believe that, does he?"

"Yes, he does," she said. "He was going on and on about it in the tent last night." It sounded incredible, but the way bugs had also been stalking and orbiting me for long periods during the day I began to believe it could be possible. And Whitewater stoutly maintained this for hundreds of miles, as it shook his customary composure and good humor.

Finally, we got to the Rausch Gap Shelter and eagerly sought the spring. We were relieved to see that even a minor trickle was flowing. When Nurse Ratchet disappeared into the woods to relieve herself I said, "Let's tell her we're quitting."

"If these bugs keep up like this," Whitewater said, "I just may." We lay

With the Troll family (Troll, Anchor, and Oblivious) on a perfect day for hiking. What a cool thing for a family to do—hike the Appalachian Trail. I bet 10 year-old Oblivious learned more that year than he ever would have in school.

there with our backpacks as headrests as she walked up.

"Do you want to hear the good news or the bad news?" I asked.

"What?" she asked.

"I've often wondered whether dropping off the trail is a long, drawn-out decision or happens on the spur-of-themoment. In my case, it's the latter. Whitewater can speak for himself."

"Shut up," she said.

"Honey, we're going back home to Tennessee," Whitewater drawled. "I've had all of these bugs I can take."

"Right, let's go," she said impatiently. But we weren't going anywhere.

"Do you know?" I said dreamily, "a sizable minority of the population never believed humans ever landed on the moon. They think it was all staged."

"Maybe it was," Whitewater said drolly.

"Well, I think it is the same with this Appalachian Trail. Everybody I've seen lately has been miserable or quitting. No way they're hiking the whole thing."

"Ya'll better not be serious," Nurse Ratchet said sternly, sounding a bit more concerned.

Finally, after about thirty minutes of hectoring and deriding us, she said, "Well, you two losers can do what you want. I'm hiking." With that off she stomped into the distance. Our dark moments of the soul soon passed and we slowly got up, hoisted our packs, and unenthusiastically trudged after her.

We hiked until dark and were able to root out 21.3 miles for the day. At the William Penn Shelter on Blue Mountain we watched 4th of July fireworks exploding in the distance. All that probably inspired my trail journal entry:

William Penn Shelter — mile 1,175

7-4-05: At the Continental Congress, which decided to rebel against mighty England, Pennsylvania's Ben Franklin famously said, "Let us all hang together, or else we shall hang separately." We hikers should keep that in mind. — **Skywalker**

We were passing by the Pennsylvania 501 shelter the next day as the weather looked threatening. Again, entropy set in with Whitewater and me, while Nurse Ratchet roused us out of our lethargy. "I'm going on," she said. "You two wimps can do whatever you want." Soon we were trailing after her.

Hiking to dusk we made it to a point in our data book that showed a spring two-tenths mile off the AT. We walked expectantly down only to find the spring empty. Finally, after walking several hundred more yards, we ran across a very small pool of barely moving, bug-infested water. We had no alternative but to get out our filters and pump laboriously.

After pitching our tents in a small, clear area Whitewater said, "Skywalker, I'm tired of watching you eat cold food. We've got an extra dinner in our pack, and I'm gonna' cook it for you." I accepted and enjoyed it heartily.

They were great company, and certainly had more to offer me in a hiking sense than I did to them. That night was fabulous. Just as we finished eating and Whitewater hung the food, a magnificent electrical storm began. It thundered and rained all night as we were safely tucked in our tents. The streams would be flowing again the next day.

After a ten-mile hike, the trail ran right through the streets of Port Clinton. The other towns in which the trail had passed straight through the streets — Damascus and Hot Springs — were hiker favorites so we had high hopes. The only restaurant in town was at the Port Clinton Hotel. We tried to walk into the restaurant, but the manager rushed up with an alarmed look on his face to say, "Excuse me. You can't come in here. Hikers eat at the bar." I was well aware of our fetid odor, but segregating us so formally was nonetheless galling.

Hikers milled around in the bar, where the service was erratic. While eating, I turned around to talk to Paparazzi, whereupon the waitress, who apparently considered herself Pamela Anderson's twin sister, cleared away my plate — including my half-eaten burger. Paparazzi again captured the situation, saying, "Remember how Damascus bills itself as the friendliest town on the trail. Well, Port Clinton is the least friendly."

A Nor'Easter tropical rain storm was forecast for the next two days, and the hotel was full. Nurse Ratchet and Whitewater were planning to hike out, while everybody else stayed put. I decided at the last minute to stay under the pavilion shed in the center of Port Clinton, which earned me no admiration from Nurse Ratchet and Whitewater. I wondered if I would ever see them again.

***

At the Pavilion I ran into the notorious Troll family for the first time. Troll was a thirty-seven-year-old from Washington state who was attempting to lead his wife, Anchor, and ten-year-old son, Oblivious, the entire length of the trail. Anchor was career Navy and always hiked behind her husband and son, thus occasioning her trail name. Oblivious was your typical happy-go-lucky ten-year-old boy who was blissfully oblivious to all problems. Their signature characteristic was the dark Scottish kilts they wore.

"Kilts are lighter, more durable, and cause fewer rashes," Troll said. "It was a no-brainer." Because of their outfits and having a ten-year-old kid bidding to thru-hike, they were among the most well-known hiking groups on the AT.

A sixty-seven-year-old psychiatrist named Chronic Fatigue Syndrome also was on hand in the pavilion. "This is my third thru-hike on the AT," he said, "and my wife calls me a repeat offender."

After a night in the pavilion I resolved to hike out with this eclectic cast, regardless of the rain. The biggest surprises in hiking ability were Chronic Fatigue Syndrome at age sixty-seven and Oblivious at age ten.

Chronic Fatigue Syndrome had picked up his name because of his constant state of exhaustion from maintaining a whirlwind pace all day. He indeed had the face of a sixty-seven-year-old, but with his erect posture and confident gait could be mistaken for an NFL running back from a distance.

But then none of this should have come as a surprise when I found out what state he was from: New Hampshire. He also added a touch of class to the trail with his considerable erudition. He could discourse at length on Freud and other worldly topics, which represented a significant elevation from the normal level of trail gossip.

Oblivious had an unusually confident and erect stride for a ten-year-old. He was always ahead of his mother, who anchored the group, and he never complained. At the end of the day he was the one who had enough energy left to dutifully go, often down steep hills, to find water. He weighed seventy-five pounds and was carrying a fifteen-pound backpack, which put his pack/body weight ratio at 20 percent; around the trail norm. The family slept in one big tent that Troll carried, and cooked dinner in one big pot that they ate out of with separate spoons. Before going to bed Troll searched their bodies closely with his headlamp for ticks.

They had started March 15, and I reckon any early observer of them back in Georgia would have been very dubious about their chances of making it this far. But they got up and out early every day and hiked long hours to make up for their relative lack of speed. It was an impressive effort to watch.

One night at the Allentown Hiking Club Shelter we sat in our sleeping bags and the discussion turned to bears. "Hopefully, everybody here is quite aware just which body part a bear eats first," I said.

"Your stomach," Troll said flatly.

"Bears don't eat you," Anchor said, sounding surprised.

"Troll," I stated in as serious tone as I could muster, "you've taken your family on an epic journey and haven't even investigated the most imminent threat to them."

"Okay, I've got it," Oblivious said. "Bears eat your legs so you can't run away."

"No, they eat your head," I lectured them. "They like dessert first."

Chronic Fatigue Syndrome was listening in on this morbid discussion and said, "Let's see Skywalker. The word in Latin for bear is 'ursu.' You have ursuphobia." With this formal diagnosis by a clinical psychologist, the adjective "ursuphobia" attached to my identity, second only to tall.

Chronic Fatigue Syndrome then said, "Just ponder this over all night, Skywalker. On a still, windless day — when you see a clump of bushes moving — you've got company."

"Jesus Christ," I said. "That sounds like the Viet Cong."

Oblivious warmed to the subject and it was clear that he was different from so many modern-day kids. In this age of cell phones and iPod's, when so many kids tune adults out, he actually enjoyed talking to adults. Finally, his father said, "Shut up, Oblivious. I'm not carrying you in my backpack tomorrow."

From there on out, whenever I would clear a hill and see the Troll family down below I would begin screaming at the top of my lungs, "Bear, bear, bear."

Oblivious would then yell back, "Everybody, cover your head."

More than once, a concerned-looking stranger would approach, to say in a hushed voice, "Excuse me, did I hear there is a bear nearby?"

"No worries," Troll would assure the frightened individual. "He just has ursophobia."

Chapter 15

"This is hell in its full glory, coming up," Chronic Fatigue Syndrome said.

We were now in eastern Pennsylvania in the worst of the rocks. Some were giant boulders that often necessitated using both hands to advance. These were usually in exposed areas, where the heat was worst in the middle of the summer. It was said that you could hear rattlesnakes under these boulders, but I never stuck around to listen. However, I once saw a big rattlesnake sunning on the boulder next to the one I was traversing. Another time I put my hand on a boulder to heave myself up and when my eyes cleared the surface of the boulder I saw my hands were less than a foot from a snake of undetermined type.

In the searing sun it was often difficult to see the white blazes on rocks. The downhills were especially dreadful. Once I ended up on the side of a hill in a huge series of boulders, with no blaze in sight. All I could do was laboriously and angrily retrace my steps, until I finally found the trail again.

But mostly this section was small, flat, sharp-edged stumble-stones for miles on end. The brand-new hiking shoes I had picked up thirteen days before at my sister's house were already severely mangled by the constant banging against sharp rocks. Because it wasn't terribly hilly it was especially frustrating. Everybody thought they should be going fast, but couldn't. Plus, my feet were hurting like hell. Up to this point I had often nursed sore feet at night, but never anything as anguishing as this.

***

Troll had a propensity to fly off the handle easily. One afternoon after a thunderstorm he arrived at a campsite in an extremely agitated state. "This Appalachian Trail is the worst designed bleeping trail I've ever been on," he ranted, his face turning crimson-red. "They constantly route it over PUD's and through rock fields."

I asked Anchor, "What's a PUD?"

"A purposeless up and down," she replied. It was said of the AT that it never left a hill unpassed and that the trail was constantly re-routed to incorporate pointless ups and downs. The AT is like some old-time religion," wrote one frustrated hiker. "It heads for the top of every mountain." However, the ATC staunchly rebutted this charge, saying that every hill the trail covered fit into a grander purpose.

As for Troll's charge that the AT was *needlessly* routed through rock fields, all I could see anywhere, both on and to the side of the trail, were rocks everywhere. I had never, ever had any idea that the wilderness could be so rocky. It was daunting, almost overwhelming.

In Pennsylvania's rocky section hikers also hit the driest forty-mile stretch on the AT. On a Sunday afternoon everybody was trying to hike all the way to Palmerton, where hikers are allowed to stay for free in the old county jail. This, of course, spurred many jokes, but the lack of water was no laughing matter. After ten miles that afternoon, with no water in sight, several of us arrived expectantly at the aptly named Bake Oven Knob Shelter. The data book listed a water source here, but the spring was a steep two hundred yards down from the shelter. "I'll go check it," Ug said. Fifteen minutes later he came back with a grim look on his face. There wasn't much anybody could do but quickly hoist our backpacks and start the forced march to Palmerton.

Nobody said anything for the next seven miles. There was no need to. We were all thinking about only one thing: water. At least it got everybody's mind off the rocks. Nobody was ever happier to enter the Palmerton jail than our hiking group of six. I don't know about prisoner standards, but by hiker standards it was actually quite lavish. There was a basketball court, showers, and bunk beds. Hikers began referring to it as the Palmerton Hilton.

And it was nice that it was so hospitable, because the hike out of Lehigh Gap outside of Palmerton is the most difficult quarter mile south of the White Mountains. It is also one of the most dangerous places on the AT. In places the trail ascends straight up the face of some steep and treacherous rocks at about a fifty- or sixty-degree angle. This rock scale had not been part of the AT when Earl Shaffer did the first thru-hike in 1948. "It really shouldn't be part of the AT," Shaffer wrote in his notoriously laconic style when he hiked it again in 1998 on the fiftieth anniversary of the first thru-hike.

For a few anxious moments when I couldn't figure out how and where to heave myself over a particular boulder, I would have agreed. Princess, a mountain climber from Colorado, scaled up with me and said, "I had no idea the AT had any climbs like that."

At the top of Blue Mountain the trail is flat as a tabletop for several miles, with one great peculiarity. The vegetation on the mountain is completely devastated from eighty-two years of zinc smelting in Palmerton. The EPA finally shut down the plant in 1980. "This is eerie," Anchor said.

"Yeah, it looks like the day after a nuclear attack," Troll agreed.

"And they told me back at the jailhouse to not even consider drinking any water around here," I said.

"You haven't got to worry about that," Troll said noting the rocky, dry conditions.

Indeed, I had brought three liters (more than six pounds) of water onto the trail this day, but was carefully conserving it.

When we descended into Wind Gap, hoping to find some water, we saw some cartons lying on the side of the trail, placed by trail angels. Our hopes soared as we approached with anticipation. But it wasn't to be, as they were all empty. Troll and Oblivious walked twenty more yards, when Troll gasped, "It's a bear. Look."

I looked all right, and in the open area, under the power lines, was the biggest bruin I have ever seen. We stood there as the bear concentrated on its line of scent. Then it seemed to perk up at the notice of us and galloped up the grassy hill and into the woods.

Troll was screaming back to Anchor, "Hurry, hurry, honey, get a picture," but she was too late.

Unlike the two standoffs I had in Shenandoah National Park, this happened so fast there was no time to panic. And, for the record, ten-year-old, 4'10," seventy-five-pound Oblivious stood directly between the bear and me.

"Was that bear looking at your head, Oblivious?" I asked.

"No, Skywalker," he replied, "he was looking at your stomach."

We walked fifty more yards down to the road, where the veteran trail angels — twenty years of doing trail magic— Gordon and Sue were waiting with their van and cold Gatorades. "This stuff is the nectar of the gods," I said savoring a cold, sixteen-ounce bottle. "I'm putting you in my will, Gordon."

"You better have a will," Troll said, "the way that bear was looking at your head."

"Ha, after your bravura attitude toward them the other night in the shelter," I responded, "I was disappointed you didn't run up and try to pet it."

"Not that bear," he replied. "That sucker weighed almost five hundred pounds (By the time we were in our sleeping bags that night we had that same bear weighing 'easily six hundred pounds!')."

"It was probably a male," Gordon said. "They're much larger and have ho-hum attitudes. I saw a smaller cub cross this road about a half hour ago."

***

The bugs were hellish. I had left the body of my tent at my sister's house to save two pounds. But without netting to protect me, I even had to fight them at night, and sleep became very difficult. And the rocks had me spooked and in excruciating pain. I began anxiously inquiring from every southbounder or experienced northbounder for details of the rocks that lay ahead.

Leroy Smith Shelter — mile 1,259

5-5-05: *Pennsylvania rocks.* — ***Paparazzi 5-5-05***: *I'd rather live on the dark side of the moon than in Pennsylvania.* — ***Hamburger***

5-5-05: *First place: one trip to Pennsylvania. Second place: three trips to Pennsylvania.* — ***Chronic Fatigue Syndrome***

I decided at this campsite that I would do my best to make it 20.4 miles to Delaware Water Gap the following day, just to finish off Pennsylvania. The trail ran through Wind Gap for the seven-mile stretch that reputedly had the worst rocks in all of Pennsylvania. At one point in a particularly vicious section called "Wolf Rocks," I became so tired and agitated that I lay down flat on my back in a rare island of rock-free dirt in the middle of the trail.

Finally, the green, soft valley of the Delaware River came into view way down below.

The Delaware Water Gap, where the Delaware River has cut through rock formations of the Appalachian Mountains, has geological significance as one of the best examples of a water gap in the United States. For AT

My backpack averaged about 30 pounds through most of the hike. The item rolled up atop the pack is my ridge rest for my sleeping bag.

hikers, it is your reward for having gutted it out through Pennsylvania. It lifted my spirits, although my screaming feet recoiled at the prospect of a steep descent. But soon we were at the Presbyterian Church Hostel in the little village of Delaware Water Gap, which marks the northern terminus of the AT in Pennsylvania.

Whitewater and Nurse Ratchet were there and all seemed forgotten after the snafu back in Port Clinton. The hostel was abuzz with hiker gossip. "Did you hear the news about the 'hiker feed' in Duncannon?" Nurse Ratchet asked.

"No."

"A hiker got hit by a train and was killed."

"Good God," I exclaimed, "what are the odds of that happening."

"Supposedly, he was drunk and had been kicked out of the Doyle Hotel," she said.

"What was his trail name?" I asked.

"Packstock."

"Packstock, huh," I tried to think. "Haven't heard that name."

"And get this Skywalker," Whitewater drawled. "A hiker in New Jersey was attacked in his sleeping bag by a bear a few days ago."

"Get outta' here," I protested.

"The bear went into a packed shelter and drug him out, but it ran away when everybody started screaming and throwing things," Whitewater reported.

Baltimore Jack, the eight-time thru-hiker ("a serial hiker"), arrived at the hostel the next morning. He was returning from the hiker-feed in Duncannon, shuttled by the trail angel Mary. He immediately revealed himself as a man of outsized reputation with an outsized ego. It was said that he often had a coterie of fifteen or twenty other hikers tagging along with him on the trail listening in rapt attention to his many tales at evening campsites, as he swigged Jack Daniels bourbon. But unlike some of the other big-name hikers, nobody had ever questioned that he had done all the miles attributed to him.

Nurse Ratchet and I listened respectfully as he gave monologues on several subjects. On New Jersey bears he related the story of a hiking companion asleep in a tent next to his own when a bear came and swatted the rain cover off his tent in one swipe. "It was pretty logical" he recounted —"like a human opening up a bag of Fritos."

He also revealed himself as a man implacably opposed in every respect to Warren Doyle, his rival for most number of thru-hikes. "He's just such a ridiculous character that I can't get into the subject at such an early hour," he said. But then he did.

"Did he ever mention that most of those twenty-seven thousand miles he likes to advertise he has done were mostly without a backpack ("slackpacking")," he dug in. "My grandmother could do it without a backpack."

Then he went off, Scout's honor, and began planning a route for Mary the trail angel to slack pack *him* that afternoon.

***

Every state on the AT is known for one thing. Pennsylvania is known for its rocks, New Hampshire for being so difficult, and Maine for its beauty. New Jersey is known for its bears.

The reason is that New Jersey has been developed to the point that there is only a narrow sliver of wilderness still extant on the western side of the state, in the Kittaninny Mountains. It is now estimated that there is at least one bear for every square mile in this part of New Jersey. And it is through this narrow corridor that the AT runs.

Because human-bear encounters have risen so sharply in recent years the word on the trail was that the state of New Jersey for the first time in many years had a "controlled hunt." The purpose was to teach bears some respect for humans.

I asked several people before getting to New Jersey just how the "controlled hunt" had gone. "They killed 844 bears in two weeks," one person had said matter-of-factly. "Everybody said it was like shooting ducks in a barrel."

But just as confidently a trail wag back in Duncannon had told me, "They called it off. The animal rights activists raised a big ruckus."

An ATC employee at headquarters in Harper's Ferry had told me that the previous year on the AT a female hiker had been in her tent when a bear grabbed the tent and dragged it and her screaming for thirty feet. And the bear attack of the previous week was the second on a hiker this year. Bears in New Jersey identify hikers with food, a New Jersey hiker had told me.

So it was bears that were primarily on my mind as 49er and I crossed the mile-long bridge that the trail follows over the historic Delaware River. Whether he noticed it or not, I had assiduously stuck with 49er that morning as he had gone about making rounds to the post office, food mart, etc. And while I usually hiked faster than 49er, in New Jersey I stayed planted right on his heels. The huge bear the Trolls and I had seen had moved away from us a lot faster than the two bears I had lone encounters with in Shenandoah National Park.

The trail took a turn for the better in New Jersey. The Sahara desert feel of Pennsylvania was gone as the hillsides became fresher and greener, compared to the scraggly, worn forests of Pennsylvania. Nurse Ratchet taught me just which berries were suitable for eating and adding valuable anti-oxidants to my diet. There were even mountain ponds that afforded ample opportunity for hydration. In short, New Jersey was a pleasant surprise.

We made it through the state bear-free in four and a half days. Just before crossing out of the state, Whitewater, Nurse Ratchet, and I ran into Knees, whom we hadn't seen since Virginia. Whitewater and Nurse Ratchet didn't want to hike with him back then because they said he bragged too much about how many miles he habitually hiked. But I was glad to see him, and we walked along chatting until his legs suddenly came out from under him and he landed on some sharp rocks.

"Can I give you a hand?' I asked.

"No, no," he said quickly. "But I've marked my legs up a bit and need to apply some first aid."

So I stayed with Whitewater and Nurse Ratchet as we crossed into New York at twilight. The terrain was proving rockier and more difficult than expected, so when we crossed a stream of dubious quality we dutifully pulled out our water filters to start pumping. Whitewater saw that an item from his backpack was missing and he hurried to go back and look for it. I sat down with Nurse Ratchet and enjoyed a Snickers Bar. Fortunately, she had retired her occasional towel-snapping manner towards me and our relationship seemed repaired.

I heard a heavy pounding sound on the other side of the ridge and flippantly remarked, "That was a bear."

"It better not be," she said in almost a reprimanding tone.

But there were more heavy thuds and I said, "No hiker takes steps that sound like that." A bear strode confidently onto the AT thirty yards in front of us. "I see it now," I reported. "Keep the conversation going."

"Oh no," Nurse Ratchet said alarmed, "it has *another* bear with it."

"Where?" I asked. And a minor panic set in with the possibility of two bears. I also noticed my food bag was out and quickly stuffed it in my backpack.

It just stared at us and Nurse Ratchet sternly shouted, "Go away, go away. No, go away now!"

I picked up a rock and began softly saying, "Can't we live together." And to Nurse Ratchet I said, "Keep talking." Finally, it moved slowly up a hill in the direction it had been going.

When it was out of sight she said, "That bear was not afraid of us."

"Wow, you scared the hell out of me when you said there was another one," I said.

"Well, the way it looked over its shoulder…" she reminded me.

"You were giving it commands like a dog," I said in admiration.

"You were talking to it like a person," she laughed. Whitewater appeared over the hill empty-handed.

"We saw a bear," Nurse Ratchet reported to him. Whitewater walked defiantly right to where we pointed out on the trail and began examining the footprints. Nurse Ratchet and I followed behind. Thirty seconds later we heard an animal tearing down a hill and looked over to our right and saw a cub, perhaps a year old, fleeing in the direction of the adult bear we had seen.

"I guess Mama just rang the dinner bell," Nurse Ratchet said. "Maybe a deer."

"Maybe a hiker," I responded.

"Hopefully, not Knees," Whitewater drawled delightedly.

Chapter 16

If Pennsylvania is not an AT hiker's least-favorite state then, chances are, New York is. The trail is not as well-blazed in the Empire State as in other states, and there seems to be a lower general level of awareness about the AT. Hikers with the theretofore "magic thumb" showed great consternation at their sudden inability to hitchhike into towns to resupply. Of course, female hikers reported no such problem. This led to improvisation. Male hikers would hide in the woods while a lone female would stick her thumb out for a ride. Everyone got great joy recounting how quickly the driver's face would change from expectant to grim when the grisly, bearded male hikers poured out of the woods asking if they could pile in along with the female.

Hiker behavior also trended downward from the etiquette displayed in the initial phases in Georgia. Peter Pan, an agreeable thirtyish female from Ohio who always seemed to be in the midst of male hikers noted, "In Georgia I got a kick out of watching guys walk deep into the woods to urinate. By the time everybody was in Virginia they would only walk about ten yards away to do it. And now, I'll be talking to a guy, and next thing you know he just turns around and takes a piss."

Morale is often low when thru-hikers arrive in New York, as completion is still way off. And any AT thru-hiker faces a basic incongruity. The first and last five hundred miles are where the trail passes through its highest elevations. But these are usually done in spring and fall, when the weather up in the mountains is cold. Meanwhile, the trail passes through its lowest elevations in the mid-Atlantic states. And this stretch is traversed in high summer, when the bugs and heat are the worst. Not coincidentally, an epidemic of "yellow-blazing" — taking highways and skipping sections — broke out in these parts.

Wawayanda Shelter — mile 1,349

7-25-05: It has come to my urgent attention that a contagion of yellow blazing has broken out amongst thru-hikers. I beseech you — Don't yellow-blaze under any circumstances. Quitting would be better. — Sky Walker

But, I would soon regret this presumptuous trail entry.

Wildcat Shelter — mile 1,361

7-26-05: *Mea culpa, mea culpa, mea Maxima culpa. One hiker has labeled me a "trail-Nazi." Another hiker has threatened to "bear-bait" my tent by spreading peanut butter all over it. I humbly repent.*

— *Sky Walker*

* * *

The AT has a reputation for not being as difficult in these Mid-Atlantic States. But a few states back I had asked a New Yorker on the trail about his home state. "You'll be surprised, actually," he said. "The trail has been relocated and it'll sucker punch you."

After Nurse Ratchet and I had received our "ursine greeting," just over the state line, we ran into a series of rocky and rugged ledges. We suddenly found ourselves stumbling and heaving ourselves over and shimmying down various rock scrambles. Maintaining backpack balance to avoid either a "header" or a backward fall was exceedingly difficult.

On a Sunday evening we were trying to hurry to make it to the shelter before dark when I pitched forward down a jagged boulder for only my third bad fall on the trail. Fortunately, it was my left arm that suffered the deep bruise. If you're going to hurt something on the AT, an arm is actually the place you'd want it to be.

But I jumped up quickly without applying the triple anti-biotic ointment, bandages, and all that Knees had done after his fall a few miles back. I didn't want to camp alone tonight out here in all these rocks, and with bears prowling around.

After finding a semi-rocky clearing near a cliff to camp for the evening, we arose early to try to make better time. But the in-your-face quality of the trail soon reasserted itself. For the next two miles the trail wandered in zig-zag fashion from one boulder obstacle course called Pinnacle Rocks to another called Cat Rocks. "This is obnoxious, is what it is," Nurse Ratchet said.

"I reckon we could tunnel underground faster than this," Whitewater added.

The unifying factor that had kept the three of us together so long was that we were all task-oriented toward doing as many miles per day as we reasonably could. But this terrain just didn't allow it.

The mid-July humidity was so heavy it was no surprise that fast-moving black clouds swooped overhead. Soon, lightning blazes began snapping. A nice couple from New Jersey was huddled under a rock and looked very puzzled as we started to ascend Mombasha High Point just as the pyrotechnics got started. It didn't take a genius to see our poor judgment in climbing a mountain during an electrical storm. We were again being "mileage greedy."

Sheets of rain were falling, and Nurse Ratchet and I stood before a steep escarpment of boulders that together were the size of a mansion. We were at a loss as to our next step. But the unflappable Whitewater enthusiastically yelled, "Follow me," and bounded over a giant boulder. We followed.

Like most summer rainstorms it ended quickly. But after descending a steep section aptly called "Agony Grind," we arrived at New York Highway 17. Our feet were throbbing, and we were frustrated. A fit-looking middle-aged fellow was waiting there beside his pickup. In the back of it was every known type of hiker food. "Hi, my name is Paddie O," he said. "I'm the local trail angel."

"Boy are we glad to see you," I said. "You are the first trail angel in two hundred miles. We were getting it every other day in the South."

He started cooking hot dogs and handing out sodas when Whitewater said, "What do we owe you?"

"You don't owe me a thing," he said merrily. "I've got a five thousand dollar trail-magic budget I set aside for this year." Then he added wistfully looking off at the mountains, "I owe this trail more than I could ever repay it. Mount Katahdin alone was the most unbelievable thing I've ever seen."

"The trail almost brought us to our knees the last two days," I said. "We were dumbfounded about New York."

"You see that telephone booth over there?" Paddie O asked.

We nodded and he said, "I'm working on getting that removed."

"Why?"

"Because people get to this roadside demoralized after all those rocks and they bail out," he explained. "Five thru-hikers in the last two days have quit right here." Chronic Fatigue Syndrome was apparently one of them on his attempt at a third thru-hike.

Nurse Ratchet had been having more problems with kidney stones, which are often caused by dehydration. Hiking in near one hundred-degree weather was exactly what the doctor had not ordered. The next morning she and Whitewater took the bus into New York City to spend three days with her aunt.

***

So I set off up Bear Mountain alone for what would be seven straight nights out in a tent. Being alone, my main concerns were bears — after the encounter a couple nights before — and losing the trail. Having other hikers around reduces the chances of both problems. The trail passed through a narrow cleft between two huge boulders, called the Lemon Squeezer. I had to remove my backpack and toss it up on the rock ledge to the left while squeezing through, turned sideways. Fortunately, the trail opened into grassy fields in Harriman State Park. There were even some great views of Seven Lakes.

The trail ascended steeply to the top of Bear Mountain, and the Manhattan skyline was visible in the distance. While chatting with a watchman at the top of Bear Mountain, I was struck by the lonely sound in my voice. I hadn't seen another person since early in the morning. Water had been tight all day, and I savored a couple cold drinks from the drink machine. A steep descent down Bear Mountain spit me out of the woods onto the large, open expansive lawn of the historic Bear Mountain Inn.

This seemed a perfect opportunity to stealth camp right there, despite the police station at the far end of the lawn. I marveled at my boldness and brilliance. It seemed too brazen to erect my tent, so at dark I just lay down on top of my sleeping bag beside the lake. That was a mistake.

The bugs were ferocious, and I soon realized that the bug population increased with proximity to the lake. However, moving away from the lake meant moving toward the police station. I moved my sleeping bag and thermarest pad twice in the middle of the night, and by morning was less impressed with my stealth-camping agility. The bugs were so atrocious that I could barely eat a couple bites of breakfast before bolting out of there in desperation.

The AT runs right through the Bear Mountain Zoo, which hikers are permitted to pass through for free. Of course, given our appearance and odor some looked at us as if we were part of the display. When I passed by the Bear's den I thought, "*What a novelty to have a fence, for once, between this four hundred-pound ursine and me.*" Actually, the bear in this zoo looked more happy-go-lucky than the six I had seen on the trail, which were going

Kent is a picturesque, bucolic New England town with graceful, old churches and inviting taverns. Unfortunately, there was absolutely nowhere to stay. Further, it was late Sunday afternoon, the grocery store was closed, and I was just about out of food. I had no idea where I was going to stay.

Finally, in desperation, I approached an elderly woman in her yard and explained my predicament. "Well, I've got a back yard where you could put up your tent," she offered.

"I would be willing to pull every weed out by hand if I really could," I said gratefully.

"No worries," she said, "and how about letting me do your laundry?" This turned me giddy, but there was one small problem: My friends.

My father used to say, "Be a pig, but don't be a hog."

I disregarded that advice and said, "Uh, I was just wondering one thing. I've been hiking with some friends."

She cut me off right there. "It's not big enough, and I don't want my yard trampled."

"Why, of course."

The Trolls were forced to hitchhike back to the trail, where they had to hike south halfway back up the mountain we had just descended in order to sleep in the shelter. Meanwhile, I was able to eat deli sandwiches and drink milkshakes until dark and then head across the street to the lady's backyard to retire for the evening.

The hike north out of Kent is eventful. The trail ascends sharply to Caleb's Peak, and then descends precipitously six hundred feet in one-third mile on exposed rock with little on which to gain traction. The scenery is beautiful running along the west bank of the Housatonic River, which the trail finally crosses.

Once over the Housatonic River the trail enters a series of deep-rock ravines and creek crossings, and I soon realized I wasn't moving as fast as expected. My goal was Pine Swamp Brook Lean-To, which was six miles away. The sun had dipped below the horizon, and I was hurrying. Yet when I crossed Connecticut 4 and saw trail angels Gordon and Sue, I didn't even consider turning down their offer of a Gatorade.

"The Trolls left about twenty minutes ago," Gordon said.

"Are they trying to make it to the next shelter?" I asked.

"No," he replied. "There is a campsite two or three miles from here."

"Good, I'll camp out with them," I said and eagerly headed off.

After a couple miles I began actively looking for the Trolls and the campsite, but somehow missed them. Now I had to make it another three miles to the shelter. The rocky, angular terrain didn't appear to offer anything in the way of camping opportunities before then.

By the time I crossed over West Cornwall Road, it was about eight-thirty, with little light left. According to my guidebook it was one and one-tenth miles to the shelter, but with a steep climb ahead. There was nowhere acceptable to drop my sleeping bag, so I bolted up the mountain without hesitating. It was a strain to make out the blazes in the flat light. After almost a half-mile of climbing, a couple of huge boulders lay in front of me. It wasn't apparent whether the trail went around, through, or over them. I didn't see a blaze and decided to try to run up and around them to the right. But, quickly it became clear it was impassable, so I turned down to go back around. I panicked and ran to the left of the huge rock, frantically looking for a blaze in the near dark.

Finally, I spotted a blaze down and to the left and ran toward it, but my stomach sank when I realized I was headed back down the mountain. I ran back up to the huge rocks and, squinting my eyes, was still unable to locate a blaze or anywhere that looked passable. Disconsolate, I quickly decided my best bet was to use the remaining bit of light to get back down the mountain by the road. My chances of an acceptable evening should be better there than on this rocky mountain.

***

But my instinct when crossing the road the first time — that there wasn't anywhere flat nearby — proved correct. It all looked inhospitable. However, peering down the windy, mountain road I saw some lights in the distance and walked toward them. My hopes were lifted when I came upon a series of modest-sized buildings.

Two middle-aged people were chatting when I approached. "Hi, is there lodging here," I inquired.

"It's a drug rehab center," one replied. "You'd have to ask the manager."

They took me to find the manager, and I explained what happened. "Yes," he said pensively, "we've had a couple lost hikers here before." Then the three of them began peppering me with questions about the AT, and I even told them about the wilderness therapy program for recovering drug addicts. Soon a dozen people were gathered excitedly around looking at me like a museum piece. With their expansive lawn and ample facilities, my prospects looked pretty good.

As politely as possible I asked the manager, "Is there anywhere around here, maybe your lawn, that I could drop my sleeping bag for the evening?"

"I'd like to say yes," he said evenly, "but I have to ask the director."

I held my breath as the manager called the director at home. It was now completely dark. When the manager started saying, "Uh, huh, yeah, okay, I see," my heart sank. He hung up and said, "The director says that because of liability reasons you can't stay on our property."

But then he added, "There is an area behind our property down by the creek where you might be able to stay."

I dutifully wandered off the lawn as several of the inhabitants commiserated with me. When I went down a hill behind their property I was able to make out with my headlight a swampy area with a creek, and I began looking for somewhere this side of awful to set up for the evening.

After locating what appeared the best spot, I wandered back up the hill looking for more solace. Two late-twentyish females jumped up and said, "God, you scared us. We thought you were a bear when we heard you."

Not in a joking mood, I asked, "Are there bears around here?"

"Oh yes-siree," one said emphatically. "Some outdoor society, I forget the name, anesthetizes troublesome bears in the Northeast and dumps them off on a mountain near here."

"Oh great," I muttered.

I finally got in my sleeping bag, knowing full well that the mosquitoes would be on the other side of awful. I wrapped myself as completely as possible so that the only exposed parts of my body were my mouth and nose. Sleep is so important to a long-distance hiker that I sometimes felt like I was trying to convince myself I was sleeping, even when I wasn't.

After about two hours I was awakened by a loud, reverberating sound, but tried to ignore it. At first I honestly thought it might be the power lines malfunctioning. Then I realized it sounded more like the snort of an angry animal. I looked up and, in the moonlight glare, caught a glimpse of a buck deer dashing away. Counseling myself that deer aren't dangerous, I tried to go back to sleep. But soon I heard a heavy animal thrashing through the brush on the far side of the creek. More wild animal calls carried through the woods.

Chalking up the sleeping effort as a failure I packed up my belongings and wandered back up the hill and onto the lawn. I looked for a place to just sprawl out, but the night-shift manager approached me. Again I explained myself, and he seemed sympathetic. But then he said he had to call the director. I braced myself as he awakened the director and explained about a lost hiker and the animal disturbances. But when he said, "I see, yes mam," my hopes dimmed.

He hung up the phone and with a more serious look said, "You were here earlier."

"Yes," I replied meekly.

"She says you can't stay on our property," he said firmly. "But there's a cemetery across the street where you can stay." I wandered over to the road, but all I saw was a steep, windy mountain road. When I went back and reported this he called someone else to find out where the cemetery is. He hung up and said, "Actually, if you follow this road down the mountain the cemetery should be on your left in a couple miles."

"What time is it?" I asked. I was trying to impress upon him the seeming inhumanity of sending a lost individual down a lonely mountain road in the middle of the night looking for a cemetery to sleep in.

"One-thirty," he replied.

I slowly hoisted my backpack, hinting at my need for just the most basic succor, but all he could say was, "Sorry."

I finally decided I had too much self-esteem for this treatment. I wasn't going to wander down a mountain road in the middle of the night looking for a cemetery, and I wasn't about to go back down to the swamp with all the heavy animals rampaging. I walked over to the very edge of the lawn and threw my sleeping bag down. My attitude was, "What the hell." I don't know if he saw me, but I lay there until six o'clock and then got out of there. I hope that lily-livered director tries to hike the AT some day.

***

The following night was somebody else's turn to be tormented. I was alone in the Limestone Spring Shelter and had gotten my head fully wrapped in my sleeping bag for bug protection, when a panicky, shirtless hiker appeared in the entrance to the shelter.

"My friend has given out," he said anxiously. "I've got to help him down the mountain."

He dropped two backpacks in the shelter and tore off with his headlight. A half hour later he was back with his friend, also shirtless, draped around his shoulders. They were policemen from New York on a week's hiking trip. When I told them about the cold spring behind the shelter, billed as Connecticut's finest, they looked as if I had mentioned the Holy Grail. The stronger one set up the sleeping pad and sleeping bag of the weaker one, and then went and retrieved water.

"That was close," he said relieved to his zombie-like friend.

In supine position the exhausted one accepted a few ministrations of water from his helping friend, and quickly fell into a deep sleep. They woke up early the next morning and hiked out at first light. I never saw them again.

**

But then sometimes things work out perfectly. Coming out of Salisbury, Connecticut, the trail goes up yet another Bear Mountain. Signs were posted all around the base of the mountain. "Warning: Due to Recent Bear Activity We Recommend Hikers Exercise Caution." However, as I neared the top of the surprisingly steep climb to the summit I ran not into a bear, but into two "hiker-friendly" women. The younger one, in her early-thirties was especially impressionable. She lobbed one softball question after another in wondrous fashion. Finally, she asked, "How do your feet stand it?" When I started to go into the mechanics of duct tape, mole skin, and the wonders of callous formation, she said, "I'm a massage therapist. Would you let me massage them at the summit?"

I struggled not to accept in overly eager fashion. But then she strained credulity by exclaiming, "Oh, you thru-hikers are so brave. Only a thru-hiker would be brave enough to let a complete stranger massage his toes." When I suggested a nearby boulder for her to ply her ministrations, she insisted, "No, the summit is what we agreed on."

"Why yes, of course," I said and dutifully trekked up to a summit that I thought would never arrive. I hadn't been so glad to see a summit since Blue Mountain on my "day from hell," back in Georgia. We sprawled out on a huge boulder overlooking the Housatonic Valley and she enthusiastically went about her task. She didn't even complain about the infamous hiker "toe cheese," guaranteed to powerfully pique one's olfactory properties.

"I love the Appalachian Trail," I said dreamily.

"I love these feet," she giggled. I don't know if she was lying, but I damn sure wasn't at that point.

Halfway through my thirty minutes of bliss, Stranger, an unflappable Kansan, arrived with a look of amazement. "Stranger," I called out to him, "You're my witness when I brag about this to everyone."

Because of the unexpected delay, Stranger and I got to the Hemlocks Lean-To just before dark. Just as I had hoped, the shelter was full of male hikers, a perfect audience for my story. From the looks on their faces when I described the foot massage it felt like I was describing a gourmet meal to a bunch of concentration camp inmates.

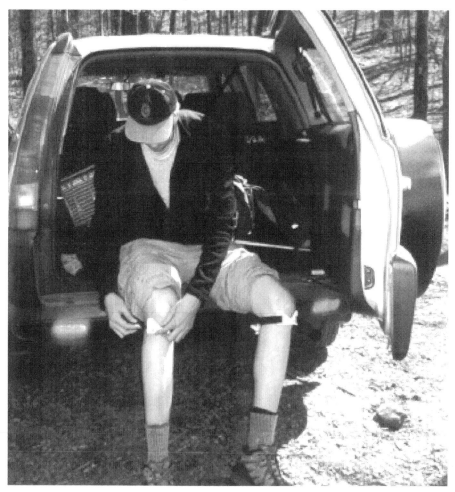

Every part of your legs take a tremendous pounding on the hike, but particularly the knees. AT veteran Warren Doyle strongly believed it is problems with the knees and feet, not ankles, that knock people off the trail. For that reason he strongly advised against wearing boots.

Chapter 17

Like many of my southern brethren, I had always imagined Massachusetts as a land of nauseating, pointy-headed snobs. I pictured it populated by latte drinkers, Kennedy aristocrats, and urban elitists with Ha-vud accents. But after walking through the rugged and scenic Berkshires in western Massachusetts, and passing through lonely, quintessential New England towns adorned with American flags, I began to hold it in a different regard. Norman Rockwell, the famous American illustrator whose paintings glorify small-town settings and rural life, had settled in nearby Stockbridge.

But of all the early American writers extolling the virtues of wilderness, the name of Henry David Thoreau rings most resoundingly. The early European settlers had been shocked at the utter denseness of forest in the new continent. Their attitude can be summed up in one word: *Hostile.*

Wild animals and darkness loomed large in this haunted imagination. One pioneer on the American continent, theologian Cotton Mather, wrote in 1707, "the Evening Wolves, the rabid and howling Wolves of the Wilderness, make havoc among you, and not leave the bones 'til morning." Perhaps their greatest fear of all was that wilderness would drag down the level of all American civilization. "The further and further a pioneer pushes into the woods," wrote Timothy Dwight, the President of Yale, "the less and less civilized man he becomes."

Given such paranoid attitudes almost universally held towards wilderness it is no wonder that the pioneers set about to conquer it. These early settlers used martial metaphors, referring to wilderness as "the enemy to be vanquished by a pioneer army." Their obsession was to clear the land and bring light to darkness. In fact, it was the chief source of pioneer pride and national ego.

But in the nineteenthth century the transcendentalists, led by Emerson and Thoreau, began to view nature reverently, even as a source of religion. Thoreau thought that if a culture or an individual lost contact with wilderness, it became weak and dull. "The forest and wilderness furnish the tonics and barks which brace mankind. It is the raw material of life," he intoned. "All good things are wild and free," he exulted.

Thoreau grew up on the eastern side of Massachusetts, in Concord, a Boston suburb. However, given his contrarian style and romantic bent, he naturally gravitated to the western side of the state, with its rougher, wilder geography.

Wild is what Thoreau got in western Massachusetts. The AT moves up mountains and down deep ravines and through swamps. The bugs and mosquitoes are nightmarish. One thru-hiker, Adrienne Hall, in her book, *A Journey North*, vividly described her Massachusetts experience:

The trail circled, skirted, and sometimes plunged directly through nearly every swamp in the state. I sank and slogged in the mud. Nearing 100 degrees, the stagnant air was itself a chore to walk through.

She continued:

The wetlands belched out swarms of bloodthirsty mosquitoes. They attacked with gusto. I was driven by a deep hatred for them. But I swore these measly little bloodsuckers would not stop me from going to Maine.

In this land of swamp and bugs I met the folksy character of Doctor Death. He was in his late forties, with a slim wiry build and thinning black hair. "I thru-hiked the trail last year," he said. "I'm thru-hiking this year, and I plan to come back and thru-hike again next year."

"How can you afford to do that?" 49'er wondered.

"I go home to Florida and eat Ramen noodles six months out of the year at twenty-five cents a pack," he said, "in order to save up enough money to come out here and eat Ramen noodles for six more months."

The following day I remarked, "It seems like we're going up and down more than at any point since Virginia."

"You can assume it's all tough from here on out," Doctor Death responded in his gravelly voice.

It was dry as a bone. The area had experienced a drought for two months and, combined with the intense heat, many streams were dry. Streams that had water took on a brackish tint, possibly unsuitable for even animals to drink.

At dusk I climbed Mount Wilcox with the Troll family to arrive at the Mount Wilcox South Lean-To after 19.7 miles for the day. We were elated to see Whitewater and Nurse Ratchet for the first time since they had gotten off the trail to visit New York City. But our greetings were truncated by a more pressing question. "Where's the water?" we anxiously asked.

"We'll see how you like it," Whitewater said. He then led us bushwhacking down a precipice as Troll and I held our breath.

There was a hole about a foot deep, with a pool of water full of leaves and debris. "Fuck this," Troll said and stormed away to tell his weary family they weren't through marching for the evening.

Meanwhile, I was staring at the hole of dirty water that Troll had so quickly rejected. I pumped my filter with maximum exertion and was finally able to get a decent supply for the night, although non-essentials like cooking and brushing teeth had to wait.

49er and Doctor Death had been with or behind us all day. We had speculated they would pull up somewhere shy of the shelter for the evening. However, right at dark they came panting and sweating up the mountain to the shelter. "We sold you short," I greeted them effusively.

"Is there water?" they asked wild-eyed and in unison.

"Just a bit," I responded. "And you can put your tents. …"

"No, the water," Doctor Death cut me off. "Now." I led them through the bushes just as Whitewater had taken Troll and me.

When Doctor Death arrived at the puddle he had just the opposite reaction of Troll. He maniacally dipped his Nalgene bottle in the hole filling it with water, leaves, and probably dirt. Forty-niner and I stood by transfixed as Doctor Death downed a full liter of the cloudy liquid.

"How is it?" 49er asked.

"It's wet," Doctor Death answered immediately. He quickly filled up again.

When we got back to the shelter I told the story of Doctor Death to Whitewater. "Yeah, ol' Doctor Death," Whitewater said, "he's all salt and vinegar."

***

Sleeping in the rocky terrain behind the shelter was again nigh impossible. The bugs attacked in the most immodest places. What I couldn't understand was how, with a stocking cap, a scarf wrapped around my ears, and ear plugs I could nonetheless hear the buzzing. It was maddening enough fighting them all day. But this gauntlet they ran you through at night could drive you over a cliff mentally.

Others were spooked by the bugs as well. When I ran into the Troll family the following evening at a campsite Anchor absolutely refused to come out of the family tent, with its netting protection.

"You look like one of those child hemophiliacs in a bubble," Doctor Death noted drolly.

The AT runs right through the streets of Dalton, Massachusetts, a charming working-class New England town right out of a Norman Rockwell scrapbook. A nice middle-aged fellow who worked at the local pharmacy permitted hikers to pitch tents in his back yard. Just where we were to use the bathroom was a question best left unasked. About eight of us were there when he pulled up in his car. He was a short, balding nondescript fellow, and very soft-spoken. "I had some luck with the lottery," he reported with a smile. "I won $100 and want you folks to have dinner with me."

He then pulled out ribs, fried chicken, potatoes, slaw, etc. to serve us dinner. Like every other hiker, I was warming to New England fast. And the best lay ahead.

***

Mount Greylock, the inspiration for the great American novel, *Moby Dick*, is the highest and most storied mountain in southern New England. Herman Melville, who lived in a nearby farmhouse called Arrowhead, had spent so much time staring at the eminence of Greylock from his second floor study that he became convinced of its likeness to a great white whale. The AT goes right over Greylock peak which is the biggest climb we had faced since central Virginia. After I scaled a steep section called Jones' Nose, the trail crisscrossed a windy, paved service road that goes to the top.

Thoreau had written vividly of getting lost on a cold, snowy day and spending the night alone ("Like most evil the difficulty is imaginary, for what's the hurry") on Greylock summit. But unlike Thoreau, I had blazes to follow. The summit was crowned with fine spruce trees, and a sixty-foot stone-tower war memorial affords visitors fine vistas including the Green Mountains, where we would soon be, to the north. Better still, Bascom Lodge was there to serve hearty meals.

It seemed more like a leisurely day at the beach than Thoreau's more pristine encounter with dense forest, snow, and complete solitude. But to me, the advantages of Bascom Lodge and the road to the top of Mount Greylock greatly outweighed the disadvantages. That's the American way: giving access to as many as possible.

Hamburger, 49er, Whitewater, Nurse Ratchet, and I crossed over into Vermont — the twelfth state — the next morning. The first one hundred miles of the AT in Vermont coincide with the famed Long Trail, the nation's oldest long-distance hiking trail. After sharing the first one hundred miles the AT veers sharply east to New Hampshire, while the Long Trail continues straight north to the Canadian border.

The section of the AT with the Long Trail was one of the most crowded sections of the entire AT. The AT had a diverse cast of hikers to be sure. But the grim task of thru-hiking had narrowed the demographics in these later states, with a definite preponderance of people in their twenties. The Long Trail, meanwhile, seemed to have the most ecumenical population imaginable. Middle-aged school teachers, accountants, engineers, day laborers, etc., were well represented in its swarm of participants. You could take a long vacation and do the Long Trail, instead of having to quit your job, as with the AT. Some use the Long Trail as a warm-up for the AT — the rule of thumb being that if you could hike it in twenty-five or fewer days, you were fleet enough to thru-hike the AT.

As in other arenas in life, gossip thrives on the AT. In fact, it's especially advantageous for hikers given that it weighs nothing. We had spent the last three states arguing about the propriety of a married couple that was spotted *en flagrante* on a couple occasions in the streams that we frequently crossed and drew water from. (I didn't see a helluva lot wrong with it considering they were married, and it was running water — others heatedly disagreed). But after several months of writing shelter register entries, discussing all conceivable subjects ad-nauseum, and making every idiotic joke imaginable within our insular community, I had noticed some of the jokes were losing their luster.

Fortunately, we were traveling with a very intelligent and witty fellow named Hamburger, who provided a new dimension to our conversations. Hamburger was a poster child for the modern global economy. He was from Hamburg, Germany, worked for an American company, and was based in Paris. Annually, he talked his company into letting him take six weeks off — he is based in France, remember — to hike a section of the AT.

"You daft Americans never cease to amaze Europeans with your foolishness," he chortled. "The Monica Lewinsky story was endless entertainment — the way the entire country was obsessed with this one man's penis."

"Well, if we're so bad," Nurse Ratchet popped back, "why are you talking about moving here?"

"I didn't say you don't have some nice parts," he replied a bit defensively.

Then it was my turn. "Is it true, as I've read, that a higher percentage of Germans have penil-implants than any other country in the world?"

"Where did you read that?" Stranger interjected to laughs from everyone.

"I would have thought Japan would be first," Nurse Ratchet commented incisively.

"What are penil implants?" Hamburger asked in a seemingly authentic display of ignorance on the subject matter.

When we explained, he laughed, "Oh, yes. I often receive e-mails from America offering these."

When Hamburger marveled at the number of American leaders who had been assassinated it was Stranger's turn. "Hey, at least we know when to take care of 'em. Ya'll couldn't even get rid of Hitler. He had to do it himself for you."

Touché.

***

The descent to Vermont Highway 9 and Bennington was a precursor for what lay ahead in New Hampshire and Maine: steep and rocky. It was on this particular descent, in fact, that Baltimore Jack was supposedly brought to heel in his bid for a record ninth thru-hike with a foot injury.

I hitchhiked into Bennington to re-supply and attend to a metastasizing wound on my arm. Lyme disease was spreading at an alarming rate among hikers, but this ended up being from a brown-recluse spider — not surprising given the swampy terrain we had recently covered. But I had been lucky with injuries so far. Before beginning the thru-hike, my doctor had ordered me to take six Advil daily to help absorb the pain from an old neck injury. The pain had flared up while hiking on many occasions to the point that I often had to awkwardly move the left backstrap of my backpack over the rim of my left shoulder onto my arm to relieve pressure. From the outset I had feared this had the potential to knock me off the trail, but it hadn't happened. And while I had lost too many toenails to count, that hadn't posed a serious problem either.

However, in Bennington I was shaken by the skeletal figure and haggard facial features that appeared before me when I looked into a mirror. Further, I felt a deep, down-to-the-bone dehydration that couldn't be remedied by a few cold glasses of water. I decided to take a "zero" day for the first time in weeks.

Whitewater and Nurse Ratchet hiked ahead, marking the end of our hiking partnership. We had been together about 60 percent of the time since Tennessee. When we had started together I had easily been able to keep up with them. Then, in the Mid-Atlantic States, Whitewater had developed an extra spring in his step that Nurse Ratchet and I had trouble matching. But in the last few weeks I had been struggling to keep up with both of them.

It made sense. Whitewater had started off at 5'9" and two hundred pounds. By losing thirty-five pounds he had strengthened himself. Nurse Ratchet had lost only a few pounds. But, as mentioned earlier, women have this magical quality of turning fat reserves into heavier, leaner muscle. On the other hand, if a person starts at 6'11" and 212 pounds and loses thirty or more pounds, his legs might be stronger, but he's weakened in some basic ways. I'd feel more of this in coming weeks.

***

Northern New England was getting prettier by the minute. The AT goes over the mountains of three prestigious ski resorts in the Green Mountain National Forest: Stratton, Bromley, and Killington.

The second day out from Bennington we summitted Stratton Mountain. The story goes that it was while sitting in a tree on the slopes of this mountain in 1921 that Benton MacKaye was suddenly struck with the idea of a trail running the length of the Appalachian Mountain Range, and covering its major peaks.

On the way up the mountain, surrounded by fine balsam trees we saw some moose scat for the first time. "You know what that is, Skywalker?" Troll asked.

"Yes," I responded, "but a moose is nothing more than an enlarged horse, right?"

"Let me tell you," Troll said, his eyes narrowing. "If you have nightmares when you're in bear country, you should be straitjacketed in moose country."

"Get outta' here," I countered.

"I'm serious," he shot back. "They will charge and trample you when the mood suits them."

"I'm glad to hear I don't have a monopoly on outdoor phobias," I said.

We hiked down only about nine hundred feet over the next three miles to the Stratton Pond Shelter. Down by the lake was a beautiful piped spring of crystal-clear, cold water. Later, in Vermont, we would come across entire spring-fed lakes; you could just dip your bottle in and drink up.

We were back in the mountains, and the bugs were no longer as invasive. Everything was perfect.

The shelter had been constructed by the Green Mountain Club, one of the oldest outdoor clubs in the country. Ninety percent of the shelters on the AT are free. However, the Green Mountain Club in Vermont and the Appalachian Mountain Club in New Hampshire and Maine usually have a caretaker who charges around six to eight dollars. Given the amount of work that goes into the construction, maintenance, privy-care, etc., it seemed reasonable to me, but not everyone agreed.

One of those who didn't agree was Lemon Meringue.

"I don't believe in paying for the use of the outdoors," she flatly said.

"I guess when you're on the cusp of completing the Triple Crown you can set your own rules," I chided her.

"And throw in some European socialist philosophy behind that as well," Troll quipped.

We all paid up, except for Lemon Meringue. She hiked out alone at dark to camp somewhere unbeknownst. Her cool aplomb was to later impress me in a variety of situations. We came across her after a couple miles the next morning, camped alone along a creek. Such are the ways of Triple Crowners.

The trail passed by the William Douglas Shelter. William Douglas was the seventeenth thru-hiker ever on the AT in 1952. He later became a U.S. Supreme Court justice in the 1960s and 1970s, and was renowned for being a firebrand in support of environmental causes.

I couldn't help but believe that the current thru-hiker population contained some future environmentalist firebrands as well. It was almost impossible to walk through the northern New England trees and picturesque landscapes and not identify with environmental causes, whatever your political stripes.

Manchester Center is another lovely, quaint northern New England town. A friend with roots in Vermont had told me that Vermont was "Mississippi North." Indeed, the people were charming and hospitable, and knowledge of the AT was high. In fact, you could say that in most of

On break at the top of Moose Mountain in New Hampshire. Thru-hiking forces you to cut breaks short and hike on low-morale days. Otherwise, you don't make it all the way to Maine in time.

northern New England a "hiking culture" exists. It made a thru-hiker feel good to be a part of some grand endeavor, rather than a freak show.

The AT out of Manchester Center climbed straight up the ski slopes of Bromley Mountain. At the top I ran into English Bob. He was a thirtyseven-year-old from England who was doing the second half of the trail this year. He had worked as a janitor for one company for most of his career, and had taken various hiking vacations in Europe over the years. English Bob was all of about 5'1," and for the next few weeks we were the hiking odd couple. With his understated British wit, and coolness in the face of adversity, he was the perfect hiking partner.

Nurse Ratchet, who had noticed my propensity to lose the trail in rocky areas, had explicitly suggested on multiple occasions, "You need a hiking partner going through the White Mountains, Skywalker." After seeing English Bob's style and pace I planned on making him that person.

***

Very little virgin forest remains in the eastern United States. It was surprising when people kept telling me this in such densely forested places as the Great Smoky Mountains, Shenandoah National Park, and Green Mountain National Forest. But consider this arresting statistic: *The USFS*

(U.S. Forest Service) has eight times as many miles of roads as the entire interstate highway system! But that statistic will soon be outdated because there are aggressive plans on the drawing board to build many, many more. After watching truck after truck motoring up and down dirt roads groaning from the weight of strapped down wood, it became clear the principal purpose of the USFS roads we frequently crossed is to haul lumber out of the woods.

Of course, some stoutly maintain that timber cutting serves a larger end. These modern foresters see trees competing with each other for the necessary water, sunlight, soil nourishment, and growing space. The death of one can be the blessing of another. Systematic cutting, forest managers assert, allows the remaining trees to grow stronger.

That sounds like a viable position. But too often this management is not done prudently, and whole areas are cleared out. What's more, the U.S. Forest Service is notorious for leasing out large tracts for timber cutting to favored customers at below market rates. These sweetheart deals have resulted in more trees being cut down than growing. *And I recently was startled to read that more greenhouse, heat-trapping gasses are emitted by cutting down trees than are emitted by every single car, truck, and airplane in the world.* Walking through the wondrous, fine whispering forests it's easy to understand why environmentalists get so up-in-arms over cutting down trees.

The environmental movement, which was so ascendant in the 1960s and 1970s, is now outmatched politically by commercial interests. In the 1980's Ronald Reagan loved to say, "Sometimes I don't think these people (environmentalists) will be happy until the White House is turned into a bird's nest." I absolutely loved Reagan, but like most people at the time, he didn't give two cents about the environment. Neither did I. We pursued money and material success in almost monolithic fashion. The environment was an issue for hard-core activists, counter-cultureniks, and the like. But as I so often observed on the AT, the environment has become the issue for the generation in their twenties, and they will have to be reckoned with. My bet is they will turn the tables in the next ten or twenty years.

***

Southbounders had been streaming by for the last couple weeks at this point. Some chose to start at Katahdin because they graduated from school in May or June, and thought hiking south would lengthen their hiking season. Others were from the North and just thought it was logical to begin there.

But a lot of us northbounders were put out by southbounders. "They think because they've already done the Mahoosucs in Maine and the Whites in New Hampshire, they know everything," complained one northbounder.

Another said, "I get the impression they think they've outsmarted us tactically."

"They'll find out how smart they are," one wit mused, "when they arrive in the most remote regions in the South during the middle of hunting season late this fall."

For my part it, certainly was easy to detect them as they approached. They not only had the swagger and sense of purpose of thru-hikers, they had the smell. They walked down the center of the trail as if everyone else was supposed to clear out of the way. When they stopped they acted as if they were doing you a favor talking to you. At shelters their body language bespoke, "Approach me at the risk of reproach." In fact, the more I saw of them the more I thought they reminded me of, well, *us*.

***

On my second-to-last day in Vermont I was following the trail through a dung-filled cow pasture, when I approached two female hikers having lunch on the edge of the pasture.

Both were in their early twenties. One was short and pigeon-toed, but cute as a button. The other was fair-haired and fair–featured, with a graceful, appealing look. "Hi, I'm Cackles and this is Box-of-Fun," the shorter one said. "We're the Joy Machine."

They had graduated from college in New York the previous year and had begun thru-hiking on March 7. Noting their early start, but delayed progress, Baltimore Jack had asked to their indignation, "What are you on — the Katahdin by Christmas plan?"

Looking up at the threatening skies I asked, "How far are you planning to go today?"

"We're going to try to make it to Thistle Hill Shelter, if there's time," they said.

"I'm a fair-weather hiker," I replied. "Do you mind if I hike along with you?"

"Sure," they replied.

Like so many others their age on the trail, the Joy Machine was brimming with youthful idealism, especially environmentalism. Cackles had that rare ability to maintain a conversation while climbing mountains, while my normally voluble self shut off on ascents. It had taken me seventeen hundred miles to figure out downhills were the best places to reply.

The trail traversed open pastures and wooded forests, and when the Thistle Hill Shelter appeared just before dark, Box-of-Fun gave me a leaping high-five. Had I not joined with them, I probably wouldn't have tried to go so far. As it was, it proved to be my last twenty-plus mile day, for reasons that would soon become very apparent.

I volunteered to hike down a steep hill to retrieve water for everybody. However, my headlight battery was running low as I bushwhacked to get to the bottom spring — the only one that still held water. I had my long legs spread-eagled to hem up the running water in the creek when I tipped over, completely backwards, into the muddy stream. When I got back up the hill to the shelter, with mud all over me, Cackles said, "You don't look like a fair-weather hiker to me."

The Joy Machine shared a tent and seemed perfectly congenial. "People have asked if we're a couple," Cackles said with her inimitable laugh, "But, actually, we both have steady boyfriends."

The following day I wound through a tree plantation at Bunker Hill that felt like a slalom course. Then the trail crossed the Connecticut River to enter Hanover, New Hampshire, a leafy New England town, dominated by the broad lawns and academic citadels of Dartmouth University. The white blazes run right by the university on its main street. This privilege may soon be gone as the desirability of hordes of sixteen-hundred-mile-ripe hikers trooping through this pristine town has been hotly debated. But it's only humane that hikers retain access to this last outpost of civilization given what lies immediately ahead.

Part IV

"In wilderness is the preservation of the world." — **Henry David Thoreau**

Lichens, wildflowers, and moss, all tough plants, suitable to the cold, windy conditions, form the Alpine landscape. And rocks dominate — rocks of every conceivable form, from tiny pebbles to gigantic boulders. Indeed, the trail in the Whites above the treeline is marked by cairns, which are piles of rocks formed by dedicated volunteers.

The view at the summit of Mount Moosilauke includes the famous Presidential Range, which lay ahead. The panorama was one of rugged bleakness. Soon English Bob and I were forced to take refuge, crouched down behind a low wall of rocks built to protect hikers from the wind.

The descent from Mount Moosilauke is considered by many to be the single most dangerous section of the entire AT. "I'm surprised more people don't get killed here," Warren Doyle had said very emphatically.

The trail is, for miles, a jumble of rocks that run parallel to a creek with several cascading waterfalls. There was nothing particularly dangerous about this, except it was laborious, picking from one rock to another. But then the trail amazingly went straight down some smooth, wet rocks with wooden ladders and steel rungs built into the rocks to aid in the descent. It required getting one's body perpendicular to the rock being descended and moving at a snail's pace. One misstep could and would result in serious injury, or even worse.

Fortunately, it was a nice day, and we reached the bottom at Kinsman Notch without incident. What is referred to in the South as a "gap" is a "notch" in New England. Gordon and Sue were at the bottom, exchanging goodbyes with the Troll family with whom they had been so close. It was a logical place to stop, for there were few places in the Whites to drive their van to meet hikers. It was their twentieth year as trail angels, and, sadly, would be Sue's last. She was placed in a nursing home three months later, ending her long career as a trail angel (and hiker before that).

The next day was an Attila bitch, pure and simple. English Bob and I spent all day going up and down, five thousand feet of three peaks. We rarely talked other than to express disbelief at what kept popping up in front of us. "Bloody hell," English Bob would softly remark when an especially nasty boulder ascent or descent would appear. "This is a cruel hoax?"

At various points trail maintainers had installed metal handholds into the rock to enable hikers to haul themselves up. Often we would throw our hiking poles up to a ledge on top of the particular rock being scaled in order to allow us use of our hands to grab a rock or tree to propel us over. The descents were even worse. Usually, they involved hanging on to some tree off to the side of the boulder and jumping down to some narrow area for a landing. These steep, rocky chutes through narrow areas jolted on my knees. For months afterwards I lived with the feeling of deeply jarred knees.

Worse yet, it began to rain, and the rock scrambles became all the more treacherous. My secret weapons were my new Vasque Trail Shoes. They have a special type of stealth glue on the soles that performed fabulously in these settings. Many times I was able to rush straight up a rock slab bent forward instead of having to go to all fours.

***

Several times along the way the Troll family had earned my admiration. But none more so than on this day. As a group, the Trolls weren't able to do as many miles as most people who had made it this far. Most who traveled at their pace had dropped out long ago.

As usual they had left from the campsite before everybody else. English Bob and I had caught up with and passed them midday. We stopped for lunch at the Eliza Brook Shelter, and they arrived twenty minutes later. "This fucking trail," Troll had shouted out, "what's with it? Straight up, straight down, all day, you never feel like you're getting anywhere."

"Welcome to the Whites," Anchor said trenchantly.

They left after only a ten-minute break at the shelter to head straight up Kinsman Mountain. English Bob and I followed a half-hour later. At the top of South Kinsman Mountain we spotted the Troll family in their inimitable Scottish kilts, laboring halfway down the mountain.

I again shouted, "Bear, bear, bear." It didn't get the usual return shouts, as they were struggling gamely down yet another rock scramble.

There were bear boxes for hikers to store their food all over the Whites, just as there had been in New Jersey. However, I had honestly wondered what bear in his or her right mind would choose to travel in this type of rocky terrain and dense forest.

It was a good thing they didn't because I had another worry: making it over the third mountain, North Kinsman, before dark. We had plenty of time, but the sky had a dark, forbidding feeling so deep in the woods. One otherwise adept hiker, Afraid of the Dark, had said, "Darkness is the ultimate reality. You have to respect it." As it began drizzling and the fog socked in, the depths of my fears stirred. Weather in the Whites is famously unpredictable. What's more I was worried about the Trolls. There was nowhere remotely hospitable to camp on this rocky, jagged mountain.

When we passed them on a ledge between rock scrambles Troll said, "Can you believe this?"

"I could if it was two o'clock in the morning," English Bob said. Even Oblivious for the first time seemed to have lost his happy-go-lucky ways. He was no longer oblivious. But there wasn't much discussion as we passed them for the second time of the day. Everybody was struggling as hard as they could with the mountain.

Finally, English Bob and I made it over and down North Kinsman, the third mountain of the day. An AMC shelter was off on a side trail and a caretaker collected our eight dollars. For this price one apparently receives a weather report. The forecast was dire.

"The one place you don't want bad weather is in the Whites," I lamented.

English Bob said, simply, "We'll ride it out mate."

"You damn British, what is it with you?" I asked. "Is it true you put Viagra in your toothpaste in order to maintain a stiff upper lip?"

That elicited a laugh. But no laughing matter was that North Kinsman Mountain, which we had just descended, was at this point completely enveloped in fog, and the rain was picking up. The Troll family was still out there somewhere in that soupy mess, and I felt a bit guilty for not having hiked along with them. I briefly considered going back up there to see if I could find them, but my chances of getting lost were as great as theirs. Besides, I was bone tired. It had taken us ten hours to hike twelve hellish miles. But it had required more effort than almost any twenty-mile day I had done. I set up my tent inside the shelter to keep me warm from the engulfing cloud, and hoped I would soon hear the Troll family's footsteps.

But the Trolls never arrived. For the first hour the next morning we expounded various theories of what could have happened to them. Finally, we came up on them camped out at the edge of Lonesome Lake. "Are ya'll self-hating, or what?" I wanted to know. Troll gleefully recounted their refusal to pay the shelter "ransom," and told of their harrowing trip by headlamp down to the edge of Lonesome Lake. There, in the pitch black dark the previous evening they had, with great relief, found the perfect camping spot, albeit right in the middle of "No Camping" signs. They had struggled over the most difficult terrain from the crack of dawn to nighttime. It was the single-most impressive one-day effort I was to witness on the AT. They had covered about fourteen miles in approximately fourteen hours.

***

Two days later English Bob and I hiked out of Franconia Notch. Bode Miller, the two-time World Cup downhill ski champion and noted free spirit, had grown up in the hamlet at the base of the mountain in a house with no electricity. By the end of the day we were to see how this area could produce such a world-class alpine athlete. The topography and terrain were ferocious, almost macabre. The trail was flat for approximately two straight steps the entire day.

It began with a steep, rocky thirty-eight hundred-foot climb straight up the face of Mount Liberty, Little Haystack, and Lincoln Mountains. This was the longest climb yet on the AT, and once again the weather seemed to be alternating between fits of rain, howling wind, and supercooled clouds. Had we known what lay ahead we might have waited for a better day. But English Bob was no summer soldier, and on this day I was his reluctant foot soldier.

When we finally cleared treeline and emerged onto the rocky, barren Franconia Ridge, its ominous nature immediately revealed itself. One book describes it as a "true alp, with peaks and crags on which lightning plays, its sides brown with scars and deep with gorges." For 3.5 miles, hikers are exposed to the harshest terrain and weather. One minute we would be in sheets of rain, next in a super-cooled cloud, and then standing in sunshine, admiring the unique, spectacular views of the far-reaching mountains and valleys below.

The Greenleaf Hut lies twelve hundred feet below Franconia Ridge, down a side trail, and has undoubtedly saved thousands of lives of unsuspecting hikers who have desperately had to bail out. Refuge back below treeline appeared tantalizingly close, but it took much longer than it appeared it should take. Every step was a laborious task, especially on the downhills.

Finally, our descent brought us to the famous krummholz, below treeline. There on a rocky slope that was the most unlikely of lounging places were several exhausted hikers taking a break. Stranger, who had the smoothest walking stride I had ever witnessed, said "That was by far the toughest hiking I've ever done."

We then went up and down rock chutes and finally arrived at the sign pointing to the Garfield Ridge Shelter. In the Whites even the side trails to the shelter were steep, rocky, and tough. My feet were screaming.

We were soon to come up on the Presidential Range — named after early presidents — the nation's greatest network of footpaths. This range is traversed not only by the AT, but by sixty other trails. By car and by foot, White Mountain National Forest gets approximately seven million visitors per year. That's more than Yellowstone and Yosemite National Parks combined.

There are those who decry this onslaught of humanity, but not me. In a nation with an obesity rate of 20 percent, full of workaholics, and a virtual obsession with money and celebrity, it seems all the more desirable for as many people as possible to share in the breathtaking beauty and challenges that White Mountain National Forest provides. And believe me they come away more impressed (and better off financially!) than from a vacation at Disney World.

The great irony is that in this age of computers, cell phones, and hyper-connectedness, *the outdoor lifestyle is growing in appeal.* A recent authoritative study of the American Sociological Review found that the average American has only two close friends, down from four in 1985. And the number of people with no close confidants soared from 10 percent in 1985 to 25 percent in 2004. People are more closely connected than ever, but apparently it isn't very authentic. On the other hand, when you are out in the middle of nowhere busting your butt with people it quickly builds trust and authentic friendship.

Late in the evening boisterous school songs rang out in the cold night air from the campsite behind the shelter. The Yale Outdoor Club was camped out there. I was extremely impressed to learn that the vast majority of incoming freshmen at universities in New England participated in outdoor orientation trips. The Yalies were planning to head southbound the next day, over what we had just covered. The group leader sauntered over to debrief us on the terrain. "Do you want something that will make you sleep well or do you want the truth?" I asked.

"We want the real deal," she said. "This is part of our character development at Yale."

"Our last three presidents went to Yale," Stranger noted. "Did they skip the White Mountains hiking portion of their education?"

"That is a matter of great debate, of course," she diplomatically responded.

Skywalker

***

The AMC (Appalachian Mountain Club) is the oldest mountaineering organization in the United States, established in the 1870s. It reportedly has a healthy six-figure budget just for search and rescue in these mountains. Its most notable accomplishment, though, is building the hut system in the White Mountains. These eight huts, built in some of the most remote places in the range, were an engineering feat of the highest magnitude, as well as a demonstration of raw manpower. In the summer they are usually full, despite prices in the eighty dollar range for a small, rectangular bunk and a modest meal.

English Bob and I struggled through relentless rocky climbs and descent to arrive at the Zealand Hut after ten miles. Our mileage was plummeting in the Whites, but that was budgeted in my schedule.

Doctor Death and a short, late-fiftyish, balding fellow named DA were among those there doing "work for stay." It was a great deal, but only a few people got to do it at each hut. Some hikers chose to hike short distances to arrive at a hut in the early afternoon and reserve one of the "work for stay" spots. When I asked the hut manager he said, "Sorry, we're full."

Then he said, "We try to entertain our guests here. Can you think of any memorable lines you've heard about the Whites." I looked at a bulletin board that read, "The weather in the Whites is like herpes, off and on."

I walked out onto the porch, discouraged, and gave English Bob the news. Just then a tide of cold wind and rain ripped through the trees. "This is serious, dangerous weather," Doctor Death said ominously,

DA looked out and said humbly, "I wonder if I'm ever going to make it out of the Whites."

DA was a district attorney from Oklahoma, doing the second half of the AT this year. We hit it off probably because we were both humbled by the circumstances. He was going to hike down a side trail the next day to re-supply and insisted on giving me one of his Lipton dinner packages. Finally, the hut manager came out after all the guests had eaten and offered to let us sleep on the floor for eight dollars, after the guests had left the dining room. We were relieved.

The next night, after an ambitious fourteen-mile hike in schizophrenic weather, we arrived at the Mitzpah Hut. Again, we were too late, and the "work for stay" spots were filled. But, eager to get relief from the cold rain, I asked the hut manager, "Could we pay you to sleep on the floor?"

This particular hut manager didn't exactly goose step, but you got the impression he could learn quickly. "The more you stay in contact with nature, the better," he replied "There is a site for tents out back." In fact, several years back, a couple hikers had frozen to death while camped out behind this hut.

"Have you seen the weather?" I asked, peeved.

"It will help you get ready for northern Maine in the fall."

"Will you be tenting out tonight?" I asked testily.

"I'm the manager," he replied flatly. Even deep in the mountains you can't escape all human hierarchies.

After a frigid evening we climbed up Mount Pierce the next morning in very poor visibility, and once again violated treeline. In fact, the next fifteen miles on the AT are the longest stretch in the entire eastern United States above treeline. We were enveloped in clouds, wind, and rain. We strained to follow the cairns. "Is there anybody else on this planet?" English Bob joked. But no joking matter it would be if one got lost out in this.

Finally, the well-known Lake of the Clouds Hut came into view. Completed in 1915, it's the most elevated and most popular hut in the Whites. I asked to do work for stay and they obliged.

I was washing dishes when the Troll family arrived in late afternoon, anxiously asking to do work for stay. The hut manager looked dubious about what to do with them so I went over to make a plea. "The thing they do best is hunt bears," I said. "They use little Oblivious' head for bait." Troll smirked, but the manager appeared confused. "Animals stay below treeline," he responded. A few minutes later the Trolls were forming an assembly line with me at the dishwasher.

A diminutive, college-age girl came in bundled up from the cold, hauling a huge, bulging knapsack. "How much does that bloody thing weigh?" I asked.

"About sixty pounds."

"Which is about sixty percent of your body weight," I said incredulously.

"My record is one hundred ten pounds," she said enthusiastically. "This is actually the easiest hut to deliver food to. They drive it up in a van to Mount Washington and we hike up to pick it up and carry it all downhill. At some of the other huts you have to carry it straight uphill."

Hamburger had told me that in the Alps the food was taken up to the huts by horseback.

But the Whites were too rugged even for horse travel.

***

Any ascent on Mount Washington must be treated with great caution. Along with Mount Denali (McKinley), in Alaska, it is the most dangerous mountain in America. Its notoriously tempestuous climate is generated from lying between the warm Gulf Stream in the Atlantic and the frigid arctic air of Canada. Changes can be sudden and deadly.

The sign at the foot of Mount Washington read:

WARNING

THE AREA AHEAD HAS THE WORST WEATHER IN AMERICA. MANY HAVE DIED FROM EXPOSURE EVEN IN THE SUMMER. TURN BACK NOW IF THE WEATHER IS BAD.

Ten-year old Oblivious leading his family up a rock scale in the White Mountains. Often the hands were as useful as the legs in New Hampshire and Maine. Everybody was amazed at the way these steep climbs and descents kept presenting themselves in front of us. The Appalachian mountain chain, while not as elevated, is consistently more inclined than either the Sierras or the Rockies.

Chapter 19

In 1951 John Keenan had graduated from high school in Charlestown, Massachusetts, and was "over the moon" about landing his first job on the Mount Washington survey crew. The first thing the other members of the survey crew told him at orientation on his very first morning was that clouds could close in very quickly. If this happened, he was told to simply stay where he was and they would come get him. At ten o'clock that first morning a sudden cloud engulfed them. The crew began calling for Keenan to come in, but he didn't. Soon up to one hundred people were out searching for him. But, alas, he was never seen again.

On the day he disappeared a cold rain was being blown by a fifty-mile per hour wind on the Presidential Range. In such situations there is almost an irresistible impulse to walk downwind. It is less miserable on your face, requires less energy, and it feels as if nature is subtly urging you in that direction. Of course, in one sense, that is all rational. But it can be fatal.

Of course, there have been other notorious tragedies as well — the most famous probably being the teenage girl, Lizzie. Her family was caught in violent gales and freezing rain while three miles from the summit. An old stone motel called the Tip Top House used to sit at the summit, and the family attempted to force march up the mountain to reach it. But as they neared the summit they were at the point of exhaustion and could go on no longer in the blinding rain. Lizzie's uncle prepared a crude windbreak to protect the family from the elements. But it wasn't to be. "She was deadly calm," her Uncle George reported, "uttered no complaint, expressed no fear, but passed silently away." Tragically, the next morning the uncle awoke and the weather had cleared. They had camped out a mere "forty rods" from the hotel.

The common denominator in most of these tragedies is sudden weather change. Future Supreme Court Justice William Douglas wrote of his ascent on Mount Washington: "I felt comfortable enough. But suddenly the wind arrived like gunshot, and I was blue with cold. There were moments when I questioned whether I would be able to reach it. The experience taught me the awful threat that Mount Washington holds for incautious hikers." Even the Native Americans were known to give Mount Washington a wide berth and view it warily. With precipitation 304 days per year, it's almost impossible to predict what lies ahead.

But as we headed laboriously up the mountain, following the cairns, the wind gales blew away the clouds we had been wallowing in the previous five days. The sun came out. Right in front of us appeared the summit, the famous weather observatory, and the visitor's center.

Mount Washington measures 6,288 feet and is the highest peak in New England. But despite that, and despite the throngs of tourists who pay to drive up the service road to see it, the summit is not especially impressive. That's probably because unlike Mount Greylock and later Mount Katahdin, which dominate their local landscapes, Mount Washington is just a bit taller than the surrounding peaks in the Presidential Range.

Despite the lucky weather break a thermometer at the top showed the temperature was only thirty-nine degrees, sans wind chill, when we summitted. But we considered ourselves lucky, because the average temperature is twenty-seven degrees, and the mountain receives 175 inches of snow per year. But the more impressive statistic is the one recorded on April 12, 1934. On that day the Weather Observatory at Mount Washington dubbed, "the sturdiest building in America" recorded gusts on two different occasions of 231 miles per hour and several gusts of 229 miles per hour. It was the strongest wind ever recorded.

After a brief stop in the somewhat forgettable visitors' center, the Trolls, Lemon Meringue, and I headed for the much tougher descent. Gusts of cold air rocked us in staccato fashion, even on this relatively good day. "The key is to get down as fast as possible to lower altitude," Lemon Meringue said. "Jesus Christ, every bloody step is demanding," I said exasperated. Indeed, the next several miles seemed to be just careful planting of feet from one boulder to another. A series of white crosses on the mountain commemorated the spot where various hikers had perished.

After a couple thousand feet of descent we stopped and took in the serene, azure sky and wide-ranging scenery. It was formidable, granite mountain summits as far as the eye could see. My mind flashed to Afghanistan, where the world's most powerful army has been unable to catch the world's most wanted terrorist. "You know," I observed, "if you consider that Afghanistan has terrain similar to this, but over much larger areas, no wonder we can't find Bin-Laden."

"You have a point, Skywalker," Lemon Meringue rejoined. "But this is what we've been waiting for and don't ruin it by talking about politics."

"I'll take the pledge," I lamely said.

"Instead, let's talk about something interesting like sex," the Triple-Crowner suggested. "Why are AT thru-hikers so shy and asexual compared to PCT and CDT hikers."

"Because the AT is a tougher trail than the PCT or CDT," interjected Pirate, an old hiking mate of hers from the PCT.

***

The sense of relief at having cleared Mount Washington was short-lived. After laboring from one rock to another, one arrives at Madison Summit and is confronted with a descent over big, loose rocks. I had never seen anything like it.

"This looks like they detonated an underground nuclear explosion here," Wilderness Bob said, observing the landscape. Each step was tentative and deliberate in order to avoid getting wedged between sharp rocks or losing one's balance. One New Hampshire hiker, Tink, told of being blown fifteen feet from one boulder to another on Mount Madison. "I honestly wondered if I was being hurled from the mountain," she recounted.

After three hours and a three thousand-foot descent, but only three trail miles, we finally arrived below treeline and some more hospitable footing. If there was one place on the entire AT a hiker could wish for good weather it probably would be this very rocky fifteen-mile stretch above treeline, encompassing Mount Washington and Mount Madison, which we had just covered. After several days of foul weather that old bitch, Lady Luck, had shined on us with two days of good weather at the single most critical point.

At dusk, at Pinkham Notch, I got lost looking for the designated campsite. I ended up wandering up some ski slopes, and while backtracking saw the perfect field to camp. However, it was ringed with "No Camping" signs. It was now completely dark and I started to set up my tent. But again I remembered my late father's words, "Be a pig, but don't be a hog." Setting up a tent was being a hog, so I just lay out my sleeping bag in this forbidden territory and spent the evening looking up at the stars.

The Pinkham Notch Outdoor Center on a Saturday morning held an atmosphere foreign to me. The masses of people setting out were almost reminiscent of people pouring out to the beach or the golf course on a Saturday in Florida or Georgia. Only in this case, everybody was headed into the high mountains for hikes of various lengths on one of the sixty trails in the White Mountain chain. Fernand Braudel, the famous French historian, theorized that geography is the most important element that influences any culture. Nobody who has hiked the White Mountains could disagree.

Wildcat Mountain had a ski lift going to its summit, and several thru-hikers had unapologetically taken it after the brutal pounding of the previous several days. Again, the trail traveled steep inclines and over ledges, and the going was slow. Unfortunately, when I reached the ski lift building at the top I didn't have the luck to see any sheepish-looking hikers unloading with their backpacks.

Time was also more of the essence now in northern New England, with the days rapidly shortening. Splashes of color were appearing in the trees. We had started in the southern Appalachians in early spring, when the forest was still mostly bare at higher altitudes. I had passed most of the summer in the Mid-Atlantic States, with its lush forest, dense vegetation, and glorious blooming flowers. Now there was a hint of autumn in the forest, with its pageantry of brilliant colors heralding the approach of winter. This perennial cycle of life and death plays out vividly in front of the long-distance hiker.

The last night in the Whites at the Imp Campsite the caretaker squinted through his glasses and asked, "Don't I know you?" He happened to be the ridge runner in the Smokies who had cussed me out on that awful third afternoon in the Smokies. We both got a good laugh out of that and it was a fitting coda to the Whites.

A helluva tough job he and all the other trail maintenance people had, indeed. And needless to say the pay was thankless.

I was relieved to finally make it to the thriving trail town of Gorham, in the rain, after eleven days covering only one hundred miles in the Whites. Remnants of Hurricane Wilma were blowing into the area, which would strand dozens of hikers in Gorham.

***

Hikers rarely get sick. All in all, it is actually a very healthy lifestyle. One obviously gets lots of exercise and fresh air, and water constitutes almost the entire liquid diet of a hiker.

But then something strange happened to all of us. A lot of us got sick at one time. It happened toward the end of our time in the Whites. Gorham resembled a sick bay.

Almost surely this stemmed from heavy exposure to humans in the huts in the Whites, after a long period of absence of such heavy exposure. The vast majority of Native American deaths came from exposure to Europeans carrying diseases for which they had no immunity. Likewise, we had lost our immunity to various viruses and bacteria after a prolonged period outside with little exposure. I spent three days bottled up in Gorham. It was the most time I spent off the trail anywhere, but it didn't get rid of my fever. It was only when I got back on the trail, and the routine of exercise and fresh air, that it cleared up.

After 16.5 surprisingly gentle miles out of Gorham I crossed into Maine, the fourteenth and final state. All along I had been telling people I was walking to Maine, and here I was. It was getting near dusk, and I squinted to make out some faded blaze down a steep rock chute. I slid down it, and struggled the next half-mile in jagged terrain, worried about beating the dark, to make it to the Carlo Col Shelter. That last half-mile would be a precursor of what lay immediately ahead.

Without these wooden steps constructed by trail volunteers, hikers would have to slide down the mountain in rainy conditions. In other places, hikers ascend and descend using metal rungs hammered into the mountain.

Chapter 20

When people debate the prettiest places on earth you often hear about the mountains, lakes, streams, rivers, and even glaciers of Patagonia in southern Chile and Argentina. Another place frequently mentioned are the windswept, grassy moors of northern Scotland. But any hiker on the AT who passes through Maine is bound to speak of it in similarly majestic terms. At 280 miles, it's the second longest state on the AT. And by the time we finished, it would be almost everybody's favorite of the fourteen.

Maine is a wilderness with more forest land than any other state on the east coast. Its sharp cliff-like climbs on silvery summits that overlook deep shimmering bodies of water tucked deep in the forest offers a solitude to stir the depths of even the most hard-bitten souls. The treks through brilliant balsam forests with moss and lichen floors create the fairylike atmosphere of a Disney movie. And the white-capped currents in rivers, which hikers often cross on foot, add a touch of flair that is absent in the previous thirteen states.

One other thing is worth noting. The AT in Maine is tough as hell. In fact, it was thoroughly debated among the hikers as to whether it or New Hampshire is more difficult. Maine has sections that border on the diabolical, with climbs straight up and down rock faces. What's more, ubiquitous roots, deep mud holes, narrow log-lined bog bridges, and cold rivers to ford are part of the program in Maine. Yet it also has areas of hospitable terrain.

But, once again, I want to emphasize that Maine is a wilderness. Thoreau, who previously had been an unabashed proponent of pure wilderness, was shocked by Maine. "It is more grim and wild than you can imagine," he wrote. "The landscape is savage." And instead of his usual exultation in the presence of nature, he felt "more lonely than you can imagine." It was in Maine that he went from being a unabashed cheerleader for wilderness to advocating a balance between civilization and wilderness. It was a shocking turnabout for a man who had previously said, "What shall we do with a man who is afraid of the woods, their solitude, and their darkness? What solution is there for him?"

At the Full Goose Shelter I set up my tent and then wandered up to the shelter to see who had arrived. Stitch was there. So was Pokey-Pikey, but his hiking partner, DA, had not arrived. I had a soft spot for DA, dating to his self-deprecating humor on that cold, grim night on the porch of the Zealand Hut in the Whites. On just a few occasions I had felt I might be in over my head on the AT. But from what I had seen with DA, and from various wry remarks he had made, it may have been more than a few occasions with him. One veteran hiker had said that this twenty-mile stretch was the toughest on the entire AT. Now it was pitch-black dark and DA had not arrived. It was hard to see where in the jagged, steep terrain a lost hiker could pitch camp.

Finally, I started yelling "DA" at the top of my lungs. In the distance I could hear him respond. All was well, so I sat down and cooked a Lipton dinner. But at the conclusion of dinner DA still hadn't arrived. "He has some serious vision problems," his hiking partner Pokey-Pikey said. I yelled out again, and once again he responded in the distance. Unfortunately, he seemed to be the same distance away as before.

We sat around and chatted for fifteen more minutes, but the whereabouts of DA seemed to be putting a damper on the conversation. I yelled out again as loud as I could, "DA, are you okay?" Again, an unintelligible response came back from seemingly the same place. Since I had arrived at the shelter first, I was the logical person to try to help him. "I'm gonna' go find him and show him the shelter," I finally said, and put on my headlight.

"Do me a favor," Stitch said. "Use my headlight. It's incredibly powerful."

Stitch's lighter lit up the dark Maine wilderness like a stadium. And after tip-toeing up and down rocky terrain for a few hundred yards, DA's responses to my calls started getting louder. When I arrived at the point of a steep climb, it sounded like he was right above me. Finally, I saw him. He was perched over a precipice the trail descended. But all he had in his hand was a backup key lighter. "I see you," I yelled up, but he kept asking my whereabouts until I was almost on him.

"Skywalker, what am I supposed to say?" he asked.

"That you bit off just a little bit more than you can chew," I said.

"This dang lighter," he said with consternation. "My main one went out, and I can't see five feet with this thing."

"Here, let me carry your pack," I said.

"No, no, I'll carry it," he insisted. "I've been standing here for an hour wondering how to take the very next step." He marveled at the glow of Stitch's lighter and within fifteen minutes we were at the shelter. His life had not been in danger, but I honestly don't see how he could have made it to the shelter in steep terrain with such poor vision and almost no light source. He probably just faced a very unpleasant night on the rocks.

Several times in the next few days he thanked me effusively. It felt good to finally be on the giving end, after having been almost exclusively on the receiving end of advice and succor from the likes of Justin, Sal Paradise, Fork Man, Whitewater, etc.

***

Mahoosuc Notch, despite being completely flat, is widely billed as the toughest single mile on the AT. House-sized granite boulders have fallen from the mountain and filled the ravine, and ice caves lie at the bottom of these boulders. For one mile the AT traverses this veritable jungle-jim of rocks.

Before I left the shelter, the caretaker asked, "Would any of you mind carrying this little eight-pound tool to Adam, the caretaker at the next shelter?" We all looked at the ground, avoiding eye contact with him. We had heard about this notch since starting in Georgia, and nobody wanted to be burdened with extra weight.

So off I went, sans eight-pound tool, and was soon staring at Mahoosuc Notch. I waited around vainly, hoping somebody would come along in either direction, but it was to be a solitary adventure.

Hiking Mahoosuc Notch seemed almost like a puzzle. For starters, hands were as useful as legs in traversing it. Every twenty or thirty yards the hiker is faced with a straight-up boulder climb, usually requiring all fours. Three different times, while squeezed between rocks, I could think of no other way of advancing myself than to take off my backpack and slide sideways between two boulders. At one point in a section aptly named "Hangman's Noose," the AT went under some low-lying boulders requiring hikers to get on the ground and scrounge forward. Being mildly claustrophobic this was definitely *the toughest ten feet on the AT*. After ninety minutes I reached the end. On average I could cover a mile in twenty or twenty-five minutes, but Mahoosuc Notch had required four times that much time.

When I reared my head out of the notch I was almost euphoric. Then I saw a fast-moving hiker coming in the opposite direction. "You must be Adam, the caretaker."

"Yes," he said, expressionless.

"Yeah, the caretaker back there tried to get somebody to carry the tool to you," I told him, "but none of us felt confident we could get through the notch with it."

"Well, that's too bad for *me*, isn't it," he said, and started down into the notch.

Next came a sixteen hundred-foot climb up Mahoosuc Arm to Old Speck Lake. It seemed odd to arrive at a large body of water *after a long climb*. It is the highest body of water in Maine.

I didn't break long because I was eager to get over Old Speck Mountain which is exposed to harsh, cold northern winds. One hiker, Swinger, had told me, "I don't really believe in God or anything like that. But at old Speck I prayed to God." As the old cliche goes, there are no atheists in foxholes. For a brief instant I even considered turning back down the mountain when the wind began to play havoc with my balance. Fortunately, the trail turned left before reaching the summit and cut along a ridge lined with the heroically resistant krummholz.

There are certain sections on the AT that an average hiker such as myself is bound to worry about. This had been one of them, and I was relieved to make the remaining five miles to Baldpate Lean-To (Maine shelters are called Lean-To's). A group of French-Canadian section hikers was happy to put national rivalries aside and offer me plentiful servings of pasta. But because they seemed so merry, with empty wine bottles lying about, I decided to tent out and not risk a chorus of lusty snoring. It was my single best night of sleep on the AT.

I needed it. The air was sharp as a knife the next morning as Wildcat, who I hadn't seen since North Carolina, and I headed straight up Bald Pate Mountain. Bald Pate is a typical example of why Maine's mountains are so difficult to negotiate. It has multiple peaks, separated by deep gorges, as Bigelow, Saddleback, and Chairback Mountains would later have. Furthermore, Bald Pate is a steep walk on glazed rock, following cairns on an exposed summit. It would have been flat-out dangerous to traverse in bad weather. I counted my lucky stars to be on Wildcat's heels on an overcast and blustery, but dry day. *Hiking in Maine was indeed an exotic brew of exhilaration and fear. But absolutely no money can buy the adventure and freedom it offers.*

A steep sixteen hundred-foot descent brought us to the Frye Notch

Lean-To. Inside, a long, gaunt figure with a stubby, gray beard lay sprawled out in his sleeping bag at noon. For a second the unspeakable occurred to Wildcat and me. But then a creaky voice came from the supine figure, "Skywalker, long time, no see."

"Yeah," I answered quizzically.

"Vertical Jerry," he finally said while rising to his elbows. "Not since Georgia."

I looked at him with astonishment. Vertical Jerry had been a strutting, healthy-looking dandy with a style and élan all his own. But what lay in front of me five months later had a gallows-like appearance.

The only question that came to mind was the obvious one, "What happened?"

"I've been stuck here for two days," he said. "It's coming out of both ends."

"You're probably dehydrated, or have giardia," I suggested, and went off to the nearby stream to retrieve some water. He hadn't talked to anybody in two days and seemed overwhelmed with emotion. Then I remembered that my doctor had sent me some Lo-Motil prescription pills to me in Hanover. I offered him a couple and said, "Believe me, these will put a cork in you like you've never had before." But I warned him, "They'll dehydrate you. Maybe only take half." He downed both as Wildcat and I looked at each other, worried.

"Have you thought about getting off the trail?" Wildcat asked. "There's a road five miles ahead."

"Yeah, that's the direction I came from," Vertical Jerry sighed. "I'm flip-flopping. I got off at Harper's Ferry, and flew to Maine. Now I'm headed south."

It was clear he had no realistic chance of making it back to Harper's Ferry before winter. In fact, in the condition he was in he'd be lucky to make it out of the wilderness period. We wished him well and left him to suffer the agonies of the damned.

The physical appearance of most thru-hikers has gone to pot by this point. Our complexions — especially the males — had gone sallow, and many of us looked like a two-iron golf club. A thru-hiker experience may not have rated with those of Cro-Magnon Man, who had life expectancies of fewer than thirty years. But it was wilderness immersion well beyond the point of healthy balance. And humans may not be alone in this regard. I recently read that bears living in the wilderness have an average life expectancy of ten to seventeen years, but those in zoos live to a mean age of twenty-five. Wilderness is indeed one of God's greatest gifts to humankind, but its essential wildness — even savageness — should not be underestimated.

The hiking pole proved to be a perfect substitute for a golf club in the wilderness. I have to admit, my set-up isn't too bad.

Chapter 21

We had seen thru-hiker wannabes bailing out all over the place for all kinds of reasons up through New York. But those still on track were now focusing like a laser beam on their daily tasks and Mount Katahdin. Everybody was taking far fewer breaks as the days got shorter. It definitely seemed like the thru-hiker completion rate had improved from the 10 percent baseline figure up to 20 or even 25 percent. Of course, some of the improvement was probably due to the wonders of modern-day lightweight gear.

The conversation deep in the woods this September often centered on what people were gonna' do back in the "real world." But Cackles of the Joy Machine often pointed out "We should refer to the 'other world,' not the 'real world.' This world out here is just as real as that other world." That was a profound point.

I was having trouble finding people to hike with here in this most isolated state. Several months of extreme exertion, weight loss, and poor sleep had finally started to take a toll. The X factor that had goaded me on to hike until dusk almost every day during the summer had gone missing. Through the first twelve states I had been passing people 80 percent of the time, but now this pattern seemed to have reversed itself.

Whitewater, 49er, Stranger, and other familiar faces had moved ahead, according to the trail registers, and I didn't feel capable of catching up. Meanwhile, I kept running into this young group of the Joy Machine, Stitch, and Foamer.

The Joy Machine fully lived up to their billing, and could be highly entertaining. Yet, I felt dated in their presence. The lingo seemed of a totally different era. Seeing my new green cap, Cackles said, "That's really pussy, man." When somebody had to perform a bowel movement in the woods, they would say, "Time to go lay a deuce."

Cackles had a cheeky flamboyance about her and thrived on being the center of attention. But like many such entertaining personalities she had a volatile side. She had a tendency to rifle harsh charges at other hikers who

{}

were out of earshot, and I began wondering if I was on the receiving end of some of her sharp invective.

I had known Stitch before ever meeting the Joy Machine. He was a good, down-to-earth guy with a bit of an all-American look to his freckly face. But he was captivated in the extreme by the Joy Machine and treated me very differently, tone of voice and all, while they were around. Foamer, a young Kentuckyite whose bug eyes and overwrought monologues earned him his trail name, also seemed to be in the thrall of the Joy Machine — but to his credit he didn't let it affect his attitude toward me. However, it inspired Stitch to consistently treat Foamer in a demeaning, even cruel, manner.

Of course, none of these things are new under the sun, as a reading of any Shakespeare play will show. But, it did show that this world we were in had some similarities to the "other world."

On a few occasions I even tried to get away from this group, and at times felt they were conspiring to do the same. But we were traveling at roughly the same speed which, more often that not, dictates hiking partners on a 2,175-mile hike.

Because of the long distances between Maine towns, hikers were forced to carry more food. Fortunately, this was offset by the frequent streams, which gave me the confidence to carry less water. But those same water sources necessitate many log walks. Often long logs had been laid lengthwise along the trail to facilitate progress in these boggy areas. It would have been a hat-in-hand horror show traversing these boggy areas without what had obviously been yeoman work on the part of volunteers. God Bless the Maine Appalachian Trail Club. But even as it was, we would often be on rickety logs over swampy areas. Stories were legion of hikers toppling over into this mud soup.

There *are no bridges on the AT in Maine* despite the fact the trail frequently crosses surging waterways. The data book showed that hikers were expected to ford in over a dozen places, and anticipation was building. The last thing I had done in Gorham was drop by the outfitters to buy some lightweight, foam shoes called "Crocks," to ford streams in. But, the first couple of streams that were listed as to be forded we were able to get over with some fancy rock-hopping. For once I found something to brag about. "I'm the best rock-hopper on the AT."

***

In Maine we were running into piles of moose scat along the trail seemingly every five minutes. And given the fact that they are vegetarians, it made one wonder at the enormous extent of their plant diet.

I was not surprised one day to come upon a couple moose, nibbling at some plants. One was smaller than the other so I tread carefully, assuming it was a mother-daughter tandem. But since moose are vegetarians, with no interest in human foods, there was none of the trickery or gamesmanship associated with bear-human encounters.

Those two moose had the gentlest dispositions of any creatures I've ever seen. However, they seem to be in the grips of a lifelong lassitude and ennui (except, of course, during mating season!). The smaller animals, on the other hand, ranging from bugs and mice to raccoons, are often raring to go on the attack. Bears, which are low to the ground, but impressively wide, seemed to be in the middle.

It's no radical theory to postulate that bigger and taller humans have to guard against being excessively laid-back and unassertive. Shorter people, on the other hand, are notoriously more aggressive. What I was witnessing there in the wilderness showed this tendency wasn't just human nature, but the natural order of all living things. When I spouted my highly unscientific theory to Swinger at the campsite that evening, he replied with amusement, "Thank you, Professor Skywalker Darwin."

***

Fred Flintstone, a fifty-eight-year-old ex-military serviceman from New York, and Steady Eddie, a sixty-eight-year-old from Minnesota, had been paired up since North Carolina. That, in fact, was where I had passed them. I had never expected either of them to make it this far, but they had combined great discipline with an innovative transportation arrangements to facilitate slackpacking.

However, this strategy became inoperative in New Hampshire and Maine, which were so isolated, with infrequent road crossings. They made up for it with great determination. Each morning they would be on the trail by seven o'clock and they took few breaks until reaching their daily destination. Steady Eddie would then quickly eat and get straight into his sleeping bag, where he stayed approximately thirteen hours per day. He spent the remaining eleven hours walking. This was in keeping with Thomas Edison's philosophy that "Genius is one percent inspiration and ninety-nine percent perspiration."

Fred Flintstone, on the other hand, was more garrulous. His military-like daytime discipline waned dramatically when it came to evening campsite conversation. At the Poplar Ridge Lean-To, on a cool, stormy fall night in the Maine wilderness, Fred Flintstone found the perfect audience to relive the late 1960s, when he was a serviceman in steamy, humid South Vietnam. And it was the steamy nightlife he remembered so fondly. "We'd go to downtown Saigon for a steam-blow and a bath job," he said.

"Didn't you say that backwards?" Swinger asked confused.

"No, goddammit," Fred Flintstone said insistently. "That's what we called it, and that's what it was."

"I always wondered why the U.S. stayed in Vietnam so long," I said.

"And get this," he enthused, "this one named Coop-Coop, with green teeth, said I was the biggest tipper in the whole damn American army."

As the old saying goes, there is no fool quite like an old fool. It began to look like this might go on all night until Swinger finally said, "We've got some big climbs ahead tomorrow. I don't have any military training, and need some sleep."

I stayed on Swinger's heels the next day for a hellish eleven miles over jagged terrain, until we finally came to the Sugarloaf Mountain Side Trail. "There's a summit house up there where hikers can sleep," he said.

"And get this," he added in an awestruck tone, "you can see Mount Katahdin up there sometimes." My feet were pleading for mercy and there was no campsite nearby, so I followed him straight up the face of this steep, rocky side trail.

Sugarloaf Mountain is Maine's second-highest mountain and biggest ski resort. We located a bubbling crystal clear, mountain spring on the way up, and finally arrived at what looked like a perfect cone peak. Fortunately, we quickly spotted the summit house and hurried over in what were almost unbearable wind gusts. The mood inside was glum as powerful gusts of wind mixed with a U-Boat silence.

"Hey, come look at this," one hiker said, "That must be Katahdin." A whole panorama of mountains lay before us, and indeed a distant peak silhouetted in the far distance seemed to distinguish itself as we stood there silently at dusk. It was a tantalizing glimpse, even if I wasn't entirely convinced that it was Mount Katahdin ("The Greatest Mountain"), still 180 miles away, that we were ogling.

Fred Flintstone and Steady Eddie arrived, but the frigid conditions inside strongly discouraged any repeat of Fred Fintstone's epic tales. The howling wind tore at the windowpanes, which made sleep difficult. I set up my tent behind a wall to gain some protection from the cold draft, but the fierce wind shook at the window panes all night. We were all up at first light the following morning, and my tent was soaked from the condensation created by warmer air colliding with cold air. We filed out silently, and I was quite happy to get back below tree line.

***

A couple days later the trail ascended three thousand feet on the Bigelow Range. Colonel Bigelow had been part of Benedict Arnold's expedition that attacked the British along this route during the revolutionary war. This was, of course, during Benedict Arnold's good ol' days as a red-blooded American patriot. Had they succeeded in this attack Canada might today be part of the United States.

My emotions were mixed. The whole AT had started off as an intense shout of freedom, and it had been anything but a disappointment. But at some point a person's appetite for the new begins to flag, and I had just about reached it. A profound fatigue greater than could be remedied by a mere good night's sleep was setting in. At this point I just wanted to make it all the way.

That night I was alone, and had to hike a half-mile off the trail in tricky terrain to find a suitably un-rocky campsite. I tried to hang a bear line, but ended up failing miserably. This meant keeping my food in the tent with me all evening, never a soothing prospect. But my biggest worry turned out not to be hungry bears, but high winds. The wind howled and shook the forest all evening as branches fell off trees, bouncing off other branches lower down. I lay cowering in my tent, completely exposed to a tree blow-down, of which I noticed there had been many.

Inevitably, I began the next day in low spirits. But then I arrived at the bottom of Little Bigelow Mountain. This was the end of Warren Doyle's Section Three of the AT, which he had labeled as the toughest of the four sections. That was good news. Better yet, as I followed the trail down a dirt road in isolated, central Maine I noticed a big camper with a picnic table set up on a side road. I gnash my teeth now trying to remember his name, but he was a member of the well-known "Billville Hiking Club." He invited me over for a picnic.

"How many hamburgers would you like?" he asked heartily. "I'll cook 'em on my grill for you."

"One would be great," I said.

"One," he said surprised. "I've never had a hiker eat just one."

Even though I had just eaten lunch 1.5 miles back, the burger had a heartiness and flavor that few besides thru-hikers and animals could appreciate. And there was just something about trail food that never quite hit the spot ("like the soup made from the shadow of a crow that starved to death"). After I devoured that burger and meekly asked for a second, he replied, "There you go, and try some of this other stuff, please." Sure enough, the table was decked out with pasta salad, desserts, candy bars, and soft drinks. He even had Advil, aspirin, and toilet paper for hikers to take. Soon, Stitch, the Joy Machine, and Foamer arrived with ineffable looks at what lay before them.

I finally headed off with a renewed vigor that, honest to God, lasted for a full day and a half.

Everybody was in buoyant spirits at the shelter that early autumn evening, and most went swimming in the nearby lake. The hot topic at the Lean-To was Warren Doyle's entry in the trail register from a couple weeks before.

West Carry Pond Lean-To — mile 1,911

9-01-05: Five Myths — Warren Doyle
1. *Iraq has weapons of mass destruction.*
2. *Saddam was connected to 9-11.*
3. *Bull moose like to become intimate with female hikers during their menstrual cycles.*
4. *Masturbation leads to blindness.*
5. *The Kennebec River is unfordable at all times.*

"That's the most entertaining journal entry I've read in two thousand miles," I exclaimed.

But fully imbued with the anti-Doyle trendiness pervading the younger hikers, Stitch spoke for the group, "That guy is nuts." And looking at me he added, "You're crazy to listen to a word he says."

"Get a life, Stitch," I responded.

Below the five myths Warren had gone on to list ten steps for fording the Kennebec River, all of which we had discussed in his class. A woman had died several years back attempting to ford the Kennebec, and there had been several other near drownings. Finally, the ATC, whether for humanitarian or liability reasons, had decided to provide a ferry with a blaze painted on it to carry hikers across the river. But the fiercely independent Doyle had said, "Remember, if you take the canoe, you haven't hiked the entire trail."

The woman who drowned had had her backpack strapped on tightly, and was unable to remove it as she was swept up by the current. Warren had demonstrated to our class how to carry our backpacks with straps loosened while fording.

I had been thinking about doing it for some time. But the first step Warren had listed was to be at the shore by seven o'clock, when you're fresh and the water from upstream hasn't been released yet. The largest dam in the Northeast is a few miles up the Kennebec from where the AT crosses it, and water is released at irregular intervals. After each release the water levels and current increase rapidly. But we were thirteen-and-a-half miles away from the Kennebec that evening, which meant we wouldn't arrive at the shores of the Kennebec until two or three o'clock the following afternoon at best.

The trail was abuzz the next day as we approached the river. Unfortunately, my statement in support of Doyle's journal entry and remarks to the effect that I might consider trying it under the right circumstances, had been turned into bold claims that I would.

At the lean-to, 3.5 miles before the Kennebec, was the following entry:

Pierce Pond Lean-To — mile 1,921

*9-16-05: **High Noon**. Skywalker meets the Kennebec. — **The Riddler***

***

The trail wove downhill, toward the river, which I began to hear surging by. Then I cleared the hilltop and the Kennebec River presented itself in full. It looked more like the Potomac River, than some of the waterways we had been able to negotiate by rock-hopping. And a cursory glance both upstream and downstream didn't reveal any significant rock outcroppings to gain traction.

The canoe ferry operator approached, and from the shore I shouted out, "Is it fordable?"

"Oh don't go committing suicide, now," he yelled back. "You see the water where you're standing, now?"

"Yeah," I replied looking at the water under my hiking shoes.

"That will be up to your waist in a half-hour," he shot back. "They just released the water from the dam upstream about twenty minutes ago."

"How deep is it?" I asked.

"Maybe twelve or fourteen feet when you get half way across," he answered. "Just last week two people tried it and ended up floating one hundred yards downstream before they were lucky to catch a rock."

I was chastened as my chance to distinguish myself among my peers was jettisoned.

Disillusioned, I joined the others in loading my backpack in the canoe. It soon became clear that he was right, as we struggled mightily to help him paddle upstream and then across the powerful, streaking currents.

Our first challenging fords came the next day in heavy rain. "Skywalker, this must be a piece of cake for you," Foamer shouted out.

"No way," I shouted back. "A high center of gravity is no good in this." As best I could tell the biggest risk was taking a step into an unknown deep spot and then toppling over. I unbuttoned my backpack straps, per Warren Doyle's advice, just in case I did fall over.

The fords often came unannounced; they weren't even listed in the guidebook. We would arrive at a wide creek or narrow river, and look left and right before somebody would spot a blaze on the far side of the water. Dutifully, everybody would pull off their hiking shoes and put on the crocks to wade across. The bottom was usually rocky, and the natural urge to hurry could cause one to careen over. In just a few days Hurricane Rita would have these streams jumping their banks and they would be anywhere from dangerous, to completely impassable.

The trail also kept coming up on rickety bog bridges and fifty-foot puddles. Hikers had a choice of splashing through the mud and water or trying to skirt around through the bushes and trees. Inevitably, our shoes and boots were filled with mud and water. I was thankful for the company. Getting lost in these rural parts, in heavy rain and with several streams to cross, would have been a grave matter.

***

Finally, three days after crossing the Kennebec, I came to Maine Highway 15. A sixtyish lady, who gave the impression of nobly performing a grim duty, gave me a ride into Monson. This was the last northbound hiker town on the AT and the entry point into the Hundred-Mile Wilderness.

Monson is another nondescript one-street town in which AT hikers resupplied, but Shaw's Boardinghouse is anything but ordinary. It is a picturesque two-story house located off the main street that has been putting up hikers for thirty years. Several rooms are available at reasonable prices, and a fabulous breakfast is served at six o'clock.

The first person I saw upon entering was Baltimore Jack. After his unexpected dropout due to injury, Evan was helping out with the late-season rush of hikers. They were full, but I agreed with his suggestion to sleep out on the lawn. It was to be about the only thing we agreed on.

Downstairs, Baltimore Jack began holding court in trademark fashion in front of a captive audience. Stitch had told him about his rival Warren Doyle's trail register entry about fording the Kennebec. But Evan didn't find it amusing. He was even threatening to hike out to the West Carry Pond Lean-To Shelter to retrieve Warren's entry and show it to the ATC Board of Directors. Apparently, Warren had been taken to task by the ATC for advocating that hikers ford the Kennebec, despite the fact that he was a board member himself.

"What's wrong with his fording the Kennebec, if he chooses to?" I asked Evan in what some took as an act of lesé majesté.

"He can ford the Kennebec all he wants," Evan fired back. "But he tries to shame and humiliate others into doing something dangerous." Well, maybe Evan had a point, but Doyle's journal entry had specifically taken issue with the idea that the Kennebec was unfordable at all times. It was all pretty esoteric stuff and the passions it aroused would show what a bubble thru-hikers live in.

"Look, he's a maverick with a bit of a swagger," I said taking a philosophical tact. "No, he's not 'a maverick with a bit of a swagger,'" Evan thundered back. "He's a fraud."

At six-thirty Baltimore Jack called out, "Silence. Jeopardy time." For the next half-hour he demonstrated a stunning command of minutiae and historical facts going back hundreds and thousands of years. The amateur Freud in me couldn't help but wonder if it all wasn't linked: eight thru-hikes in nine years, heavy drinker, chain-smoker, fixation on Jeopardy trivia, obsession with Warren Doyle. A classic addictive personality.

He had joked, "I'm a drunk with a hiking problem." Humor was his saving grace.

Fresh fruit is a delicacy to a hiker. It always was a hoped-for item when we happened to encounter a "trail angel."

Chapter 22

The remnants of Hurricane Rita blew a powerful storm into the area, pouring sheets of rain all night, with no letup the next morning. We glumly realized it would be practically insane to head out as Wilma lashed the area all day. Meanwhile, Baltimore Jack gave us a brief primer on the streams to be forded in the 100 Mile Wilderness. "Watch out for the Little Wilson," he said in words that would soon gain great significance for us. "It can be a problem after heavy storms."

The Shaws dutifully shuttled us back to the trailhead early the next morning, where the sign said:

YOU ARE ABOUT TO ENTER THE 100 MILE WILDERNESS. YOU SHOULD HAVE 10 DAYS OF FOOD TO COMPLETE THIS JOURNEY.

I had about a seven-day supply, which I thought would be sufficient. My backpack now weighed forty pounds, the most ever. This was a far cry from the low twenties it weighed back in Georgia. I felt myself swaying and "back heavy" the first couple rock climbs. It immediately became clear that the trail conditions had changed dramatically in just thirty-six hours. In the wake of the powerful storm, long stretches of puddles and thick mud presented themselves right in the middle of the trail. Hikers were trying all manners of bushwhacking, straddling, and the like. Still our feet and socks were a mess after one mile, with ninety-nine more to go. Travel was slowed dramatically, and I quickly began wondering if I had brought enough food.

One reason I wanted to hang with a group was to avoid getting lost in the most isolated stretch in the entire eastern United States. But with my long, gangly physique I consistently had trouble keeping up with people in rocky, wet, and muddy areas. And that was to be the case on this day as the trail traversed around ponds and over slippery slate rock and through quagmires. Fortunately, the Maine Appalachian Trail Club (MATC) had once again done a fantastic job blazing the trail, even in the most remote wilderness areas.

Leeman Brook Lean-To — mile 2,064

9-19-05: *Has anybody seen the fountain of youth? — **Skywalker***

* * *

A short, middle-age man with a clipped moustache appeared from the opposite direction. It was surprising to see a southbound hiker this time of the year. As usual, I planned to debrief him on what lay ahead, but he beat me to the punch. "Hi, I'm Cocomo. You might want to go back with me," he said flatly. He had a frozen, stunned look on his face.

"I just left from Monson," I said, confused.

"Those streams up ahead are dangerous," he stated succinctly. "I almost drowned in the Big Wilson yesterday." His face looked ashen.

"How high was it?" I asked anxiously.

"At one point it was over my head, and I thought I was going to die. Thankfully, the current washed my backpack ashore downstream."

"Did you make it across?" I asked.

"No, I slept on the south bank and this morning the current was still so powerful I decided to turn around," he said matter-of-factly.

"Is that the only fordable stream ahead?"

"No," he answered. "This big, burly guy just saved my life getting me back over the Little Wilson, just ahead."

"So you don't recommend that we try to get over the Little Wilson or Big Wilson today," I pressed him.

"No way," he flatly replied. This was not going at all according to plan, and again I wondered about my seven-day food supply.

"So where are you headed?" I asked.

"Monson."

"Are you thru-hiking?"

"I was," he sighed.

"Well, God, I hate seeing it end like this for you," I said, more in amazement than anything.

"Yep," he said looking down. And off he went, south, with a grim look on his face.

I later heard he had decided to attempt an AT thru-hike to recover from the tragic death of his twenty-one-year-old daughter. On this day he indeed did return to Shaw's in Monson, where he had been just a couple days before this. There, the Shaws and Baltimore Jack had apparently tried to break through his adamant refusal to get back on the trail. After a few days they succeeded. He went back out and eventually completed his thru-hike.

Soon I cleared a hilltop and saw the Joy Machine, Hit Man, and the Honeymooners (thru-hiking on their honeymoon — damn risky) among others. They were standing on the edge of the Little Wilson, a narrow, but surging, body of water. It was only about ten yards wide. I looked over and saw a blaze on the other side. This was where we were supposed to cross.

"Did ya'll meet Cocomo back there?" I asked.

"Yes, I felt sorry for him," Cackles said.

"What about us," I responded. "How in the world are we supposed to get across?'

"This looks like home for the evening for us," the male Honeymooner said. "We're going to hope it goes down enough by morning."

A compact-looking fellow said, "I just led Cocomo back across by hand; both of us nearly went down. That current is powerful." One look at this burly fella' told me that if he had any trouble with it I would be foolhardy to try. He finally said, "I'm going to try a horse trail somebody mentioned."

"I'll tag along if you don't mind," I said.

"Sure."

I couldn't see where the horse trail went, but followed him anyway. We walked down the bank of the cascading river, but soon the path we were on ran into dense brush. He cut up the hill, going away from the river and next thing I knew we were bushwhacking. "Is this the horse path?" I asked perplexed.

"I don't know what it is, but there has to be a route through here somewhere," he said calmly. We kept slashing until we came up upon foliage so dense a moose might have avoided it. And it was supposed to be almost two miles to get to some railroad track that would cross this river, and then a trek back up to the trail.

"I'm sorry, man," I said. "I'm just gonna' go back."

"No problem, brother," he said pleasantly. "Only you know what's good for yourself." At the moment even that was doubtful.

***

When I finally made it back to the group at the bank of the Little Wilson Trail, they all smiled knowingly as I related the tale. Fortunately,

Stitch and Swinger had just built a log bridge a few hundred yards downstream to get across.

But then, for one of the few times on the trail, a bold impulse, the desire to do more than get from point A to point B, seized me. Perhaps it was because I considered myself a good rock-hopper, or maybe it was because my other attempt at boldness, fording the Kennebec, had been foiled. "See that spot right there," I pointed to an area right before the water tumbled over and down some rocks. "That doesn't look as torrential. I'm going to try to get across there."

I quickly swapped out my hiking shoes for my crocks. As I was walking down the bank to enter the surging stream I suddenly stopped. "I'm just gonna' go without my backpack to test it out." It was to prove to be the single wisest decision I made the entire time on the AT, if not my whole life.

When I stepped in I first noticed how rocky and uneven the surface was. It was tempting to try to hurry across, but that was surely a bad idea. The uneven footing and unrelenting current were the essence of the challenge. The water was mountain-ice cold.

I picked out a big rock about fifteen yards downstream that I was planning to dive for in case I got swept up by the current. On the fourth step my foot went an extra two feet deeper than expected, and suddenly the water was above my waist. A loud, collective groan emanated from my audience perched on the bank, as they wondered where the water would be on them. Meanwhile, I wondered where the water would be on my next step. Fortunately, with my hiking pole I was able to probe and get a better idea of what lay ahead. Finally, I got to within a few feet of a big rock on the far side and flung myself on it and crawled out of the Little Wilson River. My audience on the far side gave me an ovation. It may have been my high moment on the AT.

But now I had to go back and retrieve my backpack. When I stepped back in, the male Honeymooner yelled over, "Try it down here and see if you can find an easier place for everybody to get across." Dutifully, I went down to where a rope had been hung across the stream. This was where the water spilled over the rock and the current seemed the strongest. I got halfway across, but the powerful current turned my legs into jelly. Everybody kept yelling, "Grab the rope." It was probably good advice, but it didn't seem a sure bet. And one look down the torrid, white-capped rapids told me it had to be a dead cinch—or else. I turned around and went back to the north bank. Then I quickly ran up to where I had crossed before.

But when I started across this time my legs again felt unsteady, and now I was tired. It seemed dangerous, so I turned around to return to the north shore after a few steps. I lost my balance at the end and had to lunge to safety on the big rock I had arrived at when I had originally crossed successfully. The fundamentals were grim. My backpack was on the south side of the Little Wilson River, and I was on the north side. And I had just failed twice in attempting to get back to the south bank.

Thank God for the log bridge Stitch and Swinger had built. Embarrassed, I hurriedly bushwhacked downstream to try to find it and get back across. After a couple hundred yards I saw where somebody had laid two narrow tree logs from the far bank of the river to a rock in the middle. My task was to jump from the north bank to one rock, and then from that rock to the big rock in the middle. Then I would crawl across the rickety log bridge. It was doable, but there was no margin for error. This far downstream the Little Wilson broadens, which means that in case of a blunder a person's chances of being helplessly swept away increased.

Cackles had come down to watch with a quizzical look on her face. "Is this the bridge Stitch built?" I yelled out to her.

"I guess," she shouted back. I executed the two jumps to the middle rock well, and then got on my knees to crawl across the two logs. They seemed somewhat steady, if not a bulwark. I carefully crawled across and was finally back on the south bank of the Little Wilson, where my backpack was after my misadventure. "You did great," Cackles consoled me, but I was torn about the whole effort.

When we got back upstream to where everybody was, I said, "There was my fifteen minutes of fame. Now it's somebody else's turn."

"How did you hurt your foot?" Hit Man, a hulking Floridian, asked. I looked down and saw blood spilling profusely out of my big toe. Undoubtedly, it was cut by one of the sharp boulders at the bottom.

The maximum effort had tired me, but everybody except the Honeymooners started back downstream with their backpacks for the log bridge, and I followed suit. I was contentedly back in my more familiar follower mode.

One by one, everybody walked carefully over the slick rock to the log bridge and got on their knees with their backpacks strapped on. "Make sure your backpacks are loosely strapped on, just in case," I called out. Box-of-

Fun was second-to-last, followed by me. She teetered over the logs very tentatively. Several times she stopped, unsure of herself on the log bridge. Just a few feet below roared powerful white torrents that would have given vertigo to anyone who focused on it for long. Finally, she made it to the rock in the middle, and then after long surveys of the terrain executed the two rock hops perfectly to the far bank.

Everybody seemed to take it for granted that I would easily re-cross the log bridge, but this time I had my backpack strapped on. Nevertheless, it came off fine, and we had finally all cleared the Little Wilson, even if it hadn't been pretty.

"All's well that ends well," said Hit Man.

"Yep," I added. "And we should be able to find a good place to camp on the banks of the Big Wilson in three miles, and then hopefully get across tomorrow morning."

"Yeah," Hit Man replied. "And we should see Stitch, Swinger, and company camped out on the banks of the Big Wilson." Surely it was impassable on this day. The next few miles everybody seemed relieved to have dodged one bullet and gotten vivid intelligence on how to handle the next powerful stream.

***

Anticipation and apprehension built as we started hearing the rush of running water getting closer. Soon we arrived at the banks of the Big Wilson. Stitch, Swinger and company were nowhere to be seen. "Let's refrain from any morbid jokes," I said, surprised.

"They must've gone across," Hit Man said. "I reckon we can make it too."

"God, wouldn't it be nice," I said. "The shelter is just a half-mile over this stream."

It was about fifty yards across, and the white-capped current was moving steadily, but not as torrentially as the Little Wilson had been. "I'll go first," Hit Man volunteered.

"No objections here," I said, having exhausted my quest for glory back at the Little Wilson.

"But I'm going to keep my hiking shoes on, instead of wearing crocks," he said, sensibly.

The big, burly Hit Man then waded in and moved steadily across as the water never got up to his waist. The Joy Machine soon followed suit with the water reaching their waist, but they did not seem shaken at all. It made a big difference when I followed, wearing my hiking shoes, although the steady current kept me intently focused.

It was 4:30 when we happily arrived at the Wilson Valley Lean-To. We had about ninety minutes of reliable sunlight remaining. Foamer was there to greet us with a Foamerism: "These long days sure are short." I scoured the immediate vicinity for somewhere to pitch a tent, but the terrain was rocky and inclined.

Then, to my amazement I noticed the Joy Machine making plans to head off, and Hit Man joined in. "How about you, Skywalker?"

"This is home for me," I said with uncharacteristic decisiveness. Off they went with a little more than an hour of sunlight left and five tough miles to the next shelter.

A southbounder arrived at dark, and Foamer and I briefed him on what lay ahead with the Big and Little Wilson Streams. "Doesn't sound any worse than what I just did," he said. "The water was up to my chest."

"Did you pass a threesome on the way here?" I asked.

"Yeah, I was going to warn them," he said, "but it was getting dark."

After an hour of hiking the following morning, Foamer and I crossed a stream that fell off down a waterfall for almost one hundred feet, just fifteen yards after it crossed the AT. After we were able to rock hop across I asked, "Do you think this is the stream that guy was talking about last night?"

"Probably so," Foamer said. "They go down fast overnight."

"Glad we waited until this morning," I said. "Fifteen feet off the trail to the right and it's all she wrote."

But a mile or so later we were eating our words, as we arrived at another cascading stream. It was only about ten yards across, so we ran up and down the banks looking in vain for a way to get across. Not in the mood to take any chances I took off my socks and put my hiking shoes back on. It was up to my thighs and the current was stiff. Halfway across, Foamer said, "See where the current hits me," pointing to just below his waist. "It's probably fallen at least a foot from when they crossed last night."

When we passed the shelter soon after, I read Cackles' entry:

Long Pond Stream Shelter — mile 2,076

9-21-05: *Fording a surging stream at night with water reaching your chest is not highly recommended. It's not even smart.* — ***Cackles***

Foamer and I then ascended seventeen hundred feet, virtually straight up the granite mass of Barren Mountain. At the summit, decked out and having an extended picnic was the Joy Machine. "How are the two nighttime forders?" I asked.

"Oh, you should have seen it," Box-of-Fun said.

"I doubt I could have," I responded, "because it was nighttime and there couldn't have been much of you poking out of the water to see."

They had forgotten to buy cheese in Monson, and I was carrying three half-pound blocks of Vermont cheese. "Ya'll deserve a morsel of cheese for your heroics," I said. Like animals catching a whiff of prey in the Maine wilderness, they hurried over.

The idea of getting caught at night out here in the rocky, mountainous wilderness loomed ever-present, and I cut my break short to reach my evening destination. The Joy Machine, meanwhile, continued lounging and gazing at the sights — a classic adrenaline hangover.

***

Howling wind and rain were back with a vengeance. At two-thirty in the afternoon we all made it to the Carl Newhall Shelter, but like an army, we appeared stalled out in the mud and fog. Getting over exposed White Cap Mountain was going to be impossible this day. And quickly it became clear it was going to be a miserable afternoon and evening. It was cool and damp, and I knew how my 6'11," now less-than-180-pound physique would respond. Further, Stitch was again carping and snapping at Foamer.

When Cackles said, "There's a campsite one and eight-tenths miles up the mountain. We're going to head on," she piqued my interest.

"I'll tag along, if it's okay," I said. Moving on would at least keep my body temperature up for the next ninety minutes. Off I went, tagging behind the Joy Machine. Cackles, as noted before, was the master of conversation while trekking up steep climbs. I just tried to keep up and not get lost in these nether regions.

We arrived at a wide open area, which we presumed to be the Sidney Tappan Campsite. Three guys had their tents set up right in the middle of the AT. "There has to be more to this campsite than this clearing," Box-of Fun said, looking around. We wandered over to the nearby camping area to inspect the terrain. "It all looks a little rocky," Box-of-Fun said, examining them.

"The clearing is cool with me," Cackles said, and I followed them out to the clearing. We put the tents up. The rain had lightened up, but we were completely exposed to a powerful, forest-shaking wind.

The Joy Machine had the good sense to cook dinner and then get in their tents for the evening by six o'clock. I, on the other hand, dithered in the dark. I even went on a sightseeing tour to the privy, despite my anemic headlamp battery. When I finally did get in my tent it was probably about eight o'clock, and I had already begun feeling chilled. Nevertheless, I was able to get comfortable until about midnight. At that time I exited my tent to relieve myself. But upon returning a strong draft began to dominate my thoughts in the "warmth" of my tent.

Over the next few hours I tried everything I could possibly conjure up to get warm, but to no avail. Not even the emergency blanket worked, as I thrashed around as if fighting a wild animal. I'd made a huge blunder in not camping over in the less-exposed trees, or down the mountain with Stitch and Foamer. The temperature was probably no less than forty degrees, but my muscles became increasingly tense. I just didn't have the body fat to stay warm in these high winds. I wondered if I would even have the energy to make it over White Cap Mountain the following day.

As I lay there listening to one roaring gust of wind after another, paranoia began to set in. When I heard some stirring in the guy's tent I yelled over, "What time is it?"

When one responded "two-thirty," my heart sank. That meant I had three or four more hours of maximum physical exertion and eerie mental torment to endure before daybreak.

Then I remembered the *privy*. In my sightseeing tour the previous night I had noticed it wasn't one of those open-air privies. It had four sides. That made it the most valuable piece of real estate in the Hundred-Mile Wilderness.

Off I went down a dark side trail and soon I came upon the privy. It wasn't big. I opened the door and sat on the toilet seat. It wasn't much bigger than an airplane bathroom, but seemed okay. I sat in there listening to the howling wind bouncing off the privy walls and began to feel more relaxed. In fact, I was marveling at my genius for improvisation during a crisis.

It was so good that I decided to go retrieve my sleeping bag and make a night of it in there. Again, I stumbled back to my tent, and a few minutes later I was back in the privy, with my sleeping bag wrapped around me.

My enthusiasm waned a bit when multiple efforts to find a sleeping position failed. It waned even more when a strong ammonia-like smell hit me. I wondered if I was getting paranoiad again or whether I was getting high off the smell. My mind started to wander, when suddenly, thank God, I came to in a cold sweat. I burst out of the privy swaying. It was all I could muster out of my shaky legs to stagger with my sleeping bag in the dark back to my tent. Fortunately, when I dove back into my tent my body had been so exercised by the entire misadventure that I was warmer and the crisis passed.

At first light when Box-of-Fun poked her head out of the tent, yawning, I asked, "Were ya'll able to sleep out here exposed to those high winds?"

"Yeah," she answered, confused as to the basis of the question.

"Another rookie mistake on my part," I then explained.

"You and your rookie mistakes, Skywalker," Cackles reprimanded me acidly. "You've gone all the way from Georgia to Maine. That excuse is getting old." She obviously had a point. However anyone who has unsuccessfully tried everything in their human power to get warm for several hours knows just how desperate the feeling is. Desperate people do desperate things.

***

Finally, I got moving, but the usual morning adrenaline lasted no more than a mile, the least ever. The climb up White Cap, which in typical Maine fashion had multiple ascents, was punishing. I was stopping every fifteen minutes in my debilitated state. "Ha, Skywalker," came a vaguely familiar voice from my rear. Looking behind me I saw Buffet and Goat for the first time in three months. They were a late-fiftyish couple who had started in late March and that I had come upon in central Virginia. After hiking with them for a couple days I had gone ahead of them, presumably for good.

But it was utterly impossible to guess whether a thru-hiker wanna-be could make it all the way or not. It reminded of my friend who worked in a nursing home who said that the every-day banter of employees included everyone guessing which patient was going to be the next to die. "It was uncanny how wrong we were," he related. "Some patients you were sure were goners would find something deep within and fight back to live for years. Others would just fall off a cliff and be gone in a wink." The same phenomenon was at work here on the AT in a less final way.

"This is bad for morale," I said to Buffet and Goat. "People I passed are all now blowing past me."

"We've enjoyed reading your journal entries," Buffet laughed. "Especially the one at the Halfway Store in Pennsylvania when you wrote one word: 'Uncle.'"

"Now I remember," I said. "You're New Hampshirites. You turn out hikers the way Brazil turns out soccer players." They laughed and continued past me, to stay ahead for good.

White Cap Mountain's frosty peak had a majestic view of uncharted lakes and the dense Maine autumn forest below. But I skipped across the granite summit in a hurry because of the powerful draft and my all-important focus on maintaining my sense of direction while above treeline. After three steep miles of rocky descent the trail leveled off.

An ATC map showed unprecedented topography. For the next sixty miles the trail is flat as a landing strip, until abruptly interrupted by the gigantic forty-two hundred foot climb up Mount Katahdin. Despite bone-weary fatigue, my morale had picked up dramatically from my awful night.

Right as the sun came out in the afternoon I found an ice-cold spring just off the trail near Mountain View Pond. That gave me a disproportionate boost, and I was able to rock-hop over the Pleasant River. Then the trail became a straightaway and I put the speedometer on maximum speed (three mph). Everything was perfect on this late-September day in the northern Maine wilderness. I was now an odds-on favorite to complete this dreamlike journey.

When I got to the shelter I told Foamer about the previous night's privy incident. "Boy, it's a good thing you didn't do that back in Georgia when people were getting trail names," he cracked. "No telling what kind of name you might have ended up with."

I made it to Mount Katahdin, the northernmost point of the AT on Sept. 27, 2005, exactly 171 days after starting at Springer Mountain in north Georgia, the southernmost point. As you can see in my face, along the way my weight dropped from 212 pounds to fewer than 180 pounds.

Chapter 23

I wandered upstream and pitched my tent along the brook. In the morning at the shelter I saw where Stitch had once again caught ten or twenty mice overnight with his mouse trap and laid them on a stump for hiker viewing. As vegetarians, the Joy Machine didn't normally approve of such things, but they made an exception in the case of rodents occupying shelters.

The next couple days this hiker convoy moved through the last part of the Wilderness at an increased clip. Periodically, we would stop at one of Maine's seemingly endless, large, shimmering lakes with names like Potawadjos, Pemsdumcock, Nahmakanta, or my favorite, Mooselookmeguntic, to take in glimpses of the imposing façade of Mount Katahdin. Unlike the first glimpse of it one hundred fifty miles back from the ski summit house, it was quite clear what we were gazing upon.

In one shelter register Paparazzi captured my thoughts well with the following entry:

Rainbow Stream Lean-To — mile 2,151

5-5-05: What is it going to be like living in a world where people don't argue incessantly about Warren Doyle, Baltimore Jack, and Wingfoot?
— Paparazzi

Finally, we got to Abol Campground and the end of the 100 Mile Wilderness.

***

I walked alone the next day along a stream running away from the mountain with the heavy mass of Katahdin looming ever larger. The forest was approaching full-golden there in late September. The blazes ran out on this side of the rushing stream, and I wandered around confused. Finally, I spotted one on the stream's far side and pondered how to get over. At last I found a log-and-rock path across and looked downstream at the white rapids of this mountain stream and the golden autumn forest. I had never seen anything like Maine. It's a jewel. It was really coming home that this whole new, intense way of life was coming to an end, and I wondered how in the world I would come down from it.

I followed the serpentine trail and entered Katahdin Stream Campground. At the ranger station they told me there was a special campsite for thru-hikers, called the Birches, for which I paid eight dollars. "What's your weather forecast for tomorrow?" I asked.

"Not at all good," he said ominously. "The hurricane-related weather is expected to get here tonight."

A group of hikers arrived right after me and said they were hitchhiking to Millinocket, twenty-seven miles away.

"Why not just do it tomorrow, after summiting?" I asked.

"Have you heard tomorrow's weather forecast?" one said, looking me in the eye.

This looked like one of those places, such as Mount Washington, where weather could be an especially critical factor. I thought of Paddy O's remarks back in New York that, "I owe that mountain more than I could ever repay."

When I got to the Birches Campsite the Joy Machine, Stitch, Hit Man, and Cactus were already cooking dinner. There was a sense of anticipation in the air, although everybody was well aware of the weather forecast. "It's hard to believe this is our last night out here," Hit Man said. But my thought process hadn't gotten that far as I was directly focused on how to scale Mount Katahdin—and the ominous weather forecast.

As I was putting up my stove I felt the first light drop. "It's raining," I reported to nobody in particular. Everybody headed to the shelter, and I got in my tent for the last time.

***

Mount Katahdin is, with the possible exception of Mount Washington, the most storied mountain east of the Rockies. In the native Abenaki language Katahdin means "pre-eminent mountain." Bamola, the god of Katahdin, was known for flinging boulders through the air and creating violent storms and blizzards to avoid human contact. Thus, it is believed that the natives never climbed Mount Katahdin before European settlers arrived.

In 1804, Charles Turner led a trekking expedition through Maine's North Woods. The explorers were shocked after bushwhacking through the flat plains to look up and see this granite monster hovering over them. They decided to ascend, and nine hours later became, apparently, the first people to summit Mount Katahdin.

None other than Henry David Thoreau was one of the next to attempt to climb Katahdin, in 1846. Struggling with the elements and the direction Thoreau later wrote, "There was clearly felt the presence of a force not bound to be kind to man. It was a place for heathenism and superstitious rites, to be inhabited by men nearer of kin to the rock and the wild animals than we." He ended up getting lost and never saw the summit. Despite that failed attempt, a spring bearing his name flows about a mile from the summit, farther up than he ever made it.

***

September 26, 2005, dawned with heavy gray, leaden skies. It's often said that the summit of Mount Katahdin is the first place in the entire United States to receive any sunlight. But not on this day. I decided to eat most of my remaining food before heading up, while everybody else hurried out to try to beat the rain. But it soon started pouring.

Each morning the rangers post the weather forecast and classify the days for suitability of hiking above treeline. Often in the fall the trail can be closed for up to two weeks. Baxter State Park closes for good on October 15 each year, and there were rumors every year, including this one, that it would close early. In short, Mt. Katahdin is an iffy proposition in bad weather. After three nice days, that's what this day was. *Damn.*

I trooped down the dirt road to the ranger station, stopping to fill my two bottles from a running stream. It was hard to imagine much running water in a forty-two hundred-foot climb. I was hoping this would be the last water I would drink from a creek for a long time. "Is the mountain open?" I asked the ranger, halfway hoping he would say no.

"Yes," he flatly said, and I meekly went about making final preparations.

I started up the AT for what I hoped would be the last time. The trail went straight up, and the wind and rain howled into my face through the narrow chute the trail formed. After a few hundred yards there was a register to sign and I glumly noted that it was filled by the names of only a few thru-hikers. Of course. Who in their right mind would try something this macabre that didn't have to? Right off the bat I began thinking about turning around and waiting to summit another day.

But I kept walking and the trail got steeper, the rain and wind got worse, and the visibility was extremely poor. My first big mistake was not putting on long-johns and my marmot jacket over my Gore-Tex and fleece jackets. Soon I was shivering and soaked.

After a steep and steady climb of two thousand-plus feet I stopped to eat a candy bar. Normally, after such a climb I would rest for at least fifteen minutes, but with wind buffeting me down the narrowly cut trail I couldn't relax. I tried hiding behind the spruce trees that lined the trail, but it provided scant comfort. I was cold and wet and either had to continue on or turn around. I headed on.

Although the first part of Katahdin is straight up, the second part is far and away the most difficult. The trail does a figure-eight around a mansion-sized boulder at which point treeline is violated. I couldn't believe what lay ahead. It was the most exposed area on the entire trail and the visibility was worse than any of the previous 169 days. Combined with the steady sheets of rain and sixty mile per hour wind gusts, I was in conditions the likes of which I had never seen in my forty-five years. My first thought was, again, that I was going to turn around. But, instinctively, I continued.

Right away the trail became hellish. First, there was a five-foot ledge to scale, and I wondered if I was going the right way. But I saw a blaze, which meant I had to get over this shelf, so I looked for a way to clear it. Finally, after a couple false starts I found a stone to use as a springboard to get over. Soon it became clear it was necessary to work for every step— with maybe fifteen yards of visibility.

Would I be able to find my way back down? All I could see on three sides were sharp boulders and steep rock walls. It felt like some Manichean version of Blindman's Bluff. The previous year a hiker had been killed when a boulder had landed on top of him.

Another ghoulish thought kept popping into my head; my old friend from Chicago, Rob Slader. His lifelong dream had been to climb K-2 in Pakistan. Finally, he had received a coveted permit from the Pakistani government to attempt the climb. Before boarding the airplane for Pakistan a reporter asked him about the perils of K-2. "I summit or I die," Rob crowed. "Either way I win."

Slader and five other members of the expedition team finally reached the summit of K-2 on a brilliant August day in 1995. They radioed down to report their success. Soon 110-mile per hour winds roared out of Manchuria and blew all six off the mountain. None survived.

Thru-hiking the AT was a several-year dream for me, but it didn't reach that level of fanaticism. The only way I could blow it was to blunder right here.

But I continued on. Finally, I made out some human forms about thirty feet in front of me. It was Thistle and Lightfoot. Lightfoot was, as his trail name suggested, quite fleet of foot. He had already summitted and was on the way down. "What's it like at the top?" I asked anxiously.

"After you get through this steep middle section the trail levels off into a tableland that is much less difficult," he replied.

"Is the wind bearable up there?" I quickly asked.

"Well," he said pensively, "you can expect high winds from here on, especially right at the summit."

Thistle, a rugged Texan, stoutly said, "We'll go up together, Skywalker."

"I'm shaking, man, I'm so cold," I said grimly. "I've got to turn around."

Grabbing me and pulling me over behind a rock wall Thistle said, "Stand here for a second and relax." I tried, but I was soaked through and shivering uncontrollably. Further, Thistle traveled at a slow, even pace which meant I would probably end up alone, and I again worried about getting lost up there and not making it down before dark. Heck, I wasn't entirely confident about getting down from where I currently stood.

"Well, I'm going," Lightfoot said.

Instinctively, I said, "Let me trail along back down with you." I was less than two miles from the summit and badly wanted to finish. But I started back down, attempting to chat with Lightfoot to slow him down a bit. Having somebody to follow in the dense fog made a big difference and soon we were back below treeline. Lightfoot soon disappeared. By the time I got to the bottom I couldn't believe the difference in rain, visibility, and wind force. It seemed almost like a normal, wet day, as opposed to the surreal conditions I had just encountered above treeline.

I went to the ranger station and asked, "What does it take to close the mountain?" Then I asked, "How do you know what in the world it is like above treeline being down here?"

But those were just the hollow words of a depressed, defeated hiker.

I was out of food and my clothes were soaked, which meant I had to find a way to Millinocket, twenty-seven miles away. The park was essentially abandoned. Mercifully, two rangers agreed to take me fifteen miles to the entrance of the park, and from there I was able to hitchhike. I was exhausted. Normally chatty to anyone considerate enough to give me a ride, I couldn't stay awake.

***

I glumly walked through Millinocket, looking for a place to stay. Fortunately, I found a room at the Appalachian Trail Inn and then ate at the Appalachian Trail Restaurant. Then I wandered around in the rain, finally locating a grocery store and then a Laundromat to dry my clothes. A general *northern* hospitality pervaded Millinocket, another decimated factory town.

I returned to the Appalachian Trail Inn with hangdog airs and ran into Mr. and Mrs. Snowman. Mrs. Snowman had started off as a thru-hiker with her husband, but was one of the unfortunate ones to drop off in Georgia. Her husband had hiked onward, while she returned to their home in Wales for several months. But now she had made the trans-Atlantic passage again to try to scale this last mountain with her thru-hiking husband.

After I recounted my day's humbling tale, Snowman said, "We are headed out at four thirty tomorrow morning. You're welcome to go with us."

"Sure, but why so early?" I wondered.

"Because we anticipate it taking all day to get all the way up and down," he replied.

"See you at four thirty," I said and buried myself in my room.

An hour later Cackles and Box-of-Fun arrived with their fathers who had picked them up at the foot of Mount Katahdin. Cackles screamed at the top of her lungs a long, drawn-out, "Weeee're thruuuu-hiiikers."

I didn't have much residual ego as a hiker, but whatever existed was now badly frayed. Somehow I felt I had badly failed a basic test as a hiker. They knocked on my door.

"My hat's off to you," I said. "That was a helluva' hike you two made today."

Cackles had a mountain-climbing background out West and had led them through the most awful circumstances to the top and down. And Box-of-Fun deserved the Hang-In-There Award. She had struggled to keep up with the fleeter-of-foot Cackles for 6.5 months and 2, 175 miles.

"When are you going to summit, Skywalker?" Cackles asked.

"October 15," I said, referring to the day that the mountain closes for the year.

"Oh, come on," she said. "Are you going out with Snowman and his wife, tomorrow?"

"At four thirty a.m., although the weather forecast, while not outright diabolical like today, is sketchy. And I sure don't want to endanger my reputation as a fair-weathered hiker."

I got about three hours sleep and headed out with Mr. and Mrs. Snowman in the pitch black on September 27, 2005. I tried to relax by focusing on deep breathing. When Snowman noted my total silence his wife said, "He's either sleeping or praying."

At the ranger station I felt a little better when I saw that the rain accumulation the previous day had been 2.25 inches. The forecast for this day was high winds again, but with skies clearing by mid-morning. After forcing down some more mediocre trail food I swallowed three Tylenol and headed off. This time I was fully bundled.

I had expected the trail to be a quagmire, but the powerful wind howling through the narrow-cut trail had mostly dried it out. Again, I slowly lumbered straight up the first two thousand feet, concentrating on every breath. After ninety minutes I stopped in the same place as the previous day to ingest a Snickers Bar for a last energy boost.

The direst recurring thought stemming from my failure the previous day was of Kutza. She was an Israeli girl who had told me a moving tale back in Virginia of hiking all the way from Georgia to Mount Katahdin in 2002, but failing on multiple occasions to ever summit because of repeatedly terrible conditions. The story had seemed incredulous at the time. But now I understood.

I reached the giant boulder where tree line begins and, shielded by the rock, forced myself to sit down and deep breathe for a few minutes. Then, bracing myself for the worst, I stepped out for the second time into the howling winds and rock faces of Mt. Katahdin.

***

The gusts were even stronger than the previous day. Again I started over the boulder fields and rock walls of Katahdin, wondering how this was going to work. Fortunately, the strong winds had started thinning out the thick fog layers, and for the first time I got a look at parts of this granite monster of a mountain. Indeed, in this middle part it seemingly went straight up. But on this second try I could see blazes.

Mr. and Mrs. Snowman had started up at first light, but I soon saw her wedged in a crevice. Seeing she was immobilized I said, "You must be mimicking my performance yesterday."

"Skywalker, please don't step on me when you pass, or on the way back down either," she replied good naturedly. "I plan to still be in this position."

"Well at least you haven't lost your sense of humor," I replied. "That's more than I could say yesterday."

I judged this was about where I had turned around the previous day, and could even see the shelf where the tableland began and the trail leveled. I had been within about 150 yards of making it there the previous day. Nonetheless, despite the high winds, which periodically buffeted me from side to side, it was a different hike on this day.

Upon reaching the tableland I could clearly see the summit of Mt. Katahdin 1.5 miles off in the distance. *Home free.* A group of hikers had gathered around the summit marker, all bundled up. It was a fairly gradual climb over a rocky, moonlike landscape straight to the summit. There may be no other mountain on earth like Mt. Katahdin; a straight-up climb through a narrowly cut trail, followed by a grueling steep section of boulders and rock walls, and then a fairly gentle ascent across a wide tableland to the summit.

The trail runs right over Thoreau Spring. I emptied out my Nalgene bottle and filled up with what has to be some of the clearest, purest water in the world.

The wind howled, with gusts of up to sixty miles per hour, as I neared the summit. My first thought was that I would just touch the weather-worn sign-post I had seen in so many photographs in trail towns and then immediately head back down to get some relief below treeline.

"Skywalker, Congratulations," Smiley said cheerfully. "Have you got your speech ready?"

"Yes," I responded. "And it reads, 'Any idiot can do it the second time.'"

"Well, you've undoubtedly set the record for hiking the entire Appalachian Trail in the least number of steps," he replied. All joking aside, that might have been true. A normal thru-hike is said to require five million steps. Perhaps I had been able to make it home in four million paces.

Fortunately, there were no rumors about my performance the previous day as had proliferated after my abandoned backpack mishap in Georgia.

"I heard you couldn't even see your hands yesterday," one hiker said.

"The truth is a lot less friendly to me," I said, and proceeded to recount the events of the previous day.

"You were smart," everybody said, and they actually seemed to mean it.

Peter Pan offered to take a couple photographs of me on the renowned weather-worn signpost at the summit. They now occupy a prominent place in my living room. Those photographs and the good company were adequate consolation, for if I had summitted the previous day there would have been no photographs or celebration at the top.

It was strange to see the signpost indicating distances to southward points, but no more references to anything north. All along the way I had eagerly scanned such signposts and markers to glean distances to various campsites, mountaintops, etc. But after spending almost six months wondering if this trail actually had an end, I had to fight the tendency to think, "Is that all?"

I then huddled behind a rock wall with a couple other bundled-up hikers. It was a strange place to celebrate, but Katahdin and Maine are places like no other. The vast panorama of lakes, mountains, and forest offered that "other-world" serenity I wouldn't be seeing again soon.

I had passed Smiley during his blazing summer of high passion in Pennsylvania, and Peter Pan in North Carolina. "The way everybody has been passing me lately," I said, "I wouldn't have had anybody to hike with soon."

"We're all glad to be here, I assure you," Peter Pan said softly.

One factor that dims the summit celebration is that the successful thru-hiker faces a rugged 5.2-mile descent. I was dragging on the way down, but my deep-boned fatigue brought up a happy coincidence. The AT was almost a perfect match for a person of my ability. Had it been any more difficult or longer I couldn't have completed it. But at no point during the 171 days had it been a disappointment. I felt challenged the whole way.

The key to my success in completing the entire trail was due to never overestimating my own abilities and rarely underestimating the difficulty of the trail. And, since I had been raring to try the AT for the preceding six years, I was able to recover from various setbacks and not stay discouraged for long.

***

At the base I went to the ranger station and had the audacity to write the imperial words of Julius Caesar in the register.

Skywalker

Mt. Katahdin Ranger Station — mile 2,174.8

9-27-05: *Veni, vidi, vici. — **Skywalker***

But then I worried that my colleagues might not realize that was tongue-in-cheek, so I added how Mt. Katahdin had brought me to my knees the previous day.

My overwhelming feeling was one, not of exultation, but rather relief. Thru-hiking the AT was an all-consuming project. My every day had been preoccupied with details that are existential to such a long-distance hike. The whole thing had been a step in the dark, and I honestly had not known how in the world it would all work out.

Other northward bound thru-hikers were arriving at the base of Mt. Katahdin, looking up expectantly. I began assuring them that all would be cool for them the next day. Of course, my giving advice on climbing Mount Katahdin is about like the captain of the Titanic giving navigation advice! I was so at ease that I didn't even worry about getting a ride out of the park until twilight. I began talking with an elderly couple who had driven from Missouri to pick up their middle-age son upon completion of his dream. They became worried as the sun began setting, and again I found myself in the odd role of providing assurance.

Finally, their son, Fido, came trooping down with an ear-to-ear grin that could have made another Missourian, Tom Sawyer, proud. They offered me a ride and we began piling our backpacks into their van. Then something occurred to me. "Fido, did you see Snowman and his wife?"

"Yeah," Fido sighed slowly. "They were still going up when I was on my way down."

We all looked at each other worried, and I said, "Do you mind if I go report it to the ranger?" I ran over and told the ranger that a couple was still on the mountain and most likely not able to get down before dark.

"Thank you," he said in a business-like manner and wrote down the details.

I ran back over and we headed out of Baxter State Park. "Wouldn't this be a great time to see a bear or a moose," I buzzed, "while in a car on the way out of the wilderness for the last time."

My mind went back to the first practice hikes in the dead of winter, as the wilderness lay dormant in a blanket of snow. In two days of hiking I

230

had seen one squirrel, and never, ever breathed air so crystal clear or heard a silence so pristine. Then, for some reason my thoughts turned to a hot, humid mid-summer afternoon somewhere in the Mid-Atlantic States. By this time of year the forest was a constant hum of buzzes, chirps, and mysterious sounds. I had been walking down the trail when I heard a rustle. A smallish animal, perhaps a woodchuck or porcupine, ran out of the trees onto the trail and turned directly toward me. Then, it scampered as fast as it inhumanly could, though still very modestly, straight down the Appalachian Trail for about thirty yards before plunging back into the trees. In the most profound way it really is another world out there, rich in its own glory.

Europe is dotted with majestic castles and citadels of high culture from its imperial past. America's past, on the other hand, is richly tied to wilderness.

I'm often asked about the AT: "Would you do it again?" The answer is a resounding yes. The ancient Greeks defined happiness as full use of your powers along lines of excellence. The Appalachian Trail and the outdoor life definitely offer the opportunity for great fulfillment and happiness.

I've traveled and lived all over the world. But like almost anybody who has hiked the Appalachian Trail, I found it to be the journey of a lifetime.

Epilogue

The first three weeks back my body went through a sort of deep-stage metamorphosis. My metabolism slowed dramatically, and I walked around with a newfound feeling of inner tranquility. A lifelong poor sleeper, all I had to do was lie down at night and I would wake up nine hours later, seemingly without having moved. This was not only due to a bone-wearying fatigue, but a profound emotional peace. My mother chortled to her friends on upon weighing me and seeing I had gained fourteen pounds in three days.

We had a party with thirty guests, including Eugene Espy, the second-ever thru-hiker back in 1951. The guests demanded a question-and-answer session from Mr. Espy and me. I started by offering a toast from the class of 2005 to the class of 1951. The great thing was the interest of people who never before had any attraction to or experience in that "other world." There is indeed something distinctive about the American DNA that perks up at the mention of wilderness.

The morning after the party I headed off on a six-hour drive to Hot Springs, North Carolina. I parked the car in front of a meter in the one-street town — teeming this past spring with northbound hikers — and headed up the main road. This time I knew where to look, and when I saw the double blaze signifying a right turn on the side of the highway rail, I was more forgiving of my mistake five months before. I headed up the mountain as fast as possible. Two things hadn't changed: I was still worried about *rain* and *bears*. After two hours *on the right trail* I arrived at the bridge I had circuitously found in May. I was now an official thru-hiker, and hitched back into Hot Springs.

The following day I passed through Erwin, Tennessee, to pick up Miss Janet, the notorious hikers' hostel owner, on the way to the annual ALDHA (Appalachian Long Distance Hikers Association) Gathering in Hanover, New Hampshire. Miss Janet thrived on trail gossip and is part of the rich tapestry of the AT, despite never having hiked more than a couple miles on it.

When I mentioned meeting Justin Maximus on the first day in the parking lot at Springer Mountain, and wondering why he was carrying such a large knife, she stopped me.

"Do you know what happened to Justin?" she asked softly.

"No," I said with eyebrows raised. "I asked a lot of people and got the impression he dropped out somewhere."

"No," she solemnly intoned. "Justin was killed in Duncannon, Pennsylvania. He got hit by a train."

She then related a witch's-brew tale of drinking, barroom brawling, and a romantic misadventure. Apparently, along the trail Justin had met a very attractive Ukrainian Girl called *Water Boy*. After striking up a trail romance with her he was scheduled to meet his girlfriend at the hiker feed in Duncannon. There everything came to a head, and he reputedly ended up in a shoving match at the Doyle Hotel. After being thrown out he had walked in front of the hotel to the train tracks and was either accidentally hit by or hurled himself in front of a train. Trail opinion tended decidedly toward the latter.

I had heard about it in Delaware Water Gap, but Justin had picked up the trail name Packstock (due to his heavy load) after we got separated, so I didn't recognize it. All the stories on the trail related to what a jerk he had made of himself in Duncannon. This brought my mind back to the first days on the trail in Georgia when he had talked so movingly of his distaste for crowds. Besides the obvious fact that his death at age twenty-eight was a tragedy, I found it extra sad that such a nice, authentic guy had died in a situation that had shown him in the absolute worst light.

***

The most-well-attended function at the Gathering, held at Dartmouth College, was the seminar on the PCT (Pacific Crest Trail). Well over 100 people showed up for it alone.

The speaker began by saying, "The PCT is the next step for AT thru-hikers."

I left Hanover and drove to Chicago with the Gypsy Sisters, two members of the Class of 2005. We were shocked at the flat expanse of wide-open plains once we finally got out of the Appalachian Mountain Chain. The Appalachians had left their mark not just on me, but on the country as a whole. It seems no accident that the Midwestern character is down-to-earth and wholesome, while the Appalachian parts are flavored with more flinty, cantankerous, hard-boiled types. Thank God for it all.

Acknowledgements

As a first-time writer, I was daunted by all the technical work required to get a book published. I had never considered a book a matter of anything beyond writing it. When I started attending author's meetings every writer seemed to have a hard-luck tale of being "battered, beaten, and abused" by a publisher. Fortunately, my experience with Indigo Publishing has been a positive one.

Publisher Henry Beers and his talented staff, including editors Joni Woolf and Rick Nolte, and graphic designer Audra George, proved to be quite service-oriented and forward-looking. Aspiring writers should be discriminate, but not deterred, by the publishing process.

Jerry Gramckow of Denver, Colorado, was also very helpful in reviewing and helping cut my bloated second draft.

Finally, my mother, Kathleen Malloy Walker, performed several thankless tasks in that memorable year of 2005, including fattening me up beforehand and afterwards, as well as sending and receiving clothing and hiker gear to and from various post offices along the way.

Suggested reading

Brill, David. *As Far as the Eye Can See*, Rutledge Hill Press, 1990.

Bruce, Dan *"Wingfoot"*. *The Thru-Hiker's Handbook*, Appalachian Trail Conference 2005.

Bryson, Bill. *A Walk in the Woods*, Broadway Books, 1998.

Chazin, Daniel D. *Appalachian Trail Data Book*, 2001.

Emblidge, David. *AT Reader*, Oxford Press, 1996.

Hall, Adrienne. *A Journey North*, AMC Books, 2000.

Hare, James. *Hiking the Appalachian Trail*, 1975 Rodale Press.

Howe, Nicholas. *Not Without Peril*, AMC Books, 2000. Luxenberg, Larry. *Walking the AT*, Stackpole Books, 1994.

Mass, Leslie. *In Beauty May She Walk*, Rock Spring Press, 2005.

Mikkalsen, Stacy. *Appalachian Trail Thru-Hiker's Companion*, Appalachian Long Distance Hiker's Association, 2001.

Nash, Roderick. *Wilderness and The American Mind*, Yale University Press, 1983.

Rubin, Robert. *Trail Years: A History of the Appalachian Trail Conference*, Appalachian Trail Conference, 2000.

Shaffer, Earl. *Walking With Spring*, Appalachian Trail Conference, 1983.

Shaffer, Earl with Bart Smith. *Calling Me Back to the Hills*, Westcliffe Publishers, 2001

Solnit, Rebecca. *Wanderlust: A History of Walking*, Viking Penguin, 2000.

Sussman, Aaron and Goode, Ruth. *The Magic of Walking*, Simon andSchuster, 1967

Made in the USA
Lexington, KY
19 January 2013